WORLDS GREAT NOVELISTS

WORLDS GREAT NOVELISTS

Kailash Puri

CYBER TECH PUBLICATIONS
4264/3, Ansari Road, Daryaganj, New Delhi-110002 (India)
Ph.: 011-23244078, 011-43559448 Fax: 011-23280028
E-Mail: cyberpublicationsdelhi@yahoo.com
Website: www.cybertechpublications.com

WORLDS GREAT NOVELISTS

Kailash Puri

First Edition 2010

Published by : Asian Offset Printers

G.S. Rawat for **Cyber Tech Publications**
4264/3, Ansari Road, Daryaganj, New Delhi-110002 (India)
Ph.: 011-23244078, 011-43559448 Fax: 011-23280028
E-Mail: cyberpublicationsdelhi@yahoo.com
Website: www.cybertechpublications.com

Preface

The novels in India is conventionally thought to have emerged in the middle of the nineteenth century. The year of the rebellion, 1857, also saw the publication of Alaler Gharer Dulal, upon which Bankimchandra Chatterji, who himself holds a lofty place in the development of the novel in India, lavished praise as a "beautiful written" work. The contemporary assessment of the merits of this wok has been more restrained, but nonetheless Alaler Gharer Dulal is thought to occupy a unique position in the history of India, and certainly Bengali, literature as "the first work in Bengali which can be described as a novel". The book covers all the great Indian novels and novelists.

Methodologically, the critique engages deconstruction to facilitate analysis of the ideological conflicts evidenced in the West Indian novel. The analysis demonstrates that the dialectical struggle between language as self- reflexive object and language as unself-conscious representation combines with the discursive force of imperialist ideology to complicate narrative construction of personhood and selfhood in the West Indian novel.

The work proceeds by examining the value of Jacques Derrida's theory of differance in the context of West Indian subject construction. Derrida's philosophical interrogations, popularised under the problematised term, deconstruction, are linked with Michel Foucault's discussions of discourse and power, effectively combining Derrida's deconstructive interrogations with Foucault's genealogical analyses.

— *Author*

CONTENTS

Preface

1. Prolofic Indian Writers 1

Mulk Raj Anand • Anjana Appachana • Baby Halder • P. K. Balakrishnan • Sarnath Banerjee • Ashok Banker • Vaikom Muhammad Basheer • Samit Basu • Malti Bedekar • Susham Bedi • H. S. Bhabra • Dharamvir Bharati • Suchitra Bhattacharya • Bibhutibhushan Bandopadhyay • Binod Bihari Verma • Sasthi Brata • Vikram Chandra • Rimi B. Chatterjee • Upamanyu Chatterjee • Bankim Chandra Chattopadhyay • Sanjeev Chattopadhyay • Sharat Chandra Chatterji • Amit Chaudhuri • Richard Crasta • Rana Dasgupta • David Davidar • Abha Dawesar • Swadesh Deepak • Anita Desai • Kiran Desai • Shashi Deshpande • Nabaneeta Dev Sen • Chitra Banerjee Divakaruni • Sonia Faleiro • Altaf Fatima • Sunil Gangopadhyay • Sagarika Ghose-Sardesai • Amitav Ghosh • R. Gopal • Hari Singh Gour • Anosh Irani • Raj Kamal Jha • Kalki Krishnamurthy • Jaswant Singh Kanwal • Datta Raghunath Kavthekar • Kesavadev • Prakash Kona • Sandilyan • Sharat Kumar • Bem Le Hunte • Amulya Malladi • Odette Mascarenhas • Anurag Mathur • Ved Mehta • Menon Marath • Pankaj Mishra • Jaishree Misra • Premendra Mitra • Jagadish Mohanty • Dhan Gopal Mukerji • Bharati Mukherjee • Suroopa Mukherjee • M. Mukundan • Anita Nair • R. K. Narayan • Ampasayya

Naveen • Shardha Ram Phillauri • Rahi Masoom Raza • Balachandra Rajan • Rajashree • Rajalakshmi • Malayattoor Ramakrishnan • Raja Rao • Anita Rau Badami • Pratibha Ray • Arundhati Roy • Dilipkumar Roy • Nayantara Sahgal • Sarojini Sahoo • Sulekha Sanyal • Krupabai Satthianadhan • Geetanjali Shree • Vikram Seth • Githa Hariharan • Akhil Sharma • Partap Sharma • Acharya Shivpujan Sahay • Jaspreet Singh • Khushwant Singh • Nanak Singh • Indra Sinha • Sivasankari • Indira Soundarajan • C P Surendran • TV Varkey • Shashi Tharoor • Harilal Upadhyay • V. Balakumaran • Ardashir Vakil • Shreekumar Varma • Yandamuri Veerendranath • Devaki Nandan Khatri • Acharya Chatursen • Manohar Shyam Joshi • Kamleshwar • Narendra Kohli • Harishankar Parsai • Phanishwar Nath 'Renu' • Jaishankar Prasad • Munshi Premchand • Rajendra Yadav • Shailesh Matiyani • Shivani • Sri Lal Sukla • Bhagwati Charan Verma • Vishnu Prabhakar • Vrindavan Lal Verma • Yashpal • Sachchidananda Hirananda Vatsyayan • Bhisham Sahni • Nirmal Verma • Rajkamal Chaudhary

Bibliography 259

Index 262

1

PROLOFIC INDIAN WRITERS

MULK RAJ ANAND

Mulk Raj Anand (December 12, 1905-September 28, 2004) was an Indian writer in English, notable for his depiction of the lives of the poorer castes in traditional Indian society. One of the pioneers of Indo-Anglian fiction, he, together with R.K. Narayan, was one of the first India-based writers in English to gain an international readership.

Life and Work

Born in Peshawar, he studied at Khalsa College, Amritsar, before moving to England where he attended University College London as an undergraduate and later Cambridge University, graduating with a PhD in 1929.

During this time he forged friendships with members of the Bloomsbury Group. He spent some time in Geneva, lecturing at the League of Nations' School of Intellectual Cooperation.

Anand's literary career was launched by family tragedy, instigated by the rigidity of the caste system. His first prose essay was a response to the suicide of an aunt, who had been excommunicated by his family for sharing a meal with a Muslim. His first main novel, *Untouchable*, published in 1935, was a chilling expose of the day-to-day life of a member of India's untouchable caste. It is the story of a single day in the life of Bakha, a toilet-cleaner, who accidentally bumps into a member of a higher caste.

Bakha searches for a salve to the tragedy of the destiny into which he was born, talking first with a Christian missionary and then with a follower of Mahatma Gandhi, but by the end of the book he concludes that it is technology, in the form of the newly introduced flush toilet that will be his saviour. While the toilet may deprive him and his family of the traditional livelihood they have had for centuries, it may also liberate them in the end by eliminating the need for a caste of toilet cleaners.

This simple book, which captured the puissance of the Punjabi and Hindi idiom in English was widely acclaimed and Anand won the reputation of being India's Charles Dickens. The introduction was written by his friend, E. M. Forster, whom he met while working on T. S. Eliot's magazine *Criterion*. In it Forster writes: "Avoiding rhetoric and circumlocution, it has gone straight to the heart of its subject and purified it"

Inevitably, Anand, who spent half his time in London and half in India, was drawn to the Indian independence movement. At the same time, he also supported freedom elsewhere around the globe and even travelled to Spain to volunteer in the Spanish Civil War. He spent World War II working as a scriptwriter for the BBC in London, where he became a friend of George Orwell.

Anand returned to India in 1946, and continued with his prodigious literary output there. His work includes poetry and essay on a wide range of subjects, as well as autobiographies and novels. Prominent among his novels are *The Village* (1939), *Across the Black Waters* (1940), *The Sword and the Sickle* (1942), all written in England, and *The Private Life of an Indian Prince* (1953), perhaps the most important of his works written in India. He also founded a literary magazine, *Marg*, and taught in various universities.

During the 1970s, he worked with the International Progress Organization (I.P.O.) on the issue of cultural self-comprehension of nations. His contribution to the conference of the I.P.O. in Innsbruck (Austria) in 1974 had a special influence on debates that later became known under the phrase of dialogue among civilizations.

Private Life of an Indian Prince, were more autobiographical in nature, and in 1950 Anand embarked on a project to write a seven-part autobiography, beginning with *Seven Summers*. One part, *Morning Face* (1968) won him the National Academy Award. Like much of his later work, it contains elements of his spiritual journey as he struggles to attain a higher sense of self-awareness. He died in Pune.

ANJANA APPACHANA

Anjana Appachana is a novelist of Indian origin who lives in the United States of America. She has written a book of short stories titled *Incantations* and a novel titled *Listening Now*.

Anjana Appachana was born in India of Kannada origin and educated at Scindia Kanya Vidyalaya, Delhi University, Jawaharlal Nehru University and Pennsylvania State University. Her first book *Incantations and Other Stories* was published in England by Virago in 1991 and in the US by Rutgers University Press in 1992. The book was reissued in India by Penguin in 2006.

The stories in it are set in the early eighties in India. One of her short stories titled "Sharmaji" was included in *Mirrorwork: Fifty Years of Indian Writing*, a collection edited by Salman Rushdie and Elizabeth West.

Appachana received the O. Henry Festival Prize and a creative writing fellowship from the National Endowment for the Arts in the US. Her first novel and second book is titled *Listening Now*, and was published by Random House in 1997. In it, six women tell the story of two lovers, Padma and Karan, spanning sixteen years. The novel is set in Bangalore, Delhi and Lucknow.

A.P. Kamath quotes her as saying that "Writing is not deemed legitimate work by anyone. They assume that it can be put aside for anything and everything—for housework, for house guests, for cooking... Now tell me, how many people who work outside the house do you know who would take time off from their work to cook a meal or do groceries or laundry or look after house guests? None, right?...That's because they work outside the house and because they have a regular income which apparently legitimizes their work." Appachana adds that a writer's life is comparatively more comfortable in America than in India. She lives in Tempe, Arizona, and has a young daughter.

BABY HALDER

Baby Halder (or Haldar) (born 1973 or 1974 in West Bengal) is an Indian housekeeper and author whose autobiography *Aalo Aandhari* or *A Life Less Ordinary* describes her harsh life. Abandoned by her mother at age 7, raised by a neglectful father and married off at age 12, she later left an abusive husband with her three children for a life as housemaid in New Delhi and then encountered several exploitative employers. Her sister was killed by her husband.

She wrote after work, using plain matter-of-fact language and writing in Bengali. Her last employer, writer and retired anthropology professor Prabodh Kumar, had encouraged her and aided in editing the book. He translated it into Hindi and this version was published in 2002. The Bengali original was published in 2004. A Malayalam version appeared in 2005 and the English translation was published in 2006. The book became a best-seller in India. Translations into French and Japanese are being planned. As of 2006, Ms. Halder continues to work at a home in Gurgaon on a sequel to her bestseller.

P. K. BALAKRISHNAN

P. K. Balakrishnan (1926-1991) Malayalam novelist critic historian. P K Balakrishnan is one of the greatest intellectuals 20th century Kerala has produced. His multifaceted interests took him through politics, journalism, public speaking and creative writing. He was a great patriot who gave up his studies for the freedom of the country. His uncompromising integrity showed that he was unfit for politics, created a turbulent journalistic career, made him a fiery public speaker and resulted in literary creations that were masterpieces in their respective field.

Balakrishnan was an intense personality. He was truthful to himself. Standing by what he thought was right brought him into confrontation with people and the establishment. While his uncompromising convictions earned him very few friends in the real sense, he was understood and appreciated by a close circle of people whom he valued. Though the man has passed on to the realms of history, his books stand testimony to the great intellectual that he was and the power of his writings.

Life

Balakrishnan was born to Panickasseri Kesavan and Mani in the small village of Edavanakkad in Eranakulam district in erstwhile Cochin state (Kerala), India, in a lower middle class family. He was the youngest of 4 children following 3 sisters. Though his father was bedridden with paralysis, his studies were not neglected. Bright in studies, he created a good impression on people around together with his mischievous cousins Kesavan, Chennan and Sekharan. The child hood flavours and the beautiful village where he lived can be caught in his novel 'Pluto'

He joined Maharajas College, Ernakulam. However, academic studies were last in his agenda. It was the time when the freedom movement had gathered momentum and there was no way the energetic boy could keep himself out of it. He wholeheartedly jumped into it. The involvement in quit India movement ended in jail.

Thus, his four eventful years in college ended without any qualification degree. Language was a gift he had and he had made prolific use of it through out his college days and subsequently mostly for political purposes. Though not formally, he had proved his mettle and the first job offer as chief editor proved that the caliber of the man was recognized. He started his formal career in journalism as Chief Editor of the daily news paper Dinaprabha,at the age of 32 years which was published, from Kozhicode. He quit after a year due to differences with the management. His journalistic career spread through the Malayalam dailies Kerala Kaumudi, Kerala Bhooshanam and Madhyamam Daily.

The Author

His studies on Chandu Menon (the first widely accepted Malayali novelist), the art of poetry studied through Kumaran Asan (the doyen of Malayalam literature) Vyasa Bharath & Ezhuthachan (the father of Malayalam poetry) and the art of the novel are unparelled works that enriched critical literature.

As a historian, he found that there was a disconnect between what the existing writings on history projected and what he saw of Kerala from the old literature, travelogues, and other first hand sources that is used to study history. In his writings he first dealt with Kerala history in the anthology 'Narayana Guru' on the great social reformer of Kerala who changed the face of its caste ridden society.

He brushes with Kerala history again to study why Tipu Sultan, an able ruler and administrator is perceived only as an aggressor and religious fanatic in our writings. The culmination of these studies over 3 decades resulted in his work on social history 'Jaathivyavasthayum Kerala Charitravum' (The Caste System and Kerala History). It is a seminal work that deals with various aspects of Kerala's history including the development of the Malayalam language.

However what catapulted him as a popular writer was his second novel 'Ini Njan Urangatte' (And Now Let Me Sleep), a novel that subsists on the Mahabharata. The book is unparalleled in its lofty language, imagery and depth and is considered one of the best classics in Indian Literature.

The novel is the story of Karna as seen through the eyes of Draupadi. It maintains the original story, epic atmosphere, events and characters which distinguishes it from other works based on Mahabharatha. This novel was quite a departure from his first novel 'Pluto' the story of his dog set in the back drop of his native village of Edavanakkad peopled by his friends and relatives.

While his extensive interests resulted in full fledged books, his numerous other interests resulted in various articles. No serious attempts were made to preserve the articles he wrote. So, many of these were lost after their first publication. Some of these were complied and published in his life time 'Mayatha Sandhyakal' (Unfading Twilights) and 'Nidra Sancharangal' (Sleep Walkings). These were combined and brought out as Balakrishnante Lekhanangal (Articles of Balakrishnan) in 2004. A subsequent collection of articles were published as 'Keraleeyathayum Mattum' (The Essence of Kerala etc.)

Works of Balakrishan

1. Narayana Guru (1954) An anthology on the great spiritual leader and social reformer of Kerala.
2. Chandu Menon-Oru Padanam (1957) (Chandu Menon-a Study) on the author of the first Malayalam novel 'Indulekha'
3. Kavyakala Kumaranasaniloode (1970) (The Art of Poetry through Kumaran Asan) on the noted doyen of Malayalam poetry Kumaran Asan
4. Ezhuthachante Kala-Chila Vyasa Bharatha Padhanangalum 1982 (The Art of Ezhuthachan), a work on the father of Malayalam literature
5. Novel-Sidhiyum Sadhanayum 1965 (Novel-Gift of Genius and Nurturing), a work on the craft of novel writing
6. Balakrishnante Lekhanangal (2004)(Articles of Balakrishnan)
7. Keraleeyatayum Mattum (2004)(The Essence of Kerala etc.) This book is a collection of 20 articles published in various periodicals over a time.
8. Pluto Priyapetta Pluto (1963) (Pluto, my dear Pluto) The story of his real life dog named after the Walt Disney counterpart
9. Ini Njan Urangatte (1973) (And now, Let me Sleep) A work originating from the great Indian epic Vyasabharatha (Mahabharata).
10. Tippu Sultan (1959) HISTORICAL BIOGRAPHY
11. Jaathivyavasthithium Keralacharithravum (1983) (The Caste system and History of Kerala). A path breaking work in kerala history.

SARNATH BANERJEE

Sarnath Banerjee (b.1972) is an Indian graphic novelist, artist and film maker. Banerjee was born in Calcutta and lives and works in Delhi, India. He studied image and communication at Goldsmiths College, University of London. His first novel, *Corridor* (2004), published by Penguin Books, India, was widely marketed as India's first graphic novel. However, it is not the first Indian graphic novel, since *River of Stories*, a graphic novel by Orijit Sen, was published in 1994. His second novel, *The Barn Owl's Wondrous Capers*, was published in 2007.

Sarnath has also provided illustrations for novels by other authors. He designed the cover for Upamanyu Chatterjee's novel, *Weight Loss*. He is the co-founder of the comics publishing house Phantomville, along with his friend Anindya Roy.

ASHOK BANKER

Ashok Kumar Banker (born February 7, 1964 in Mumbai, India) is a novelist and short story writer living in Mumbai, India. He has written professionally since his early teens, and has worked as a door-to-door surveyor for market research firms, a print journalist, columnist, scriptwriter for television series and documentaries, and in advertising.

Career

Known either as "Ashok Banker" or "Ashok K. Banker", he worked as a successful freelance journalist and columnist for several years, breaking front-page news for publications such as The Times of India, Mumbai, and cover stories for Outlook magazine, New Delhi.

Banker is a contemporary Indian novelist often counted among the significant literary names in post-colonial Indian literature. He is also known as a reviewer and commentator on contemporary Indian literature, and as a candid essayist with a particular focus on media hypocrisy in India, and the western racial bias against South Asian writers.

Banker has published in several genres, ranging from contemporary fiction about urban life in India to multi-volume mythological epics, as well as science fiction, fantasy, and cross-genre works. His first three novels to be published were crime thrillers, claimed to be the first written by an Indian novelist in English. They gained him widespread attention and a reputation for being a crime novelist that has clung to him despite his not having written crime novels since, though he has written short crime fiction, some of which involves characters from the novels. The stories of his "*Devi*" series are short works featuring avatars of the Hindu goddess Devi, and have appeared in various science fiction, fantasy, and horror magazines.

Three of his novels contain autobiographical elements and are closely related to one another. His first novel (though the fourth published) *Vertigo* is about a man struggling to make a successful career and home life in Bombay (the former name of Mumbai). *Byculla Boy* takes its name from the Byculla suburb of Bombay where he and his mother grew up. *Beautiful Ugly* and the complementary documentary of the same title are a tribute to his mother, portraying the tragic events of her life.

Having completed a six-volume retelling in English of the Indian epic of the *Ramayana* that has gained him worldwide attention, he is working on a nine-volume adaptation of the *Mahabharata*. These are intended to be part of a larger sequence dealing with the major myths of India, along with two yet-to-be published series that will more clearly blend myth with science fiction tropes and quantum mechanics. *The Krishna Coriolis* is to tell the life of Krishna beyond the *Mahabharata*, and *The Ganesa Palindrome* is to be set in the present and far future and focus on Ganesha, Kalki, and the end of the Day of Brahma.

Banker also has plans for *The Epic India* saga, a series of historical novels presenting the last 2500 years of Indian history from the perspective of the Indian people. He's also said to be working on an alternate history series titled "The Indus Saga" set in an alternate world wherein Indian scientists discover the scientific basis for the legendary 'dev-astras' (divine weapons) described in ancient Vedic texts and a group of Indian Freedom Fighters led by Mahatma Gandhi uses the dev-astras to change the course of World War II, gain India's freedom from the British Empire, and make India, China and Japan the dominant world powers by the turn of the 21st century. Another project by the prolific author is a graphic novel adaptation of his "Devi" tales, being developed for a major New York comic publisher.

Another project by the prolific author is a graphic novel series titled "Becoming Kali" scheduled to be published by Vertigo Comics (and not Virgin Comics as mistakenly reported by some bloggers). The Vertigo Comics series is edited by Karen Berger, Assistant Edited by Pornsak Pichetsotte, illustrated by Peter Gross, and is scheduled to begin publication in mid-2008.

Banker was earlier known as a columnist, well-known for his attacks on the celebrity-obsessed mass media. He used to write a weekly column in the Mumbai daily, Mid-Day, called "Cut The Hype", in which, as the column title suggests, he used to deflate several media celebrities as well as mock the media obsession with celebrityhood itself. In May 1998, he claimed to have discovered a new novelist, one Sunil Sawle who had received a big advance. The following week in his next "Cut The Hype" column, he claimed that he had set it all up to expose the publicity-obsessed nature of the media. He ostentatiously repudiates any desire to have publicity.

He was a prolific literary critic and reviewer, known for his candour and bluntness in reviewing books by Indian authors. His views often veered from the outright derogatory to effusive praise. He is one of few contemporary Indian authors writing in English to be included in prestigious anthologies such as *The Vintage Book of Modern Indian Literature* and *The Picador Book of Modern Indian Literature*.

His unorthodox views include the rejection of all media that is sponsored by advertising or corporate promotion as being 'unreliable' and 'editorially compromised'. According to a note posted on his official website, he is in the process of launching a 'community portal' with free blogs, email, forums, and even an ambitious "Indiapedia" project modelled on Wikipedia, with the intent of furthering information on Indian culture, history, mythology and literature without outside commercial support. More details are posted on his official website Epic India.

He is also said to be working on several film projects, including an untitled film according to the director, Michael Radford (of "1984" and "Il Postino" fame).

He wrote a short non-fiction book about Bollywood entitled *Bollywood: The Pocket Essential* (2001).

Bibliography

His previously published works include:

- *Amazing Adventure at Chotta Sheher* (1992)
- *The Iron Bra* (1993)
- *Murder & Champagne* (1993)
- *Ten Dead Admen* (1993)
- *Vertigo* (1993)
- *Byculla Boy* (1994)
- *The Missing Parents Mystery* (1994)
- *A Mouthful of Sky* (1995-96)
- *Bad Karma* (1998)
- *Brandwarriors* (1999)
- *Bombay Times a.k.a. "Swing City"* (2000)
- *Vortal* (2000-01)
- *The Pocket Essential Bollywood* (2001)

The Ramayana Series

- *Prince of Ayodhya* (2003)
- *Siege of Mithila* (2003)
- *Demons of Chitrakut* (2004)
- *Armies of Hanuman* (2005)
- *Bridge of Rama* (2005)
- *King of Ayodhya* (2006)

Collected as Omnibus Volumes

- PRINCE OF DHARMA

- PRINCE IN EXILE
- PRINCE AT WAR

Other Works

- *A Mouthful of Sky*-TV Series created and written by Banker (1995-96)
- *Bad Karma* Online serial (first published on Top Write Corner website) (1998)
- *Brandwarriors* Magazine series published in ad magazine edited by Anil Thakraney (1999)
- *Bombay Times* (2000) (a.k.a. "Swing City") Online serial published on Rediff.com
- *Vortal* (2000-01) Multimedia serial published in CD-Rom magazine "Mahazine"

Forthcoming

- The Krishnavatara Series
- Dance of Govinda
- Slayer of Kamsa
- Flute of Vrindavan
- Throne of Dwarka
- Field of Kurukshetra
- Chariot of Arjuna
- Coils of Ananta
- Lord of Vaikunta
- The Mahabharata
- The Seeds Of War
- The Children Of Midnight
- As The Blind King Watched
- Brothers In Exile
- While War Lords Speak Of Peace
- Upon This Crimson Field
- When The Blue God Awakens
- Beyond Black, White, and Grey

- The Age of Kali
- Becoming Kali (DC/Vertigo Comics, 2008)

VAIKOM MUHAMMAD BASHEER

Vaikom Muhammad Basheer (b. at Thalayolaparambu in Vaikom, 21 January 1908; d. at Beypore in Calicut, 5 July 1994) was a Malayalam fiction writer. He was a humanist, freedom fighter, novelist and short story writer. He was awarded the prestigious Padma Sri in 1982.

Early Life

Basheer, born in the village of Thalayolapparampu in northern Travancore, was the eldest child of devout Muslim parents. His father was in the timber business as a contractor, but the business did not do well enough for his large family to live in anything approaching luxury. After beginning his education at the local Malayalam medium school, he was sent to the English medium school in Vaikom, five miles away. While at school he fell under the spell of Mahatma Gandhi. He started wearing Khadar, inspired by the swadesi ideals. When Gandhi came to Vaikom to participate in the Vaikom Satyagraham (1924) Basheer went to see him. He managed to climb on to the car in which Gandhi travelled and touch his hand, a fond memory Basheer mentioned in many of his writings. He used to visit Gandhi's satyagrahashramam at Vaikom daily. He got punished for going late to school for this.

Freedom Struggle Involvement before Journey

He resolved to join the fight for an Independent India, leaving school to do so while he was in the fifth form. Part of his purpose in joining the Indian National Congress was to help ensure that there was some Muslim representation in the pan-Indian movement.

Since there was no active independence movement in Travancore or Kochi – being princely states – he went to Kozhikode to take part in the Salt Satyagraha in 1930. His group was arrested before they could participate in the satyagraha. At the police station, they were beaten up and later remanded at Kozhikode sub-jail. Basheer was sentenced to three months imprisonment and sent to Kannur prison. He became inspired by stories of heroism by revolutionaries like Bhagat Singh, Sukhdev and Rajguru, who were executed while he was in Kannur jail. He and about 600 political prisoners then at Kannur were released after the Gandhi-Irwin pact of March 1931. Freed from prison, he organised an anti-British movement and edited a revolutionary journal, *Ujjivanam* ('Uprising'). A warrant was issued for his arrest and he left Kerala.

Journey

After leaving Kerala, he embarked upon a long journey that took him across the length and breadth of India and to many places in Asia and Africa, a journey which spanned seven years, doing whatever work that seemed likely to keep him from starvation. His occupations ranged from that of a loom fitter, fortune teller, cook, newspaper seller, fruit seller, sports goods agent, accountant, watchman, cowman, hotel manager to living as an ascetic with Hindu saints and Sufi mystics in their hermitages in Himalayas and in the Ganga basin, following their customs and practices, for more than five years. There were times when, with no water to drink, without any food to eat, he came face to face with death.

After the Journey

After the journey, when returned to Kerala (1936–1937) – where he chose to live for the rest of his life – he found that his family had gone bankrupt. He tried to make a living as a sports goods agent in Ernakulam. After a bicycle accident, he lost the job, and wandered searching for a new one. He walked into the office of a newspaper 'Jayakesari' whose editor was also its sole employee. He did not have a position to offer, but offered to pay money if Basheer wrote a story for the paper. Basheer wrote his first story *Ente Thankam* (which was later published in the collection *Vishappu* under the name *Thankam*) at his request; the main character of the story based on a woman he saw everyday coming to draw water at a public water pipe in front of his residence.

Following this, he became a full time writer. During this period, he was near starvation most of the time, He struggled to pay rent and could not find money even for ink, paper and stamps, yet he wrote prolifically, stories, poems and political essays and sent them to various newspapers and publishers, for which he was rarely paid. (This scenario is described in detail in many of his works). He continued to contribute to the Independence movement through his articles for newspapers, most of them attacking Sir C. P. Ramaswami Iyer, the Dewan of Travancore. Basheer was resident in a small single room in a hotel at Ernakulam, which was part of Kochi princely state.

The Travancore State Congress was fighting for responsible government, and most of its leaders frequented Ernakulam to escape from the Travancore's police. Basheer and companions were under constant surveillance of spies of both states. Basheer's short-book *Hathabhaagyayaaya ente naadu* (My ill-fated motherland) and one act play *Pattathinte Pekkinaavu* (The terrible nightmare of Pattam) were banned in Travancore, and a warrant issued for his arrest if he entered Travancore. His house at Thalayolapparambu was searched and his mother and siblings harassed; Travancore police threatened to break his right arm to prevent his writing.

His works during the period appeared in many publications, of which he kept clippings. After his meeting with M. P. Paul, he was offered lodging at Paul's tutorial college, and also supervised the mess at the college. When Paul's tutorial shifted to Kottayam, Basheer also went to Kottayam. It was during a meeting of writers *Sahitheesakhyam* at Kottayam that Basheer read his draft of *Baalyakaalasakhi*.

Imprisonment and After

At Kottayam (1941–42), he was arrested and put in a police station lock-up, and later shifted to another lock up in Kollam Kasba police station. The stories he heard from policemen and prisoners there appeared in later works, and he wrote a few stories while at the lock-up itself. He spent a long time in lockup awaiting trial, and after trial was sentenced to two years and six months imprisonment. He was sent to

Thiruvananthapuram central jail. While at jail, he forbid M. P. Paul from publishing *Baalyakaalasakhi*. He wrote *Premalekhanam* (1943) while serving his term and published it on his release. *Baalyakaalasakhi* was published in 1944 after further revisions, with an introduction by Paul.

He then made a career as a writer, initially publishing the works himself and carrying them to homes in order to sell them. He ran two bookstalls in Ernakulam, Circle Bookhouse and later, Basheer's bookstall.

Once India achieved control of its destiny after obtaining Independence from British rule, he showed no further interest in active politics, though concerns over morality and political integrity are present all over his works.

Well into his forties, he surprised many of his acquaintances by marrying a woman much younger than him (Fabi Basheer) and settling down to a life of quiet domesticity with his wife and two children, Anees and Shahina, in Beypore, on the southern edge of Kozhikode.

During this period he also had to suffer from mental illness and was twice admitted to mental sanatoriums. He wrote one of his most famous works, *Paaththummaayude aadu* (Pathumma's Goat), while undergoing treatment in a mental hospital in Thrissur. The second spell of paranoia occurred after his marriage when he had settled down at Beypore. He recovered both times, and continued his writings.

He died in Beypore, on 5 July 1994.

Basheer is fondly called as Beypore Sultan (Sultan of Beypore). Though his works have been translated to English and eighteen Indian Languages, the peculiarity of the language he uses makes the translations lose a lot of sheen.

Writing Style

Language: Basheer is known for his unconventional style of language. He did not differentiate between literary language and the language spoken by the commons and did not care about the grammatical correctness of his sentences. Initially, even his publishers were unappreciative of the beauty of this language; they edited out or modified conversations. Basheer was outraged to find his original writings transcripted into "standardized" Malayalam, devoid of freshness and natural flow, and he forced them to publish the original one instead of the edited one. Basheer's brother Abdul Khader was a malayalam teacher.

Ones while reading one of the stories, he asked Basheer, "where are Aakhyas and aakhyathas (related with malayalam grammar) in this...?".Basheer shouted at him saying that "I am writing in normal malayalam, how people speaks and you don't try to find your stupid 'aakhya and aakhyaada' in this"!. This points out to the writing style of basheer, without taking care of any grammar, but only in his own village language.

Basheer's contempt for grammatical correctness is exemplified by his statement *Ninte Lodukkoos Aakhyaadam!* ("Your 'silly stupid' grammar!") to his brother, who sermonizes him about the importance of grammar (*Paaththummaayude aadu*).

Themes

An astute observer of human character, he skilfully combined humour and pathos in his works. Love, hunger and poverty are recurring themes in his works. There is enormous variety in them–of narrative style, of presentation, of philosophical content, of social comment and commitment. His association with India's Freedom Struggle, the experiences during his long travels and the conditions that existed in Kerala, particularly in the neighbourhood of his home and among the Muslim community – all had a major impact on them. Politics and prison, homosexuality, all were grist to his mill. All of Basheer's love stories have found their way into the hearts of readers; perhaps no other writer has had such an influence on the way Malayalis view of love. The major theme of all Basheer stories is love and humanity. In the story "Muchittu kalikkarente Makal", when sainaba comes out of the water after stealing the Bananas, the mandan Muthappa says only one thing: "Sainaba go home and dry your hair else may fall sick." This fine thread of humanism can be experienced in almost all his stories.

Autobiographical Element

One contrast among his works is between those that are primarily autobiographical as far as events and characters are concerned and those that are the product of the author's imagination. This is not to say that a novel or a story will always fall clearly into one category or another; the percentage of factual truth varies considerably. Whatever the case, a book published as fiction is to be read as such, in contrast with one published as 'memoirs'.

Works

Almost all of Basheer's writing can be seen as falling under the heading of prose fiction–short stories and novels, though there is also a one-act play and volumes of essays and reminiscences. Basheer's fiction is very varied and full of contrasts. There are poignant situations as well as merrier ones – and commonly both in the same narrative. There are among his output realistic stories and tales of the supernatural. There are purely narrative pieces and others which have the quality of poems in prose. In all, a superficially simple style conceals a great subtlety of expression.

His literary career started off with the novel *Premalekhanam*, a humorous love story between Keshavan Nair–a young bank employee and an upper caste Hindu (Nair)– and Saramma–an unemployed Christian woman. Hidden underneath the hilarious dialogues we can see a sharp criticism of religious conservatism, dowry and similar conventions existing in society. This was followed by the novel *Baalyakaalasakhi*– a tragic love story between Majeed and Suhra–which is among the most important novels in Malayalam literature in spite of its relatively small size (75 pages), and is commonly agreed upon as his magnum opus work. In his foreword to *Baalyakaalasakhi*, *Jeevithathil Ninnum Oru Aedu* (A Page From Life), M. P. Paul brings out the beauty of this novel, and how it is different from run-of-the-mill love stories.

The autobiographical *Janmadinam* ("Birthday", 1945) is about a writer struggling to feed himself on his birthday. While many of the stories present situations to which the average reader can easily relate, the darker, seamier side of human existence also finds a major place, as in the novel *Shabdangal* ("Voices", 1947), which faced heavy criticism for violence and vulgarity.

Ntuppuppaakkoraanaendaarnnu ("Me Gran'dad 'ad an Elephant", 1951) is a fierce attack on the superstitious practices that existed among Muslims.

Its protagonist is Kunjupathumma, a naive, innocent and illiterate village belle. She falls in love with an educated, progressive, city-bred man, Nisaar Ahamed. Illiteracy is fertile soil for superstitions, and the novel is about education enlightening people and making them shed age-old conventions. *Velichathinentoru velicham* (a crude translation can be 'brightness is very bright!') one of the most quoted Basheer phrases occurs in *Ntuppuppaakkoraanaendaarnnu*. People boast of the glory of days past, their "grandfather's elephants", but that is just a ploy to hide their shortcomings.

Mathilukal ("Walls") deals with prison life in the pre-independence days. It is a novel of sad irony set against a turbulent political backdrop. The novelist falls in love with a woman sentenced for life who is separated from him by insurmountable walls. They exchange love-promises standing on two sides of a wall, only to be separated without even being able to say good-bye. Before he "met" Naraayani, the loneliness and freedomlessness of prison life was killing Basheer; but when the orders for his release arrive he loudly protests, "Who needs freedom? Outside is an even bigger jail." The novel was later made into a film (MATHILUKAL, 1989) by Adoor Gopalakrishnan with Mammootty playing Basheer.

Sthalaththe Pradhaana Divyan, Aanavaariyum Ponkurishum, Muccheettukalikkarante makal and *Ettukaali Mammoonju* featured the life of real life characters in his native village of Thalayolaparambu (regarded as *Sthalam* in these works).

Awards

- Padma Sri(1982)

- Kendra Sahitya Academy Fellowship
- Kerala Sahitya Academy Fellowship
- Lalithambika Antharjanam Award(1992)
- Muttathu Varkki Award (1993) (Paaththummaayude Aadu)
- Vallathol Award (1993)

Published Works

Novels

1. *Premalekhanam* [The love letter] (1943).
2. *Baalyakaalasakhi* [Childhood friend] (1944).
3. *Shabdangal* [Voices] (1947).
4. *Ntuppuppaakkoraanaendaarnnu* [Me gran'dad 'ad an elephant] (1951).
5. *Maranaththinte Nizhalil* [In the shadow of death] (1951).
6. *Muchcheettukalikkaarante Makal* [The daughter of the card-shark] (1951).
7. *Sthalaththe Pradhaana Divyan* [The principal divine of the place] (1953).
8. *Aanavaariyum Ponkurishum* [Elephant scooper and Golden cross] (1953).
9. *Jeevithanizhalppaadukal* [The shadows of life] (1954).
10. *Paaththummaayude Aadu* [Paaththumma's goat] (1959).
11. *Mathilukal* [Walls] (basis for a film (1989) by Adoor Gopalakrishnan) (1965).
12. *Thaaraa Specials* (1968).
13. *Maanthrikapoochcha* [The magic cat] (1968).

Short Stories

1. *Janmadinam* [Birthday] (1945).
2. *Ormakkurippu* [Jottings from memory] (1946).
3. *Anargha nimisham* [Invaluable instant] (See *Anal Haq)* (1946).
4. *Viddikalude Swargam* [Fools' paradise] (1948).

5. *Paavappettavarudaey Vaeshya* [The courtesan of the poor] (1952).
6. *Vishwavikhkhyaathamaaya Mookku* [The world-renowned nose] (1954).
7. *Vishappu* [Hunger] (1954).
8. *Oru Bhagavadgeethayum Kuraey Mulakalum* [A Bhagavadgeetha and some breasts] (Short stories) (1967).
9. *Aanappooda* [Elephant-hair] (1975).
10. *Chirikkunna Marappaava* [The laughing wooden doll] (1975).
11. *Bhoomiyudaey Avakaashikal* [The inheritors of the earth] (1977).
12. *Shinkidimunkan* (1991).
13. *Yaa Ilaahi!* [Oh God!] (published posthumously) (1997).

Others

1. *Kathaabeejam* [Story seed] (Play) (1945).
2. *Nerum Nunayum* [Truth and lie] (Commentary and letters) (1969).
3. *Ormmayudaey Arakal* [The cells of memory] (Commentary and reminiscences) (1973).
4. *Anuraagaththintaey Dhinangal* [The days of desire] (Diary; originally titled *Kaamukantaey diary* [The diary of the paramour] and changed later on the suggestion of M. T. Vasudevan Nair) (1983).
5. *Bhaargavinilayam* [The house named Bhaargavi] (Screenplay for a film (1964) by A. Vincent which is credited as the first horror cinema in malayalam; adapted from the short story *Neelavelichcham* [The blue glow]) (1985).
6. *M. P. Paul* (Reminiscences of his friendship with M. P. Paul) (1991).
7. *Cheviyorkkuka! Anthimakaahalam!!* [Hark! The final clarion-call!!] (Speech) (1992).

SAMIT BASU

Samit Basu is the author of *The Simoqin Prophecies*, *The Manticore's Secret* and *The Unwaba Revelations*, the three parts of The GameWorld Trilogy, a fantasy trilogy published by Penguin Books, India. He currently lives and works in Delhi, India.

Biography

Born December 14th, 1979, Basu grew up in Calcutta, where he studied at Don Bosco School, and later Presidency College, Kolkata, where he obtained a degree in Economics. He dropped out of the Indian Institute of Management, Ahmedabad and then went on to complete a course in broadcasting and documentary filmmaking at the University of Westminster, London.

Writing Career

The Simoqin Prophecies was written when Basu was 22 and published when he was 23, making him one of India's youngest successful authors. In 2003, Basu was in *Outlook* magazine's list of 16 Indian achievers under 25. He has contributed to *The Harper Collins Anthology of New Indian Writing* (2004). He has also written short stories for children, which appear in the *Puffin Book of Bedtime stories* (2005), the *Puffin Book of Funny Stories* (2005) and 'Seven Science Fiction Stories' (Scholastic India, 2006).

In 2006, Basu published a series of articles and interviews on Indian speculative fiction called *The Trousers of Time: Possible futures of Indian speculative fiction in English* on a fellowship from Sarai In 2007, Basu contributed to 'Superhero!', a collection of stories about Indian superheroes published by Scholastic India and was declared, along with other prominent young Indians such as Rahul Gandhi and Vidya Balan, one of India's most promising 'Emerging Indians' by a survey conducted by IMRB and The Week magazine, India.

The Simoqin Prophecies, written in English, has been published in Swedish by Ordbilder, and German (from Piper Verlag) and Spanish translations of the GameWorld trilogy are on their way. Apart from his novel writing, Basu is a popular columnist, scriptwriter, documentary filmmaker and freelance journalist writing on travel, film, books and pop culture. He also runs a popular weblog. Basu has also started writing comics for Virgin Comics. His initial projects with them are Devi (#3-#10) and The Tall Tales of Vishnu Sharma based on the Panchatantra

Writing Style

Basu follows a unique writing style in the GameWorld trilogy. There are innumerable allusions to literary works from all over the world, including fantasy fiction and other fiction, to tales of superheroes and occasionally even to movies. He draws inspiration heavily from Indian and Greek mythology, Indian folklore and modern fantasy fiction works. This medley of ideas creates a comic and absurd world. Basu liberally uses puns, tangential references, and situational humour to augment the hilarity. At the same time, the text is interspersed with pithy observations and revelations.

MALTI BEDEKAR

Malti Bedekar (nee Vibhavari Shirurkar) (born 1905) was the first feminist Marathi author. She was the daughter of the progressive thinker and educator Anant Khare, whom she writes about in her semi-autobiographical novel *Kharemaster*. Her first work was *Kalyanche Nishwas* (The Sighs of Buds), a collection of short stories in which she frankly discussed issues such as premarital sex, a woman's right to set up her own household alone, and dowry. The stories were considered far too bold for 1930s India and a storm of outrage followed, including threats to the anonymous author. It was not till 1946 that Malti, now a married woman, revealed her real name. She married the novelist Vishram Bedekar in the early 1940s (she was his second wife) and busied herself getting a Ph.D. in Sanskrit. In 1950 she published *Bali* (The Victim), the story of a 'criminal' tribe and the impact of Gandhi's ideas on them. This was followed by *Kharemaster* and her last work, *Shabari*, the story of a woman trapped in a stifling marriage.

Works

- *Kalyanche Nishwas* 1933
- *Hindolyavar* 1933
- *Bali* 1950
- *Gharala Muklelya Striya*
- *Kharemaster* 1953. Published in English translation by Stree, an imprint of Bhatkal and Sen
- *Shabari* 1956

SUSHAM BEDI

Susham Bedi (born July 1, 1945) is a leading South Asian (Indian) author of novels, short stories and poetry, currently living in the United States. She is a professor of Hindi language and literature at the department of Middle Eastern and Asian Languages and Cultures (MEALAC) at Columbia University in New York. She writes predominantly about the experiences of Indians in the South Asian diaspora, focusing on psychological and 'interior' cultural conflicts. Unlike other prominent Indian American novelists she writes mainly in Hindi rather than in English. She has been widely translated into English, French, Dutch and other languages by artists, academics, and students.

She was an actress in India in the 1960s and early 1970s. More recently in the United States she has appeared on such shows as "True Crime: New York City", "Third Watch", and "Law and Order: Special Victims Unit", and in movies such as "The Guru" (2002) and "ABCD" (1999). She is the mother of the actress Purva Bedi.

In 2007 she was awarded 100,000 Rupees by Uttar Pradesh Hindi Sansthan for her contributions to Hindi language and literature.

In January, 2006 she was honoured by Sahitya Academy in Delhi for her contributions to Hindi literature.

Early Career

Susham Bedi began her writing career in high school and college, entering local competitions and writing articles and stories for magazines. She also worked as an actress and commentator on Indian television in the late-1960s and 1970s.

She attended Delhi University and Punjab University in India and taught Hindi literature. Her Ph.D. dissertation was published in 1984 as *Innovation and Experimentation in Contemporary Hindi Drama* by Parag publications in India.

From 1974 to 1979 she wrote for *The Times of India* as one of their correspondents from Brussels, Belgium. In 1979 she came to the United States with her husband.

Academic Career

Susham Bedi has been involved in exploring questions of identity, authenticity, and transformation, in her cultural criticism and academic work, and these themes are reflected as well in her fiction writing. She is the author of eight major Hindi language novels, as well as collections of Hindi short stories and poetry. These have been widely translated and have been the subject of academic dissertations and debates on the South Asian diaspora experience.

She has also been involved in Hindi language pedagogical research and has developed original reading and listening comprehension materials in Hindi. Many of these materials are available on the internet. Her "Using Authentic Materials in the Language Classroom: A Case in Hindi" was included in the anthology *Teaching and Acquisition of South Asian Languages* (University of Pennsylvania Press).

From 1990 to 1991, she contributed to a BBC weekly programme, *Letters from Abroad,* in which she discussed day to day issues about life in New York.

Fiction Writing

Her most well-known novel is *Havan* (1989), which was translated into English by David Rubin and published by Heinemann International under the title *The Fire Sacrifice* in 1993.

Her novels and short stories often feature female protagonists who are in the process of negotiating new identities which are neither fully old nor new, often finding identity and strength in the impurities in their lives. Bedi's narrative focus tends to be on the negotiative and transformative process itself, the pain and tragedy of cultural loss, but also the sense of hope and opportunity in forging new and stronger identities if one is willing to endure the transformative process. Her works are thus located squarely in the South Asian diaspora and immigrant experience.

Recent Writing

In mid-2006, the National Publishing House, Delhi, published her *Portrait of Mira* in English (translated by David Rubin) along with the second edition of *The Fire Sacrifice.*

In 2007 her second short story collection, entitled *Sarak ki Laya* (*Rhythm of the Road*), was published by National Publishing House.

Currently, she is working on her 8th novel, entitled *Maine Nata Tora* (*I Broke the Ties*).

Bibliography

Novels and Short Stories

- *Portrait of Mira*
- *Morche (Battlefronts)*
- *Shabdon Ki Khirkiyan*
- *Nava Bhum Ki Ras-katha (Epic of the New Land)*
- *Gatha Amerbel Ki (Song of the Amerbel)*
- *Itar, (The Other)*
- *Chiriya Aur Cheel* (The Sparrow and the Kite: Short Story Collection)
- *Katra Dar Katra (Drop by Drop)*
- *Lautna, (Returning)*
- *Havan (The Fire Sacrifice)*

Cultural and Critical Works

- *Kahan Hai Mera Gher (What is Home to me?)*

- *Diaspora me Hindi sahitya (Hindi Literature in the Diaspora: State and Direction)*
- "Quest for Identity: Grappling for the Literary Self in the Diaspora" Hindi
- *Hindi Natya Prayog Ke Sandarbh Men (Innovation and Experimentation in Hindi Drama)*

Pedagogy

- "Bhasha Shikshan: Anubhav, Soch aur Chunotiyan (Teaching Language: Experience, Thoughts and Challenges)"
- "Two Sides of a Coin: Linguistic and Cultural Aspects of a Language" *Hindi*
- "Using Authentic Materials in the Language Classroom: A Case at Hand." Published in the anthology *The Learning and Acquisition of South Asian Languages*
- "Culturally Authentic Situation Cards for the Teaching and Testing of South Asian Languages
- "Sunna-Samajhna: Listening Comprehension in Hindi
- "Authentic Materials for Developing Reading Comprehension in Hindi

Acting Career

Susham Bedi has appeared on "True Crime: New York City", "Third Watch", and "Law & Order: Special Victims Unit", and in movies such as "The Guru" (2002) and "ABCD" (1999).

Other

- Her high school certificate and passport list her birthday as 26 July, 1945, though she celebrates 1 July as her real birthday.
- The actress Purva Bedi is her daughter.

H. S. BHABRA

Hargurchet Singh Bhabra (June 7, 1955-June 1, 2000) was a British Asian writer and broadcaster who settled in Canada.

Bhabra was born in Mumbai, India and moved to England with his family in 1957. The family eventually settled in Beare Green, Surrey. From 1966 to 1973, Bhabra attended Reigate Grammar School. He was the only boy of Asian origin in the school, was highly regarded by his teachers, and an accomplished actor in school productions such as *Much Ado about Nothing*. Regarded by his teachers as the most exceptional member of an exceptional year, he won a scholarship to Trinity College, Oxford where he studied English Literature.

Publication

Bhabra worked for six years in international banking in the City of London. In 1984, he resigned to complete *Gestures*, a novel on which he had been working for years. He travelled and worked as a correspondent for a few years, which provided material for his career as a writer of fiction, under his own name and also as A M Kabal and John Ford. *Gestures* won a Betty Trask Award in 1987. It has been described thus: "With extraordinary force and subtlety, Gestures conducts the 'funeral rite over an entire way of life... a liberal, human, European culture which has finally disappeared'. The lines could stand as an epitaph for Bhabra himself. Infused with his own erudition, elegance and empathy, it was also-and to a great degree-an expression of his own sense of displacement." Indeed, although he published in quick succession three thrillers — *The Adversary* (1986) and *Bad Money* (1987), and *Zero Yield* — the next few years were spent largely on travels to Egypt, Mexico and Latin America.

The United States

In 1989, Bhabra was awarded the first Fulbright Chandler Fellowship in Spy and Detective Fiction Writing. This prize included a post as writer-in-residence at the University of California, Los Angeles for one year. Bhabra stayed on in Los Angeles from 1991 to 1993, hoping to earn money as a scriptwriter. That did not work out, however, though his fund of esoteric knowledge did help him win a handsome sum as a contestant on a television quiz show, *Jeopardy*, an accomplishment of which he remained proud. While there, he also developed an obsession with climbing bridges, which led to his arrest while making an assault on the Golden Gate, San Francisco. Bhabra also taught at Amherst College in Massachusetts.

Canada

In 1994 Bhabra joined his parents in Toronto, the city to which they had moved after the retirement of his father. In Canada, Bhabra was perceived as an Asian-Canadian writer and broadcaster. He taught at the Humber School for Writers at Humber College and then joined TV Ontario where he held several positions including host of the book programme *Imprint* in 1997. Knowledgeable and intelligent, Bhabra's interests ranged from food and fashion to films and books. He later became the show's producer, but left it in 1999 as a result of artistic differences with his co-host. After leaving TVOntario in 1999, Bhabra experienced financial difficulties, and debilitating writer's block.

The next year was hard financially, and Bhabra struggled to make ends meet with occasional freelance television and magazine work. He was sustained by the support of his partner, Vee Ledson, daughter of educator Sidney Ledson. Bhabra had encouraged Ledson to pursue her dream of running her own school, Laurel Academy, which she established in Toronto in 1995. The rest of the time he concentrated on plans for an ambitious fiction trilogy: plans which ultimately came to nothing.

On 1 June 2000, a week before his 45th birthday, he killed himself by jumping off the Prince Edward Viaduct on Toronto's Bloor Street. His death contributed to the argument for the Luminous Veil, a suicide barrier fence over the viaduct. In 2003, the Luminous Veil was finally completed and in the same year *Gestures* was reprinted.

DHARAMVIR BHARATI

Dr. Dharamvir Bharati (December 25, 1926-September 4, 1997), was an Indian writer. Dr Dharamvir Bharati made a deep impact on Hindi literature and is considered to be one of the most renowned Hindi poet and writer of India. His novel

"Gunahon ka Devtaa" became an evergreen classic. Andha Yug, his drama set in the time immediately after the Mahabharata war, is another classic that is enacted very often in public by various drama groups. Dr. Bharati's "Suraj ka Satwan Ghoda" is considered a unique experiment in story telling and was made into a national award winning movie of the same name in 1992 by Shyam Benegal. "Kanupriya", "Thanda Loha", "Saat Geet Varsh" and "Sapana Abhi Bhi" are amongst his most popular works of poetry.

He was born in Allahabad to Shri. Chiranji Lal and Smt. Chanda devi. The only other sibling he had was his younger sister, Dr. Veerbala. The family underwent considerable financial hardships after the father died early. Bharati did his MA in Hindi from Allahabad University in 1946 and won the "Chintamani Ghosh Award" for securing highest marks in Hindi. He was the sub-editor for magazines "Abhudaya" and Sangam" during this period. Later he completed his Ph.D. In 1954 under Dr. Dhirendra Verma on the topic of "Siddha Sahitya", and was appointed lecturer in Hindi in Allahabad University. 1950s were the most creative period in the life of Dr. Bharati and he wrote many novels, dramas, poetry, essays, and criticisms during this phase.

In 1960 he was appointed as Chief-Editor of the popular Hindi weekly magazine Dharmayug brought out by the Times of India Group, and moved to Bombay. He remained the Editor of Dharmayug till 1987. During this long phase the magazine became the most popular Hindi weekly of the country and established new heightes in Hindi Journalism. As a field reporter, Dr. Bharati personally covered the Indo-Pak war that resulted in the liberation of Bangladesh.

Honours: In 1972, Dr. Bharati was awarded Padm Shree by the Government of India. He was also honored by "Rajendra Prasad Shikhar Samman", Bharat Bharati Samman", "Maharashtra Gaurav", "Kaudiya Nyas" and "Vyasa Samman".

Dr. Bharati had one sister (Dr. Veerbala). He married (1954) and later divorced Mrs. Kanta Bharati with whom he had a daughter Parmita. Few years later he remarried and had a son Kinshuk Bharati and a daughter Pragya Bharati with Mrs. Pushpa Bharati. Dr. Bharati developed heart ailment and died after a brief illness.

Prominent Works

Suraj Ka Satvan Ghoda (The Seventh Steed of the Sun): A short novella, that may also be viewed as a set of connected mini-narratives, it can also be considered one of the foremost instances of metafiction in twentieth century Hindi literature. The protagonist is a young man named Manik Mulla who recounts these tales to his friends. The name of the work is an allusion to Hindu mythology where in the chariot of the Sun-God Surya is said to be drawn by seven horses.

Andha Yug (The Age of Blindness): Structured on events in the Mahabharata, it is a powerful metaphorical work.

SUCHITRA BHATTACHARYA

Suchitra Bhattacharya (born 10 January 1950 in Bhagalpur, Bihar) is an Indian novelist.

Suchitra Bhattacharya was interested in writing from her childhood. After graduating from Calcutta University she married and took a break from writing. She returned to writing with short stories written in the late seventies (1978-1979). She started writing novels in the mid eighties. Within a decade, especially after publication of the novel *Kacher Dewal* (Glass Wall), she became one of the major writers of Bengal.

Her writing focuses on contemporary social issues. She is a perceptive observer of the changing urban milieu and her writing closely examines the contemporary Bengali middle class. Crisis in human relationships and the changing values of the present era along with degeneration of the moral fibre of the society in the backdrop of globalisation and consumerism are depicted in her prose. Exploitations and sufferings of women regardless of their social or economic identities find a distinct voice in her writing. While she is famous for her writing on women's issues, she does not consider herself as a feminist. She took up many odd jobs in her early youth and finally joined the public service which she left in 2004 to become a fulltime writer. Her long career is reflected in many of her stories and novels.

Over the past two decades, Suchitra has written about 24 novels and a large number of short stories in different leading Bangla literary magazines. Some of her acclaimed novels are *Kachher Manush* (Close to Me), *Dahan* (The Burning), *Kacher Dewal*, *Hemonter Pakhi*, *Neel Ghurni*, *Aleek Shukh*, *Gabhir Ashukh* (A Grave Illness), *Uro Megh*, *Chhera Taar*, *Alochhaya*, *Anyo Basanto*, *Parabas*, *Palabar Path Nei*, *Aami Raikishori*, *Rangin Pritibi* and *Jalchhobi* among others. Her novels and short stories have been translated into many Indian languages such as Hindi, Tamil, Telugu, Malayalam, Oriya, Marathi, Gujarati, Punjabi and English. She also writes novels and short stories for children. Her novel *Dahana* was made into a movie by famous Bengali director, Rituparno Ghosh.

Suchitra has received several awards which include the Bhuban Mohini Medal from Calcutta University in 2004, the Nanjanagudu Thirumalamba National Award from Bangalore in 1996, the Katha Award 1997 from Delhi, the Tarashankar Award in 2000 from Kolkata, the Dwijendralal Award in 2001 from Kalyani, the Sharat Puroshkar in 2002 from Bhagalpur, as well as the Bharat Nirman Award, Sahitya Setu Award and Shailajananda Smriti Puroshkar in 2004.

BIBHUTIBHUSHAN BANDOPADHYAY

Bibhutibhushan Bandopadhyay was a Bengali novelist and writer. His most well known book is the autobiographical novel *Pather Panchali* (The story of the road), incorporated (along with *Aparajito*, the sequel) into the memorable film trilogy by Satyajit Ray.

Life

Bibhutibhushan was born on 12 September 1894 at his maternal uncle's house in Ghoshpara-Muratipur village, in the 24 Parganas of Bengal (now in West Bengal, India). His father, Mahananda Bandyopadhyay, was a Sanskrit scholar and a *Kathak*, one who tells stories for a living.

Bibhutibhushan's early days were spent in abject poverty. Nevertheless, he fought his way to complete his undergraduate degree in history, although he could not afford to enroll for the postgraduate course at the University of Calcutta. The economic burden of his family rested squarely on his shoulders. He had married in the meantime, but his wife, Gouri Devi, died in childbirth after only a year of conjugal life. The tragic theme of death and loneliness is a recurrent factor in Bibhutibhushan's early writings.

Before he became a writer, Bibhutibhushan took up various jobs to make ends meet. He taught school, became a secretary, managed an estate. Finally, in 1921 he published his first short story, "Upekshita," in *Probashi*, one of the leading literary magazines of Bengal at that time. However, it was not until 1928, when his first novel, *Pather Panchali* (also known in English as *Song of the Little Road*), was published, that Bibhutibhushan got critical attention. With *Pather Panchali* Bibhutibhushan became, instantly, a prominent name in Bengali literature. At the age of forty six, Bibhutibhushan married Rama Chattopadhayay. Their only son Taradas was born in 1947.

Bibhutibhushan had a stout constitution and walked miles in the woods every day. He usually took his notebook with him and loved to write surrounded by the wilderness.

On 1 November, 1950, Bibhutibhushan died of a heart attack while staying at Ghatshila. He was fifty-six.

Critical Acclaim

Pather Panchali is considered to be Bibhutibhushan's masterpiece. It has been included in the ICSE syllabus for students choosing to study Bengali. He has 16 novels and over two hundred short stories to his credit.

Humayun Azad opined that the novel is superior to its cinematic rendition. This is not necessarily a commonly held view, as the Apu Trilogy is considered to be among the finest films in the history of cinema. However, the unavailability of a proper translation of *Pather Panchali* makes it an issue hard for the English-speaking audience to resolve: the available translation is a truncated version of the novel. Martin Seymour-Smith, in his *Guide to Modern World Literature* (1973), calls Bandopadhyay (he uses the form Banerji) "perhaps the best of all modern Indian novelists" and says "probably nothing in twentieth-century Indian literature, in prose or poetry, comes to the level of *Pather Panchali*" .

Bibhutibhushan's works are mostly concerned with the lives of people from rural Bengal. His writings come alive with vibrant and thoroughly normal characters from the countryside.

Bibhutibhusan was an outstanding creator of adventure literature for adoloscent children. His *Chander Pahar, Hira Manik Jwale* and *Maraner Donka Baje* are adventure stories with young Bengali protagonists who visit exotic places like African jungles, the Richtersveldt mountains, Kalahari Desert, the ruins of ancient Hindu imperial cities in Indochinese islands, China during the Second Sino-Japanese War. His adventure stories build on the adventure spirit of children and also explores the adventurous nature of his own and his intimate love of nature and the whole world's people, places and cultures.

Works

Complete list of novels:

- *Pather Panchali* (Song of the Road)
- *Aparajito* (Unvanquished; sequel to *Pather Panchali*)
- *Aranyak* (In the Forest)
- *Chander Pahar* (Mountain of the Moon)
- *Heera Manik Jwale*
- *Maraner Danka Baje*
- *Adarsha Hindu Hotel*
- *Ichhamati*
- *Dristi Pradeep*
- *Debjan*
- *Bipiner Sangsar*
- *Anubartan*

- *Ashani Sanket*
- *Kedar Raja*
- *Dampati*
- *Sundarbane Sat Batsar*
- *Dui Bari*
- *Mismider Kabach*

Some short story collections:

- *MeghaMallar*
- *Mauriphool*
- *Jatrabadol*

BINOD BIHARI VERMA

Binod Bihari Verma (1937-2003) was a Maithili literateur by soul, medical doctor by profession and a defence officer by career. He is most noted for his pioneering work on Panjis, which are ancient genealogical charts, *Maithili Karna Kayasthak Panjik Sarvekshan*. He is also known for his depiction of rural poor of the Mithila region in his writings. During his lifetime, he worked as a medical officer in the Indian Army, as a lecturer in a Dental College, and as a Private Medical practitioner. He simultaneously carried on his literary works by independent publishing and in various magazines *viz.* Mithila Mihir and Karnamrit. He had command over a number of languages including Urdu, Sanskrit, Oriya, Assamese and Bengali and scripts of various Indian languages *viz.* old Maithili, Assamese, Gurmukhi, Oriya and Nepali.

Biography

Early Life and Education: Binod Bihari Vema was born in Baur, District Darbhanga, Bihar on 3 Dec 1937 to a Maithil Karna Kayasth landlord Rameshwar Lal Das and Yogmaya Devi. His father, Rameshwar Lal Das, was a freedom fighter, a prominent Gandhian and tireless worker for the upliftment of the poor, and he inculcated these values in his children as well. These values are also reflected in the writings of Dr. Verma. He lived with his brother Anand Kishore Lal Das, as a joint family. After finishing his primary school, which was at the Rasiyari village (across the mighty Kamla Balan)-there being no primary school in his village, he moved with his father and uncle to various places in South Bihar (now Jharkhand) who were trying to spread Gandhiji's message of achieving freedom through self reliance and nonviolence in the remote tribal areas of Chaibasa, Ranchi, and Singhbhum areas of South Bihar.

He developed a close bonding with the tribal children of these places which gave him a rare understanding of the lot of the poor and the underprivileged and which is depicted so picturesquely in his writings. His sojourn in the villages and the tribal areas also gave him an insight into the diversities of human nature which was reflected in his writings. He initially studied at the District School, Chaibasa. He finished his secondary schooling at the missionary school of St. John's at Ranchi. He studied his senior secondary school at Langat Singh College, Muzaffarpur. Subsequently he joined the Darbhanga Medical College and graduated in 1962.

Army Life

In 1962, in the heady days of Chinese invasion (Sino-Indian War) Dr Verma joined the Indian Army and was commissioned into the Army Medical Corps in 1963. The service life gave him ample opportunity to visit remote far flung border areas and gave him a rare insight into the lives of the people of Himachal Pradesh, Sikkim, Punjab, Assam and Goa among others. He was in effect, a life long student of the culture and language of all the various peoples he came in contact with. He tried to understand their language and read their folk tales and poetry. All these issues are vividly imbibed in his writings.

In 1984, he opted for permanent commission in the army. He fought in the Indo-Pakistani War of 1965, was involved in the Operation Bluestar in 1984 and the IPKF operations in Sri Lanka in 1988-1990, where he commanded the 404 Field Ambulance at Vavuniya. His dynamic leadership and clinical skills in these conflicts won him respect both from the men he commanded and from his seniors. He was greatly admired for his integrity and honesty. He took premature retirement from active army service in 1990, partly disillusioned with the war in Sri Lanka.

Later Life and Death

Subsequent to his retirement Dr Verma settled in Bhubaneswar, Orissa where he started his clinical practice and undertook literary tasks with renewed vigour. Post 1990 was his most prolific literary phase with regular publishing of novels, biographies, and contributions to Maithili magazines. During this period he regularly visited local libraries, met various Oriya and Maithili literary figures and was generally involved in academic activities. He taught Biochemistry in a Dental College in Bhubaneswar. In 1999 he was diagnosed to be suffering from prostate cancer. After this period his literary work was interrupted frequently due to illness. He died on 09 November 2003 at Bangalore, fighting a long battle with cancer.

Life as a Writer

Career Overview: Dr. Verma began writing with descriptive stories and essays of the life and people around him form his school and college days. Subsequently, he came under the influence of Prof. Radha Krishna Choudhary, historian and writer, and his writings increasingly depicted poor and their lifestyle being disrupted by modernization.

His works are known for subtle depiction of poverty and the richness of the culture of common folk in the form of folk songs. In this he was influenced by Maxim Gorky. Under the guidance of Choudhary, he started the major study and research work of Panjis which culminated in his first published book Maithili Karna Kayasthak Panjik Sarvekshan in 1973. After this there was a lull in his literary work till he retired from the army in 1989.

He began collecting and publishing his older works. He turned his attention to biographies and wrote the biographies of his mentor, Radha Krishna Choudhary, Sriram Sharma Acharya, and George Abraham Grierson. With the advent of

Internet in India, he took to the new medium early and created a forum for online literary discussions, however due to his illness, he had to leave it prematurely.

Early Writings

Verma began writing stories and poems in his high school days. These centred around the various people whom he met in real life. They contained vivid depiction of the life of the poor in post independent India.

They also contained pieces which depicted his various experiences in school *viz.* dissection of a frog as zoology practical class. He also wrote poems which were patriotic and motivational. These works were published in various school magazines and occasionally in Mithila Mihir.

Mithila Mihir Short Stories

After this phase he began contributing regularly to various Maithili magazines, primarily, Mithila Mihir. They involved depiction of rural life. These were subsequently published as a short story collection Balanak Bonihar O Pallavi. He also wrote a social novel, Nayanmani during this period which was published in serial format in Mithila Mihir. This was subsequently published as a novel.

Panjik Sarvekshan

In 1973, he published his magnum opus, Maithili Karna Kayasthak Panjik Sarvekshan. This work was a culmination of months of extensive research on the fast disappearing ancient genealogical charts. It exemplifies both his research and literary skills. It remains the only surviving record of certain groups of Panjis, which have now disappeared. In this work, his association with Radha Krishna Choudhary, came to the fore.

Later Works

Subsequent to Maithili Karna Kayasthak Panjik Sarvekshan, there came a long hiatus in his literary life. He again started writing and publishing after 1990, after his retirement from the Army. He published his previous works as collections. He also started contributing frequently to Karnamrit, a new maithili magazine, as Mithila Mihir had stopped being published.

He researched extensively on folks songs of mithila, the life and contribution of George Abraham Grierson, the biography of Radha Krishna Choudhary, and the literary history of Maithili. These culminated in various articles in the Karnamrit as well as various published books.

Pen Names

- Vinod
- Vinod Gopal

Marriage & Children

- Married to Pratibha Verma at Patori Village (Saharsa Distt), Bihar on 4 July 1965 in a traditional Maithil wedding
- Children: Three daughters and Two sons
    * Archana Verma: Daughter
    * Sharad Verma: Son
    * Varuna Verma: Daughter
    * Savita Verma: Daughter
    * Rohit Verma: Son

Major Influences

- George Abraham Grierson-British administrator of Darbhanga in 19th century, lover of maithili folklore and literature, writer of grammar of modern maithili
- Radha Krishna Choudhary-Noted historian, president of ICHR, leftist thinker, and Maithili writer
- Shriram Sharma Acharya-Saint and yogi based at Haridwar, spread the message of Gayatri Mantra
- Brij Kishore Verma "Manipadma"-Maithili literateur, winner of Sahitya Akademi award

Life Time Interests and Researches

- Life and works of Sir George Abraham Grierson

- Folklore of Dalits and other backward castes and their contribution to modern maithili
- Buddhist Studies with the special relation of Ancient Mithila with Tibet
- Astrology
- Mithila Painting and depiction of modern village life in Mithila Paintings
- Study of Maithili Literature
- Maithili proverbs, idioms and folk songs
- Vaishnavism in Mithila

Places Where Posted While in Army

- Panjim/Goa: Medical Officer, Military Hospital Panjim (See images at Arts Ideas)
- Ambala, Haryana: Medical Officer, Military Hospital Ambala
- Shimla, Himachal Pradesh :Arts Ideas on Google Pages and Images of Shimla at Arts Ideas
- Sugar Sector, Himachal Pradesh (Indo-China Border)
- Saharanpur, Uttar Pradesh: Regimental Medical Officer, Remount Vetererinary Corps Centre
- Allahabad, Uttar Pradesh: Recruiting Medical Officer, Branch Recruiting Office Allahabad
- Varanasi, Uttar Pradesh
- North Sikkim
- Varanasi (Second Tenure), Uttar Pradesh
- Kapurthala, Punjab: Medical Officer, Section Hospital Kapurthala
- Jalandhar, Punjab: Medical Officer, Military Hospital Jalandhar
- Tezpur, Assam: Officer Commanding, 56 Field Medical Stores Depot
- Vavuniya, Srilanka: Commanding Officer, 404 Field Ambulance

Places Where Stayed in Civilian Life

- Darbhanga
- Chaibasa
- Ranchi
- Saharsa
- Bhubaneswar

Major Works

- Maithili Karna Kayasthak Panjik Sarvekshan-a Survey of the Panjis of the Karan Kayasthas of Mithila. 1973. Madhubani.
- Nayanmani A novel describing the rural scene in Post Independence Bihar. Initially published in parts in "Mithila Mihir" from February 1968 to April 1968.1997. Bhubaneswar.
- Balanak Bonihar O Pallavi-Short Story collection on the village life of Mithila on the banks of the Kosi River and its tributaries. 1994. Bhubaneswar.
- Tapasa vai Ganga-Biography of renowned historian Prof. Radha Krishna Choudhary. 1995. Bhubaneswar.
- Adim Purkha-Translation of Sahitya Akademi award winner oriya novelist Gopinath Mohanty's work "Dadi Burha".2001.Sahitya Akademi, New Delhi.
- Vedmurti Taponishth Sri Ram Sharma Acharya-Biography of Shriram Sharma Acharya. 2005. Bhubaneswar.

Articles

- Maithili Language: An Introduction
- Tradition of music in Mithilia
- Maharsi Sri Aurobindo on Vidyapati
- Life and Works of Acharya Surendra Jha 'Suman"
- Concerns in 2002 as *Current Concerns*
- The Festival Of Bata Savitri
- Folk Songs
- Book Reviews written in 2002

SASTHI BRATA

Sasthi Brata (birthname : Sasthibrata Chakravarti) is an Indo-Anglian writer of fiction. He was educated at Calcutta Boys' School, Kolkata and then at Presidency College, Kolkata. He lives in England.

Books written by him:

- *My God Died Young*
- *Confessions of an Indian Woman Eater*
- *India: Lotus in the Labyrinth Land*
- *Traitor to India: A search for home*
- *India: The Perpetual Paradox*

VIKRAM CHANDRA

Vikram Chandra is an Indian writer who has won awards and critical acclaim for his novels and short stories. He is married to writer Melanie Abrams, who, like Chandra, teaches creative writing at the University of California, Berkeley. Chandra currently divides his time between Mumbai (Bombay), India and Oakland, California.

Family Background

Chandra was born in New Delhi in 1961. His father, Navin Chandra, is a retired executive. His mother, Kamna Chandra, has written several Hindi films and plays; her most notable works include the films *Prem Rog* and *1942: A Love Story*. One of his sisters, Tanuja Chandra, is a filmmaker and screenwriter who has directed several films, including *Sur* and *Sangharsh*. His other sister, Anupama Chopra, is a film critic and consulting editor for India's NDTV.

Education

Chandra received his high school education at Mayo College in Ajmer, Rajasthan, and attended St. Xavier's College in Mumbai. As an undergraduate student, he transferred to the United States. He graduated from Pomona College in Claremont, California, with a magna cum laude B.A. in English (concentration in Creative Writing). Chandra then attended film school at Columbia University in New York, leaving halfway through to begin work on his first novel. He received his M.A. from The Writing Seminars at Johns Hopkins in 1987.

List of Works

- *Red Earth and Pouring Rain*, Chandra's first novel, was inspired by the autobiography of James Skinner, a legendary nineteenth century Anglo-Indian soldier. The novel was written over several years at the writing programmes at Johns Hopkins University and the University of Houston. It was published in 1995 by Penguin Books in India; by Faber and Faber in the UK; and by Little, Brown in the United States. *Red Earth and Pouring Rain* received outstanding critical acclaim, and it won both the Commonwealth Writers Prize for Best First Book and the David Higham Prize for Fiction. The novel is named after a poem from the *Kuruntokai*, an anthology of Classical Tamil love poems.
- *Love and Longing in Bombay*, a collection of short stories, was published in 1997 by the same publishers as *Red Earth and Pouring Rain*. This collection of stories won the Commonwealth Writers Prize for Best Book (Eurasia region), was short-listed for the Guardian Fiction Prize, and was well received by international press and media.
- In 2000, Vikram served as co-writer, with Suketu Mehta, for *Mission Kashmir*, a Bollywood movie directed by his brother-in-law, the award-winning director Vidhu Vinod Chopra, and starring Hrithik Roshan.
- *Sacred Games*, Vikram Chandra's most recent novel, was published in 2006. Set in a sprawling Mumbai, it features Sartaj Singh, a policeman who first appeared in *Love and Longing in Bombay*. Over 900 pages long, *Sacred Games* was one of the year's most anticipated new novels and was the subject of a bidding war amongst the leading publishers in India, the UK, and the US.

RIMI B. CHATTERJEE

Rimi B. Chatterjee is an author based in Kolkata (earlier Calcutta), India. She was born in Belfast in 1969, grew up in England, and later came to live in India. She studied at Jadavpur University, Kolkata and at Oxford University, where she did a D.Phil. in the area of book history titled 'A History of the Trade to South Asia of Macmillan and Company and Oxford University Press, 1875-1900'.

Biography

Rimi B. Chatterjee got her D.Phil in 1997 and returned to India. She began working in 1998 as an editor with Bhatkal and Sen, a small publishing house which produces scholarly titles in English and Bengali in the social sciences and in gender studies under the imprints 'Samya' and 'Stree'. There she oversaw authors like Kancha Ilaiah, Bani Basu and Gail Omvedt. She contributed to the process of translating into English, several important works by women such as Sulekha Sanyal's *Nabankur* (*The Seedling*), Manikuntala Sen's *Shediner Kotha* (*In Search of Freedom*) and Jyotirmoyee Devi's *The Impermanence of Lies*. She also published a translation of *Titu MIr*, a novella by Mahasweta Devi for Seagull Books, Kolkata, which was shortlisted for the 2001 Crossword Book Award for translation.

She began her career as an academic at the Indian Institute of Technology Kharagpur in 2000, then moved to the Centre for Studies in Social Sciences, Calcutta, where she was a fellow from 2003 to 2004. Much of the writing of her history of Oxford University Press was done there. She also published a translation of Abanindranath Tagore's autobiography *Apon Katha* (as *Apon Katha: My Story*) in 2004. The following year her novel *Signal Red* appeared. She now teaches English at Jadavpur University.

Books

Histories: While in the UK she gathered material from various archives on the histories of Macmillan and Oxford University Press and their relationship with India, Pakistan,

Bangladesh and Burma covering the period up to 1947. The data on Oxford University Press is mostly hitherto unpublished archival material from confidential records generated by the Press. Her book *Empires of the Mind: A History of the Oxford University Press in India During the Raj* is the first in-depth account of a large-scale European publisher interacting with Indian markets and authors, and raises several significant questions about the nature of the colonial encounter in India though the medium of print, particularly in the later stages of British Rule.

For instance, in the case of Oxford University Press, its status as an academic press that had supported several key Indological publishing ventures in the mid-nineteenth century gave it a cachet in the eyes of Indians that other presses could not have, and it was seen as pro-India as a result. At the same time its self-imposed custodianship of Indological study was questioned, not just by nationalist groups but also by many of its own authors. Furthermore, Oxford University Press often tried to tone down the imperialism of key authors such as Vincent Smith. These findings go against more 'hegemonic' readings of Indian encounters with print, by scholars such as Gauri Vishwanathan .

Empires of the Mind won the SHARP deLong Prize for 2007, an international academic prize awarded annually by the Society for the History of Authorship, Reading and Publishing for outstanding work in the history of the book.

A second history, tracing the very different interactions of Macmillan and Company with Indian cultures of print, is on the way. This is based likewise on unpublished material from the Macmillan archives and will deal with the genesis and reception of iconic series such as Pyari Charan Sarkar's Books of Reading, which helped teach a whole generation of Bengalis how to read English.

Novels and Stories

The City of Love is a historical novel set against the spice trade in sixteenth century India ten years after Vasco da Gama's landfall at Calicut in 1498. The story begins in 1510 with the fall of Malaka to the Portuguese under Afonso de Albuquerque and ends in 1540 with Sher Shah Suri's capture of Bengal. Much of the action takes place in and near Chittagong and Gaur. The four main characters are Fernando Almenara, a Spanish spice trader who is forced to join a pirate ship, Daud Suleiman ibn Majid Al Basri, a pirate turned politician, Chandu, the son of a Shaivite priest who becomes by a twist of fate a Sufi qawwal, and Bajja, a tribal girl who becomes a spiritual leader and eventually turns her back on the world. Other minor characters include a Sufi pir and a Tantric wise woman, Dhumavati. All the characters are in search of the City of Love, which is similar to the concept of Prem Nagar in Baul and Vaishnav thought and the Ashqabad of the Sufis.

Signal Red is a science fiction novel set in the near future in a world where totalitarian Hindutva-style politics has gained control of India. It is about an Indian defence scientist working in a semi-secret state laboratory, who gradually discovers that his work is being used to develop highly unethical weapons. At first he tries to ignore the ethical implications of what he does, but eventually starts to question his bosses and go against the rules. He then discovers the extent of the rot in the system that controls him, and his own weapons are turned against him.

A short story, 'The Key to All the Worlds', appeared in *Superhero: The Fabulous Adventures of Rocket Kumar and Other Indian Superheroes*, published by Scholastic India in 2007.[ISBN 81-7655-821-4]

UPAMANYU CHATTERJEE

Upamanyu Chatterjee (born 1959) is an Indian author and administrator, notable for his work set in the milieu of the Indian Administrative Service, especially his novel English August.

Born in Patna, Bihar, Chatterjee was educated at St. Xavier's School and St. Stephen's College, in Delhi. He joined the Indian Administrative Service in 1983.

Following the success of his first novel, he lived as Writer in Residence at the University of Kent for the academic year that started in 1990. In 1998, he was appointed Director (Languages) in the Ministry of Human Resource Development of the Government of India.

Chatterjee has written a handful of short stories of which "The Assassination of Indira Gandhi" and "Watching Them" are particularly noteworthy. His best-selling novel, *English, August: An Indian story* (subsequently made into a major film), was published in 1988 and has since been reprinted several times. A review in Punch described the book as *"Beautifully written ... English, August is a marvelously intelligent and entertaining novel, and especially for anyone curious about modern India"*. The novel follows Agastya Sen-a young westernized Indian civil servant whose imagination is dominated by women, literature and soft drugs. This vivid account of "real India" by the young officer posted to the small provincial town of Madna is "a funny, wryly observed account of Agastya Sen's year in the sticks", as described by a reviewer in the Observer. His second novel, *The Last Burden*, appeared in 1993. This novel recreates life in an Indian family at the end of the twentieth century. *The Mammaries of the Welfare State* was published at the end of 2000 as a sequel to *English, August.* His latest novel, Weight Loss, a dark comedy, was published in 2006.

Anjana Sharma equates Upamanyu's vision of humanity with W.B. Yeats. She writes, "Eighty years apart, cultures, civilisations, even craft and temperament apart, Yeats and Chatterjee share an identical vision of a de-centred, de-natured world." Dr. Mukul Dikshit opines that Chatterjee has, for the first time, focussed on a "new class" of Westernised Urban Indians that was hitherto ignored in the Regional as well as the English Fiction of India. He declares that Chatterjee's imagination is as fertile as Kafka's; his tragic sense is as keen as Camus's; his understanding of the absurd-comic (farce) in life is at par with Milan Kundera and Saul Bellow.

BANKIM CHANDRA CHATTOPADHYAY

Bankim Chandra Chatterjee (27 June 1838-8 April 1894) ('Chattopadhyay' in the original Bengali; 'Chatterjee' as spelt by the British) was a Bengali poet, novelist, essayist and journalist, most famous as the author of Vande Mataram or Bande Mataram, that inspired the freedom fighters of India, and was later declared the National Song of India.

Life

Chattopadhyay was born in the village Kanthalpura in Naihati, the youngest of three brothers, to Yadav (or Jadab) Chandra Chattopadhyaya and Durgadebi. His family was orthodox, and his father, a government official who went on to become the Deputy Collector of Midnapur. One of his brothers, Sanjeeb Chandra Chatterjee, was also a novelist and his known for his famous book "Palamau". He was educated at the Mohsin College in Hooghly and later at the Presidency College, graduating with a degree in Arts in 1857. He was one of the first two graduates of the University of Calcutta. He later obtained a degree in Law as well, in 1869.

Appointed Deputy Collector, like his father, of Jessore, Chatterjee went on to become a Deputy Magistrate, retiring from government service in 1891. His years at work were peppered with incidents that brought him into conflict with the ruling British of the time. However, he was made a Companion, Order of the Indian Empire in 1894.

Married at the young age of eleven, his first wife died in 1859. He later married Rajalakshmi Devi. They had three daughters.

Literature

Chatterjee, following the model of Ishwarchandra Gupta, began his literary career as a writer of verse. He soon realized, however, that his talents lay in other directions, and turned to fiction. His first attempt was a novel in Bengali submitted for a declared prize. He did not win the prize, and the novelette was never published. His first fiction to appear in print was *Rajmohan's Wife*. It was written in English and was probably a translation of the novelette submitted for the prize. *Durgeshnondini*, his first Bengali romance and the first ever novel in Bengali, was published in 1865.

Kapalkundala (1866) is Chatterjee's first major publication. The heroine of this novel, named after the mendicant woman in Bhavabhuti's *Malatimadhava*, is modelled partly after Kalidasa's Shakuntala and partly after Shakespeare's *Miranda*. He had chosen Dariapur in Contai Subdivision as the background of this famous novel.

His next romance, *Mrinalini* (1869), marks his first attempt to set his story against a larger historical context. This book marks the shift from Chatterjee's early career, in which he was strictly a writer of romances, to a later period in which he aimed to simulate the intellect of the Bengali speaking people and bring about a cultural revival through a campaign to improve Bengali literature. He began publishing a monthly literary magazine *Bangodarshan* in April 1872, the first edition of which was filled almost entirely with his own work. The magazine carried serialized novels, stories, humorous sketches, historical and miscellaneous essays, informative articles, religious discourses, literary criticisms and reviews. *Vishabriksha* (The Poison Tree, 1873) the first novel of Chatterjee's to appear serially in *Bangodarshan*.

Bangodarshan went out of circulation after 4 years. It was later revived by his brother, Sanjeeb Chandra Chatterjee.

Chatterjee's next major novel was *Chandrasekhar* (1877), which contains two largely unrelated parallel plots. Although the scene is once shifted back to eighteenth century, the novel is not historical. His next novel, *Rajani* (1877), followed the autobiographical technique of Wilkie Collins' "A Woman in White". The title role, a blind girl, was modelled after Edward Bulwer-Lytton's Nydia in "The Last Days of Pompeii". In *Krishnakanter Uil* (Krishnakanta's Will, 1878) Chatterjee produced the work of his that comes closest to resembling a western novel. The plot is somewhat akin to that of Poison Tree.

The only novel of Chatterjee's that can truly be considered historical fiction is *Rajsimha* (1881, rewritten and enlarged 1893). *Anandamath* (The mission house of Felicity, 1882) is a political novel which depicts a Sannyasi (Brahmin ascetic) army fighting Indian Muslims who are in the employ of the East India Company. The book calls for the rise of Brahmin/Hindu nationalism but, ironically, concludes with a character accepting British Empire as a necessity. The novel was also the source of the song "Vande Mataram" (I worship the Mother) which, set to music by Rabindranath Tagore, was taken up by many secular nationalists. The novel is loosely based on the time of the Sannyasi Rebellion, however in the actual rebellion, Hindus sannyasis and Muslim fakirs both rebelled against the British East India Company. The novel first appeared in serial form in *Bangadarshan*.

Chatterjee's next novel, *Devi Chaudhurani*, was published in 1884. His final novel, *Sitaram* (1886), tells the story of a Hindu chief rebelling against Muslim rule.

Chatterjee's humorous sketches are his best known works other than his novels. *Kamalakanter Daptar* (From the Desk of Kamalakanta, 1875; enlarged as *Kamalakanta*, 1885) contains half humorous and half serious sketches, somewhat on the model of De Quincey's Confessions of an English Opium-Eater.

Some critics, like Pramathnath Bishi, consider Chatterjee as the best novelist in Bangla literature. They believe that few writers in world literature have excelled in both philosophy and art as Bankim has done. They argue that in a colonised nation Bankim could not overlook politics. He was one of the first intellectuals who wrote in a British colony, accepting and rejecting the status at the same time. Bishi also rejects the division of Bankim in 'Bankim the artist' and 'Bankim the moralist'-for Bankim must be read as a whole. The artist in Bankim cannot be understood unless you understand him as a moralist and vice versa.

Trivia

- Ramakrishna Paramahamsa and Chatterjee were good friends, and both enjoyed humour. Once, the former, playing on the meaning of Bankim (Either *Bright Side of the Moon* or *A Little Bent*), asked him what it was that had bent him. Chatterjee replied that it was the kick from the Englishman's shoe.

- After the *Vishabriksha* (*The Poison Tree*) was published in 1873, The Times of London observed:

  "Have you read the Poison Tree of Bankim Chandra Chatterjee?"
- When Bipin Chandra Pal decided to start a patriotic journal in August 1906, he named it Bande Mataram, after Chatterjee's song. Lala Lajpat Rai also published a journal of the same name.

Bibliography

Fiction

- *Durgeshnondini* (March 1865)
- *Kapalkundala* (1866)
- *Mrinalini* (1869)
- *Vishabriksha* (The Poison Tree, 1873)
- *Indira* (1873, revised 1893)
- *Jugalanguriya* (1874)
- *Radharani* (1876, enlarged 1893)
- *Chandrasekhar* (1877)
- *Kamalakanter Daptar* (From the Desk of Kamlakanta, 1875)
- *Rajni* (1877)
- *Krishnakanter Uil* (Krishnakanta's Will, 1878)
- *Rajsimha* (1882)
- *Anandamath* (1882)
- *Devi Chaudhurani* (1884)
- *Kamalakanta* (1885)
- *Sitaram* (March 1887)
- *Muchiram Gurer Jivancharita* (The Life of Muchiram Gur)

Religious Commentaries

- *Krishna Charitra* (History of Krishna, 1886)
- *Dharmatattva* (Principles of Religion, 1888)

- *Devatattva* (Principles of Divinity, Published Posthumously)
- *Srimadvagavat Gita*, a Commentary on the Bhagavad Gita (1902-Published Posthumously)

Poetry Collections

- *Lalita O Manas* (1858)

Essays

- *Lok Rahasya* (Essays on Society, 1874, enlarged 1888)
- *Bijnan Rahasya* (Essays on Science, 1875)
- *Bichitra Prabandha* (Assorted Essays), Vol 1 (1876) and Vol 2 (1892)
- *Samya* (Equality, 1879)

SANJEEV CHATTOPADHYAY

Sanjeev Chattopadhyay (born February 28, 1936 in Kolkata, India) is a fiction writer.

Sanjeev Chattopadhyay is best known and read for his witty and humorous fiction. During the 1970s and 1980s, he was the most widely read Bengali author. His style is easily recognized by his use of short satirical sentences mixed with frequent English words and very lively language.

Education

He studied chemistry at the Scottish Church College, Calcutta .

Body of Work

The plots of his fiction, set amidst Calcutta families, endeared him to the readers. Within the confines of these homes, he challenges the moral values of the fast-changing Calcutta middle class. Chattopadhyay frequently uses old men as his protagonists. These aged characters create the spiritual and philosophical edge found in his memorable novels *Lotakambala* (The Blanket and Quilt) and *Shakha Prasakha* (Branches). His most famous novella *Svetapatharera tebila* (The Ivory Table) is an example of his characteristic style of story-telling which mixes tension, dilemma, curiosity, pity, humor, and satire. He has written fiction for children and continues to write for magazines and newspapers.

SHARAT CHANDRA CHATTERJI

Sharat Chandra Chatterji, also known as Sarat Chandra Chattopadhyay or Sharat Chandra Chatterjee (15 September 1876-16 January 1938) was an author from India. He was one of the the most popular Bengali novelists of early part of the 20th century.

Background and Writing

Swagato Ganguly (2005) and Sreejata Guha (2002) both note that Sarat Chandra was born into poverty in Debanandapur, Hooghly, India. Though his family was occasionally supported by other family members, Saratchandra's lack of financial stability would influence his writing in years to come. Although he began as a fine arts student, Chatterji left his studies due to his persistent state of poverty. He got his early education residing at his paternal uncle's (Pishemosai) house.

His work represented rural Bengali society and he often wrote against social superstitions and oppression. For a short period, he was a *sannyasi*, a Hindu ascetic who abandons the material and social worlds. His first published story was, 'Mandir'.

He died in Kolkata of liver cancer in 1938.

Works

- *Baradidi*, 1907
- *Bindur Chhele*, 1913
- *Parinita/Parineeta*, 1914
- *Biraj Bou*, 1914
- *Ramer Shumoti*, 1914
- *Palli Shomaj*, 1916
- *Arakhsanya*, 1916

- *Debdas/Devdas*, 1917 (written in 1901)
- *Choritrohin*, 1917
- *Srikanto*, (4 parts, 1917, 1918, 1927, 1933)
- *Datta*, 1917-19
- *Grihodaho*, 1919
- *Dena Paona*, 1923
- *Pather Dabi*, 1926
- *Ses Prasna*, 1931.

Films

His works have been made into numerous films, particularly *Devdas* and *Parineeta*.

Select Awards and Degrees

- Kuntolin (For Mandir)
- D-Lit (Given by University of Dhaka, now in Bangladesh)

General

- Ganguly, Swagato. "Introduction." In *Parineeta* by Saratchandra Chattopadhyay. New Delhi: Penguin Books, 2005. (English translation)
- Guha, Sreejata. "Introduction." In *Devdas* by Saratchandra Chattopadhyay. New Delhi: Penguin Books, 2002. (English translation)
- Roy, Gopalchandra. *Saratchandra*, Ananda Publishers Pvt. Ltd., Kolkata
- *Sarat Rachanabali*, Ananda Publishers Pvt. Ltd., Kolkata
- Prithwindra Mukherjee. "Introduction" in *Mahesh et autres nouvelles* by Saratchandra Chatterji. Paris: Unesco/Gallimard, 1978. (French translation of *Mahesh*, *Bindur chhele* and *Mejdidi* by Prithwindra Mukherjee. Foreword by Jean Filliozat)

Textbooks

- *Golpo Songroho* (Collected Stories), the national text book of B.A. (pass and subsidiary) course of Bangladesh, published by University of Dhaka in 1979 (reprint in 1986).

- *Bangla Sahitya* (Bengali Literature), the national text book of intermediate (college) level of Bangladesh published in 1996 by all educational boards.

AMIT CHAUDHURI

Amit Chaudhuri (born 1962) is an internationally recognised Indian English author.

Life

Amit Chaudhuri was born in Calcutta and grew up in Bombay. He has written numerous novels, short stories, poems and critical essays in English, but is probably best known for his book *Freedom Song*. He attended University College London, Balliol College, Oxford and has also been a writer-in-residence at Wolfson College.

His novels have won several major awards and he has received international critical acclaim. His latest book is a collection of poems entitled *St. Cyril Road and Other Poems*, and in 2004 he edited *The Vintage Book of Modern Indian Literature*.

Amit Chaudhuri is also an acclaimed Indian classical musician. He is currently a creative writing tutor at the University of East Anglia.

On March 18, 2008, he was included in the panel for the Man Booker International Prize 2009, alongside writer Jane Smiley and essayist Andrey Kurkov.

Awards

- 1991 Betty Trask Award and Commonwealth Writers Prize for Best First Book for *A Strange and Sublime Address*
- 1994 Encore Award for *Afternoon Raag*
- 2000 Los Angeles Times Book Prize for *A New World*
- 2002 Sahitya Akademi Award for *A New World*

Works

Novels

- *A Strange and Sublime Address* (1991)
- *Afternoon Raag* (1993)
- *Freedom Song* (Picador, 1998) excerpt
- *A New World* (Picador, 2000)

Short Stories

- *Real Time: Stories and a reminiscence* (2002)

Poetry

- *St. Cyril Road and Other Poems* (Penguin, 2005)

Non-fiction

- *D. H. Lawrence and 'Difference': Postcoloniality and the Poetry of the Present* (Oxford, 2003)
- *Small Orange Flags* (Seagull, 2003) reviwed

RICHARD CRASTA

Richard Crasta, born in Bangalore, India, is an Indian writer who grew up in Mangalore, has lived in the United States for twenty years, mostly in the New York metropolitan region, and now spends much of his time in Asia. His works include the comic and frankly sexual coming of age novel *The Revised Kamasutra* (published in seven languages and ten countries to date) and nonfiction and essay collections like *Impressing the Whites*; *Beauty Queens, Children and the Death of Sex* the semi-fictional *What We All Need*, and *The Killing of an Author*.

He is known for his fierce anti-establishment style and his humour; a short sampler of his work was titled *The Unauthorized India* Kurt Vonnegut, who was mentioned in the dedication to the American edition of his novel, described his novel as "very funny."

Works

- The Revised Kamasutra: A Novel of Colonialism and Desire

- Impressing the Whites: The New International Slavery
- Beauty Queens, Children and the Death of Sex
- What We All Need: An Anti-Terrorist Book of Incompletions, Unsafe Love, and Writing While Brown
- Fathers, Rebels and Dreamers
- The Killing of an Author: Jackie Kennedy, Sonny Pfizer, Seven Little Ayatollahs and a Suicide Pact (formal launch April 2008)

RANA DASGUPTA

Rana Dasgupta (born November 5, 1971 in Canterbury, England) is a British-Indian writer. He grew up in Cambridge, England and studied at Balliol College, Oxford, the Conservatoire Darius Milhaud in Aix-en-Provence, and the University of Wisconsin-Madison. He lives in Delhi, India.

His first novel, *Tokyo Cancelled* (2005), was an examination of the forces and experiences of globalization. Billed as a modern-day *Canterbury Tales*, thirteen passengers stuck overnight in an airport tell thirteen stories from different cities in the world, stories that resemble contemporary fairytales, mythic and surreal.

The tales add up to a broad exploration of 21st century forms of life, which includes billionaires, film stars, migrant labourers, illegal immigrants and sailors. *Tokyo Cancelled* was shortlisted for the 2005 John Llewellyn Rhys Prize.

Dasgupta's upcoming novel, *Solo*, set primarily in Bulgaria, will appear in spring 2009.

DAVID DAVIDAR

David Davidar is an author and publisher. He was educated at Madras (now Chennai) and Harvard University (where he obtained a diploma in publishing). In 1985, while still in his mid-twenties, he became one of the founding members of Penguin in India, where he edited or published authors like Kiran Desai, Arundhati Roy, Vikram Seth, Vikram Chandra, Rohinton Mistry, Salman Rushdie, Upamanyu Chatterjee,

Khushwant Singh, R.K. Narayan, Shobhaa De, Romila Thapar, Shashi Tharoor, Suketu Mehta, William Dalrymple, Mohsin Hamid and Ramachandra Guha.

In 2004 he was transferred to Penguin Books in Canada, where the authors he publishes include Philip Roth, Khaled Hosseini, John le Carre, Alice Munro (in paperback), Stuart McLean, Margaret Macmillan, Joseph Boyden, Zadie Smith, Hisham Matar, Adrienne Clarkson, Michael Ignatieff and John Ralston Saul. In the 1980s, he worked for such magazines as Gentleman, GFQ, TV & Video World, Technocrat & Business Computer.

Davidar is the author of the novel *The House of Blue Mangoes*, which was published in 2002. It was translated into 16 languages and was a New York Times Notable Book and a Book Sense Pick. His new novel, *The Solitude of Emperors*, was launched in September 2007. His wife, Rachna, was recently hired to manage the forthcoming Toronto location of the Winnipeg-based bookstore chain McNally Robinson.

ABHA DAWESAR

Abha Dawesar (born January 1, 1974) is an Indian novelist writing in English. Dawesar is a Harvard graduate and lives in New York.

Novels

- *Miniplanner* (2000) (published in India by Penguin Books under the title *The Three of Us*)
- *Babyji* (2005) (winner of the Stonewall Book Award and Lambda Literary Award, 2006)
- *That Summer in Paris* (2006)

SWADESH DEEPAK

Swadesh Deepak (1942-) is a popular Indian playwright, novelist and short-story writer. Deepak has been active on the Hindi literary scene since the mid 1960s and is best known for *Court Martial,* a pathbreaking play that he published in 1991. Deepak's most recent book is *Maine Mandu Nahin Dekha,* a volume of memoirs. Deepak's work has appeared in all major literary periodicals of India, and he has more than 15 published titles to his credit. Several of his works have been staged and made into television programmes.

Deepak holds masters degrees in both Hindi and English. For twenty-six years, he taught English literature at Ambala's Gandhi Memorial College.

Writings

Swadesh Deepak found his literary expression first as a short story writer and then as a novelist and playwright. He has experimented with many forms of prose, and is well-known for his unique style.

Short Stories

The first collection of stories that Deepak published in the 1973 was *Ashwarohi* (The Rider), which marks the birth of his grim, dark storytelling style on the literary scene. Over the next few years, Deepak wrote some of his most popular stories—*Aheri, Mara Hua Pakshi, Maatam, Jaihind, Kyunki Main Use Jaanta Nahin, Kisi Ek Ped Ka Naam Lo, Kyunki Hawa Padh Nahin Sakti, Tamaasha* and *Paapi Pet*, to name just a few. Deepak also published two novels in Hindi, *Number 57 Squadron* and *Mayapot* (The Phantom Ship). The latter evoked mixed response from readers and critics. A collection of the finest stories of Swadesh Deepak, titled *Pratinidhi Kahaniyan* (Representative Stories) was published in the mid 1980s.

Plays

Swadesh Deepak was widely recognized as one of the finest playwrights in the country after the publication of *Court Martial*. The play hits hard the roots of casteism in the Indian Army. *Court Martial* has been staged close to 2000 times in India by well-known Indian theatre directors Ranjeet Kapoor, Arvind Gaur and Usha Ganguli. It has been translated into many Indian languages and has won Deepak many an award. Deepak regards *Court Martial* as his best-known work, but not the best. His other prominent plays include *Sabse Udaas Kavita* directed by Arvind Gaur (premiered by the Asmita Theatre group), *Jalta Hua Rath* (The Chariot in Flames) and Kal Kothari (first directed by Arvind Gaur—Asmita Theatre).

Reviews

- "Tight pace of Court Martial... not to be missed."-Kavita Nagpal (Hindustan Times)
- "Arvind Gaur's hard hitting realism... his intelligent approach... strong play by Swadesh Deepak."-Aruna Ahluwalia (E. News)
- "Kudos to Court Martial... a drama that goes beyond the limits of drama."-(The Indian Express)
- "The Asmita team has created a marvelous piece of theatre out of a wonderful script... don't miss it. The time spent watching the play is well worth it."-Smita Nirula (The Pioneer)
- "Stealing the scene with revolt as the theme... Court Martial is an engrossing display of theatre for social awareness."-Sushama Chadha (The Times of India)
- "Excellent acting, live and memorable... worth a see."-Ajeet Rai (Nav Bharat Times)
- "Excellent Performance by Deepak Dobrial as Captain Vikash Roy... Swadesh Deepak's brilliant script... memorable production by the Asmita team."-Romesh Chandra (The Hindu)

Memoirs

In the early 1990s, Deepak showed severe symptoms of Bipolar disorder, a condition that was diagnosed only a couple of suicide attempts and many frightful months later. He was under medication for a long time, and took many years to recover.

Around 2001, he began documenting those fateful years spent *in the darkroom of his mind.* These memoirs were first serialized in *Kathadesh*, a leading Hindi monthly, and later published as a book, *Maine Mandu Nahin Dekha* (Rajkamal Prakashan). Deepak's memoirs triggered widespread debate—

both for their innovative form, and their depiction of the way in which mental illness is perceived in India. The book won Deepak as many admirers as foes, with many putting even the suffering behind the book under the scanner.

Despite the volley of sharp-edged comments that it ensued, *Maine Maandu Nahin Dekha* is a work unlike any other published in recent times. It is special because it is a grotesque first-hand account of how this disorder destroys logic in a systematic fashion. And it is Deepak's precise, bare-bones language—almost poetical in most portions—that lends authenticity to the text.

The Loaded Gun

Deepak's works are characterized by their tragic, dark endings. His characters find death as a constant companion, and often succumb to it. Often, critics have suggested that Deepak walks alongside his characters with a loaded gun—recoiled and ready to fire. Maybe, one can trace the beginnings of Deepak's present mental ordeal to the dark stories that he was writing even in the early 1970s. Perhaps, it is no coincidence that Deepak's favourite authors are Sylvia Plath and Virginia Woolf, who succumbed to mental agony themselves.

The Return of the Storyteller

After a self-proclaimed abstinence from writing short stories lasting many years, Deepak returned to the form in the early 2000s. Some of his stories written during the period carry the echo of *Maine Mandu Nahin Dekha*. *Bagugoshe* was a fine story that he published a few years back.

Awards and Honours

Swadesh Deepak has won many awards for his powerful writings. Recently, he won the *Sur Puraskar,* the highest literary award conferred by the Government of Haryana, the state of his residence. He participated in the World Hindi Conference organized in Suriname. Deepak is one of the few playwrights to win the *Sangeet Natak Akademi Award,* the most prestigious award conferred to a performing artist in India. He is, undoubtedly, the best-known writer that Haryana has produced, and one of finest in his generation.

Tragic Developments

In early 2006, Deepak showed symptoms of acute depression related to Bipolar disorder. He had suffered a cardiac attack in 2004, but had shown considerable improvement eversince. On June 2 2006, Deepak left home for his routine morning walk, and went missing. All attempts to trace him have shown little results.

ANITA DESAI

Anita Mazumdar Desai (born June 24, 1937) is an Indian novelist and Emeritus John E. Burchard Professor of Humanities at the Massachusetts Institute of Technology. She has been shortlisted for the Booker prize three times. Her daughter, the author Kiran Desai, is the winner of the 2006 Booker prize.

Background

Born as Anita Mazumdar to a German mother, Toni Nime, and a Bengali businessman, D. N. Mazumdar in Mussoorie, India. She grew up speaking German at home and Bengali, Urdu, Hindi and English outside the house. She first learned to read and write in English at school and as a result it became her "literary language". Despite German being her first language she did not visit Germany until later in life as an adult. She was a student at Queen Mary's Higher Secondary School in Delhi and received her B.A. in English literature in 1957 from the University of Delhi Miranda House. The following year she married Ashvin Desai, a businessman. They raised four children. Daughter Kiran was born in Chandigarh and spent her childhood years in Bombay, on Alatamont Road. She recalls that as children they were taken to Thal (near Alibaug) for weekends, and this is where Anita Desai set her novel *Village by the Sea*.

Career

She published her first novel in 1963, *Cry The Peacock*. She considers *Clear Light Of Day* (1980) her most autobiographical work as it is set during her coming of age and also in the same neighbourhood in which she grew up. In 1984 she published *In Custody*-about an Urdu poet in his declining days-which was shortlisted for the Booker Prize. In 1993 she became a creative writing teacher at Massachusetts Institute of Technology). Her latest novel published in 2004, *The Zigzag Way*, is set in 20th-century Mexico.

Desai has taught at Mount Holyoke College and Smith College. She is a Fellow of the Royal Society of Literature, the American Academy of Arts and Letters, and of Girton College, Cambridge University.

Film

In 1993 Merchant Ivory Productions released *In Custody*, directed by Ismail Merchant, with a screenplay by Shahrukh Husain. It won the 1994 President of India Gold Medal for Best Picture and stars the noted actors Shashi Kapoor, Shabana Azmi and Om Puri.

Awards

- 1978-National Academy of Letters Award-*Fire on the Mountain*
- 1978-Winifred Holtby Memorial Prize-*Fire on the Mountain*
- 1980-Shortlisted, Booker Prize for Fiction-*Clear Light of Day*
- 1983-Guardian Children's Fiction Prize-*The Village By The Sea*
- 1984-Shortlisted, Booker Prize for Fiction-*In Custody*
- 1993-Neil Gunn Prize
- 1999-Shortlisted, Booker Prize for Fiction:

Fasting, Feasting

- 2000-Alberto Moravia Prize for Literature (Italy)

Selected Works

- *The Zigzag Way* (2004)

- *Diamond Dust and Other Stories* (2000)
- *Fasting, Feasting* (1999)
- *Journey to Ithaca* (1995)
- *Baumgartner's Bombay* (1988)
- *In Custody* (1984)
- *The Village By The Sea* (1982)
- *Clear Light of Day* (1980)
- *Games at Twilight* (1978)
- *Fire on the Mountain* (1977)
- *Cry, The Peacock* (1963)

KIRAN DESAI

Kiran Desai (born 3 September 1971) is an Indian author who is a citizen of India and a Permanent Resident of the United States. Her novel *The Inheritance of Loss* won the 2006 Man Booker Prize and the National Book Critics Circle Fiction Award. She is the daughter of the noted author Anita Desai.

Early Life and Education

Kiran Desai was born in New Delhi, India, and lived there until she was 14. She and her mother then lived in England for a year, and finally moved to the United States where she studied creative writing at Bennington College, Hollins University and Columbia University.

Awards and Recognition

Her first novel, *Hullabaloo in the Guava Orchard*, was published in 1998 and received accolades from such notable figures as Salman Rushdie. It went on to win the Betty Trask Award, a prize given by the Society of Authors for the best new novels by citizens of the Commonwealth of Nations under the age of 35.

Her second book, *The Inheritance of Loss*, (2006) has been widely praised by critics throughout Asia, Europe and the United States and won the 2006 Man Booker Prize as well as the 2006 National Book Critics Circle Fiction Award.

In September 2007 she was a guest on *Private Passions*, the biographical music discussion programme hosted by Michael Berkeley on BBC Radio 3.

Bibliography

- *Hullabaloo in the Guava Orchard*, Faber and Faber
- *The Inheritance of Loss*

SHASHI DESHPANDE

Shashi Deshpande (b.1938), is an award-winning Indian novelist. She is the second daughter of famous Kannada dramatist and writer Shriranga. She was born in Karnataka and educated in Bombay (now Mumbai) and Bangalore. Deshpande has degrees in Economics and Law. When she was living in Mumbai she did a course on journalism at the Bharatiya Vidya Bhavan and worked for a couple of months as a journalist for the magazine 'Onlooker' . She published her first collection of short stories in 1978, and her first novel, 'The Dark Holds No Terror', in 1980. She is a winner of the Sahitya Akademi Award for the novel 'That Long Silence'. Her works also include children's books. Till date, Shashi Deshpande has worked on four children's books and six novels, besides several perceptive essays, now available in a volume entitled 'Writing from the Margin & Other Essays'.

Books

Her books include:

- *The Binding Vine*
- *Matter of Time*
- *That Long Silence*

NABANEETA DEV SEN

Nabaneeta Dev Sen (Bengali: *Nôbonita Deb Shen*) (b.1938) is a Bengali writer from India.

Early Life

Sen was born in Calcutta, to the poet-couple Narendra Dev and Radharani Devi. She graduated from Presidency College and took her M.A. from Jadavpur University, Calcutta, A.M with Distinction from Harvard University and Ph. D from Indiana University. She did post-doctoral research at the University of California at Berkeley, USA, at Newnham College, Cambridge University, UK, and was UGC Senior Fellow at Delhi University. Besides Bengali and English she reads several languages-Hindi, Oriya, Assamese, French, German, Sanskrit, Hebrew, etc.-and has recently retired as Professor of Comparative Literature at Jadavpur University, Calcutta. She has been working with the treatment of women in the world epics and the treatment of epic poetry by rural women in India. She has just been nominated as the JP Naik Distinguished Fellow at the Centre of Women's Development Studies, New Delhi, 2003-2005, where she is translating Chandrabati's sixteenth century Bengali Ramayana text into English with a critical introduction and annotations.

Career

Nabaneeta has been a writer in residence at several international Artists' Colonies such as Yaddo and MacDowell Colony in the USA, Bellaggio in Italy, and the Mishkenot Sha'ananim in Jerusalem. She has been a visiting professor, and a visiting creative writer at different times at several universities in the USA (Harvard, Cornell, Rutgers, Columbia, Smith College, Chicago, etc), Canada (Toronto, York, British Columbia), Mexico, England, Germany, France and Japan. She has delivered the Radhakrishnan Memorial Lecture series (1996-97) at Oxford University on epic poetry.

She has held the Maytag Chair of Creative Writing and Comparative Literature at Colorado College 1988-89, and represented herself and her country in many international conferences, both academic and literary, including the Festival of India USA 1986, the Frankfurt Book Fair 1993 and the Munich Book Week 2002. She has held important executive positions in International academic bodies like the International Comparative Literature Association (1973-79), and The International Association of Semiotic and Structural Studies (1989-94), been the Vice President of Indian National

Comparative Literature Association, Chief editor of Bengali in the Macmillan's Modern Indian Novel Series, Member of the Jury of important literary awards like the Jnanpith, Saraswati Samman, Kabir Samman, Rabindra Puraskar etc. She is now the Vice President of the Bangiya Sahitya Parishat.

She has received many National awards and Honours from all over India, including the Central Sahitya Akademi Award, the Mahadevi Verma Award, the Bharatiya Bhasha Parishad Award, the Harmony Award, and the President's award, Padmashri. Nabaneeta Dev Sen is the founder president of West Bengal Women Writers' Association "Soi" Nabaneeta lives in Kolkata, in her parental house Bhalo-Basa, where she was born, now declared a Heritage Building. She has two daughters Antara and Nandana, with former husband, economist Amartya Sen, and one adopted daughter, Srabasti.

Publications

Her first collection of poems, *Pratham Pratyay*, was published in 1959. In her novels, which often use women as the central characters, Sen deals with a wide variety of social, political, and psychological problems: the role of the intellectuals in the Naxalite movement (*Ami Anupam*,1976); the identity crisis of the Indian writing in English (1977); the identity crisis of second generation NRIs (*Swabhumi*, 1985); the breakdown of the joint family; life in *sheet sahasik hemantalok* (old age homes) (1988); homosexuality (*Bamabodhini*, 1995); facing AIDS (*Maya raye gelo* 1999, *Ural* 2002); *Albratos* (child abuse); obsession; uprootedness, immigration and exile. Her short stories and travelogues are a rare combination of fine humour, deep human concern, and high intellect, which has made her a unique figure in the Bangla literary scene.

Her first short story collection was *Monsieur Hulor Holiday* (1980). Travelogues like *Karuna tomar kon path diye*, *Truckbaahane Myakmahane* have become classics in Bengali literature and are getting translated into other Indian languages.. She is one of the most well-loved children's authors in Bangla, for her sensitive, beautiful fairy tales and adventure stories, where girls are the heroes. She has also written prize-winning one act plays. Her works have been anthologised in many languages within India and abroad.

Nabaneeta Dev Sen has published more than 80 books in Bengali: poetry, novels, short stories, plays, literary criticism, personal essays, travelogues, humour writing, translations and children's literature. Her first collection of poems "Pratham Pratyay" was published in 1959. Nabaneeta deals with a wide variety of social, political, psychological problems like the role of the intellectuals in the Naxalite movement, (Ami Anupam, 1976), identity crisis of the Indian writing in English (1977), that of the second generation NRIs (1985), breakdown of the joint family, life in old age homes (1988), homosexuality (1995), facing AIDS (1999,2002), child abuse, and obsession, uprootedness, immigration and exile in her novels, often using women as her central characters.

Her short stories and travelogues are a rare combination of fine humour, deep human concern, and high intellect, which has made her a unique figure in the Bangla literary scene. Her first short story collection was "Monsieur Hulor Holiday" (1980). Travelogues like "Karuna tomar kon path diye" and "Truckbaahane Myakmahane" have become classics in Bengali literature.

She is a well-known children's authors in Bengali for her fairy tales and adventure stories, where girls are the heroes. She also has written prize-winning one-act plays.

Recognition

She was a writer in residence at several international Artists' Colonies like Yaddo and MacDowell, in the USA, Bellaggio in Italy, the Mishkenot in Jerusalem.

She has been a visiting professor, and a visiting creative writer at different times at several universities of U.S. (Harvard, Cornell, Rutgers, Columbia, Smith College, Chicago, etc), the UK, Canada (Toronto, York, British Columbia), Mexico, Germany, France, and Japan. She delivered the Radhakrishnan Memorial Lecture series (1996-97) at Oxford University on epic poetry. She held the Maytag Chair of Creative Writing and

Comparative Literature at Colorado College 1988-89, represented herself and her country in many international conferences, both academic and literary, including the Festival of India USA 1986, the Frankfurt Book Fair 1993 and the Munich Book Week 2002.

She received many awards for her contribution in creative and academic writings including President's award Padmashree and Sahitya Academy.

Nabaneeta lives in Kolkata, in her parental house Bhalo-Basa, where she was born, now declared a Heritage Building. She has two daughters, Antara and Nandana, with former husband, Nobel Prize winning economist Amartya Sen, and one adopted daughter, Srabasti.

CHITRA BANERJEE DIVAKARUNI

Chitra Banerjee Divakaruni (1956-) is an Indian-American author, poet, and professor of English at The University of Houston Creative Writing Programme.

Background

Divakaruni was born Chitralekha Banerjee in Kolkata, India. She received her B.A. from the University of Calcutta in 1976. That same year, she went to the United States to attend Wright State University where she received her Master's degree. She received her Ph.D. from the University of California, Berkeley in 1985 (Christopher Marlowe was the subject of her doctoral dissertation).

Career

She has taught at Foothill College in Los Altos, California. She has also worked as a babysitter, a store clerk, a bread slicer, a dining hall attendant, and in laboratories. She now lives in Texas, where she teaches at The University of Houston Creative Writing Programme. Divakaruni is also a co-founder and former president of a helpline for South Asian women who are dealing with various forms of abuse from others. The organization, *Maitri*, was founded in 1991.

Works

Fiction: Divakaruni's work has been published in over 50 magazines, including The Atlantic Monthly, Harper's and The New Yorker and her writing has been included in over 30 anthologies. While many of her novels are written for adults, she has also written the first two books in a juvenile fantasy series called The Brotherhood of the Conch which, like many of her adult novels, takes place in India (as well as other parts of Asia and the Middle East) and draws on the culture and folklore of that region.

Her next work will be a re-telling of the Indian epic, *The Mahabharata* told from the female characters' perspective.

Film and Television

Her novel, *The Mistress of Spices*, was released as the film *The Mistress of Spices* in 2005. It is directed by Paul Mayeda Berges, with a script by Berges and his wife, Gurinder Chadha. The film stars Aishwarya Rai.

In addition, her novel *Sister of my Heart* was made into a television series in Tamil and aired in India, as *Anbulla Snegithiye (Loving Friend).*

Bibliography

- Fiction
  - *The Palace of Illusions: A Novel* (2008)
  - *The Mirror of Fire and Dreaming Book Two of the Brotherhood of the Conch* (2005)
  - *Queen of Dreams (novel)* (2004)
  - *The Conch Bearer (novel) Book One of the Brotherhood of the Conch* (2003)
  - *Neela: Victory Song (novel)* (2002)
  - *The Vine of Desire (novel)* (2002)
  - *The Unknown Errors of our Lives (novel)* (2001)
  - *Sister of My Heart (novel)* (1999)
  - *Leaving Yuba City (novel)* (1997)

  * *The Mistress of Spices* (1997)
  * *Arranged Marriage: Stories* (1995)
  * *Black Candle (novel)* (1991)
  * *The Reason for Nasturiums (novel)* (1990)
- Poetry
  * *Leaving Yuba City* (1997)
  * *Black Candle* (1991)
  * *The Reason for Nasturtiums* (1990)
- Anthologies
  * *California Uncovered: Stories for the 21st Century* (2004)

Quote

"Badly and tentatively I began writing early poems. You think I'm being modest but I'm not. I destroyed those sentimental and bad poems recently so no archivist could find them."-Chitra Divakaruni.

Awards

- 1997: The Allen Ginsberg Poetry Prize and the Pushcart Prize for *Leaving Yuba City: New and Selected Poems.*
- 1997: Los Angeles Times Best Book for *Mistress of Spices.*
- 1995: The American Book Award for *Arranged Marriage: Stories.*
- PEN Oakland/Josephine Miles Literary Award for *Arranged Marriage: Stories.*
- Bay Area Book Reviewers Award for Fiction for *Arranged Marriage: Stories.*
- PEN Oakland/Josephine Miles Literary Award
- 2000 National Book Award judge.

SONIA FALEIRO

Sonia Faleiro is an award-winning Indian journalist and writer. She was born in Goa and has lived in New Delhi and Edinburgh. She is currently based in Mumbai.

The Girl (Viking, 2006) is her first novel, and was published to critical acclaim. A short story, 'Stupid', is featured in *First Proof : The Penguin Book of New Writing From India* II. Her short story 'Outkast D'Souza' appears in *Reflected in Water: Writings on Goa*in November, 2006.

She is currently writing her second book, a non-fiction account of Mumbai's dance bars, due for publication in 2008.

Sonia's non-fiction has appeared in India Today, The Indian Express, The Hindustan Times, Third World Resurgence, Tehelka, Time Out, Himal, Maxim, Marie Claire, Elle, and Travel +Leisure. She is Writer-at-Large, Tehelka, and Contributing Editor, Vogue (India).

Journalism

Her reportage includes a six-part series on the bar dancers of Mumbai; The Dying of the Evening Stars; a six-part series on India's domestic workers; The Other Half, and extensive writings on the farmers suicides in Vidarbha; Death of a Son, Grandson, and All of Life's Dreams.

Award

She is the recipient of the CNN Young Journalist Award 2006.

Books

- The Girl, Penguin Viking
- "Stupid", First Proof : The Penguin Book of New Writing From India II
- "Outkast D'Souza", Reflected in Water: Writings on Goa, Penguin

ALTAF FATIMA

Altaf Fatima (born 1929 in Lucknow, India) is an Urdu novelist. Her novel Dastak Na Do (The One Who Did Not Ask) is regarded has enjoyed the most success and is widely regarded as one of the defining works in the Urdu language. An adaptation was presented on Pakistan television and an abridged translation was serialised by the prestigious Karachi monthly, Herald.

Life and Career7

Early Life: Altaf Fatima was the second of four children born in a Muslim household in Lucknow, India, to Fazle Mohammad Amin and his wife Jahan Mumtaz.

Later Life

She is currently resident in Lahore, Pakistan. She now lives a retired life and has discontinued her literary works.

Additional Information

Altaf Fatima's novel Dastak Na Do has been translated into English by Rukhsana Ahmed.

Works

Novels

- *Nishaan-i-Mehfil*
- *Dastak Naa Do (The One Who Did Not Ask)*
- *Chulta Musafir*
- *Khwabger*

Collection of Short Stories

- *Woh Jisay Chaha Gaya*
- *Jub Diwaaren Girya Kurti Hain*
- *Taar-i-Unkaboot*

Translations

- *To Kill A Mocking Bird* into Urdu
- *Barrey Aadmi, Aur Unke Nazariyat,* a collection of political essays

SUNIL GANGOPADHYAY

Sunil Gangopadhyay was born on 7 September 1934 in Faridpur in what is now Bangladesh is an Indian poet. Sunil obtained his Master's degree in Bengali from the University of Calcutta in 1954. He has been associated with the Ananda

Bazar group, a major publishing house in Kolkata, for many years, and after serving five years as the Vice President he is currently the President of the Sahitya Akademi.

Author of well over 200 books, Sunil is a prolific writer who has excelled in different genres but declares poetry to be his "first love". He was the founder editor of *Krittibas,* a seminal poetry magazine that became a platform for a new generation of poets experimenting with many new forms in poetic themes, rhythms, and words. His *Nikhilesh* and *Neera* series of poems (some of which have been translated as *For You, Neera* and *Murmur in the Woods*) have been extremely popular.

As in poetry, Sunil is known for his unique style in prose. *Arjun, Pratidwandi,* filmed by Satyajit Ray (English title: *The Adversary*), *Aranyer Din-Raatri* (*The Days and Nights of the Forest,* also filmed by Satyajit Ray), *Abar Aranya* (filmed by Gautam Ghosh), *Ekaa ebong Koyekjon* are some of his well known works of fiction. His historical fiction *Sei Somoy* (translated into English by Aruna Chakravorty as *Those Days*) received the Indian Sahitya Akademi award in 1985. *Sei Somoy* continues to be a best seller more than a decade after its first publication. The same is true for *Pratham Alo* (also translated recently by Aruna Chakravorty as *First Light*), another best selling historical fiction and *Purbo-Paschim,* a raw depiction of the partition and its aftermath seen through the eyes of three generations of Bengalis in West Bengal, Bangladesh and elsewhere. He is also the winner of the Bankim Puraskar (1982), and the Ananda Puraskar (twice).

Sunil has written (and still writes) in many other genres including travelogues, children's fiction, short stories, features, and essays. Among his pen-names are: Nil Lohit, Sanatan Pathak, and Nil Upadhyay.

Though he has written all types of children's fiction, one character created by him that stands out above the rest, is Kakababu, the crippled adventurist, accompanied by his young adult nephew Shantu, and his friend Jojo. Since 1974, Sunil Gangopadhyay has written over 35 novels of this popular series, most of which appeared in Anandamela magazine.

Some Books

- Aranyer Din Ratri
- Sei Samay
- Rokto
- Arjun
- Purush
- Agniputro
- Sorol Satya
- Byaktigoto
- Pratidwandi
- Mohaprithibi
- Roktomangsho
- Atmoprokash, his first novel
- Bandhubandhab, unusual work on friendship
- Purba-Paschim (1, 2), epic book on east and west Bengal
- Jeeban Je Rakam
- Ardhek Manobi
- Bondhubandhob
- Atmoprokash-the first prosaic writing of Sunil, who originally was poet only.
- Kakababu Series-The best in the adventures....

SAGARIKA GHOSE-SARDESAI

Sagarika Ghose is an Indian journalist, author and television personality.

Ghose received her bachelor's degree in history from St. Stephen's College, Delhi. A recipient of the Rhodes Scholarship, she gained a bachelor's in modern history from Magdalen College and an M.Phil from St Antony's College at Oxford. She has been a journalist in India since 1991 and has worked at the The Times Of India, Outlook magazine and The Indian Express. She is currently a (2006) senior editor and prime time anchor on the news network CNN-IBN.

In 2004 she became the first woman to anchor the popular BBC programme *Question Time India.* She is also the author of the novel *The Gin Drinkers,* published in 1998. Her second novel *Blind Faith* was published in 2006 by HarperCollins.

She is married to a well-known television personality Rajdeep Sardesai, son of cricketer Dileep Sardesai, and has two children, Ishan and Tarini. She is the daughter of Bhaskar Ghose, erstwhile Director General of Doordarshan, the Indian public television network. Her two illustrious aunts include Ruma Pal, former justice of the Supreme Court and Arundhati Ghose, former ambassador and diplomat.

AMITAV GHOSH

Amitav Ghosh (born 1956), is an Indian-Bengali author and literary critic known for his work in the English language.

Ghosh was born in Kolkata and was educated at The Doon School (where he was a younger contemporary of Vikram Seth); St. Stephen's College, Delhi; Delhi University; and the University of Oxford, where he was awarded a Ph.D. in social anthropology. Apparently Ghosh once showed Seth some of his poetry, prompting Seth to advise him to stick to prose.

Ghosh lives in New York with his wife, Deborah Baker, author of the Laura Riding biography *In Extremis: The Life of Laura Riding* (1993) and a senior editor at Little, Brown and Company. They have two children, Lila and Nayan. In 1999, Ghosh joined the faculty at Queens College, City University of New York as Distinguished Professor in Comparative Literature. He has also been a visiting professor to the English department of Harvard University since 2005. Ghosh has recently purchased a property in Goa and is returning to India. He is working on a trilogy to be published by Penguin Books India.

Ghosh's latest work of fiction, *The Hungry Tide,* was published in April 2004. His other novels are *The Circle of Reason* (1986), *The Shadow Lines* (1990), *The Calcutta Chromosome* (1995) and *The Glass Palace* (2000). The *Shadow Lines* won the Sahitya Akademi Award, India's most prestigious literary award. The *Calcutta Chromosome* won the Arthur C.

Clarke Award for 1997. Ghosh's fiction is characterised by strong themes that may be somewhat identified with postcolonialism but is difficult to label. His topics are unique and personal; some of his appeal lies in his ability to weave "Indo-nostalgic" elements into more serious themes.

Ghosh has also written *In an Antique Land* (1992), *Dancing in Cambodia, At Large in Burma* (1998), *Countdown* (1999), and *The Imam and the Indian* (2002, a large collection of essays on different themes such as fundamentalism, history of the novel, Egyptian culture, and literature). He was awarded the Padma Shri by the Indian government in 2007.

R. GOPAL

R.Gopal also known as Nakkeran Gopal is a famous journalist who publishes a famous magazine called Nakkeran. He has also published several controversial books and magazines.

HARI SINGH GOUR

Hari Singh Gour, also known as Sir Hari Singh Gour and Dr. Hari Singh Gour, was a distinguished lawyer, jurist, educationist, social reformer, poet, and novelist. He was one of the greatest visionaries of education of this century on the Indian subcontinent and even on a global scale. Gour was Vice Chancellor of the University of Delhi and Nagpur University, founder and Vice Chancellor of the University of Sagar, Deputy President of the Indian Legislative Assembly, an Indian Delegate to the Joint Parliamentary Committee, a Member of the Royal Commission on the Indian Constitution (popularly known as the Simon Commission), and a Fellow of the Royal Society of Literature.

Early Years

Hari Singh Gour was born on November 26, 1870 in a poor family near Sagar, India. The family had to be supported by Hari Singh's eldest brother who provided an allowance of 50 rupees per month. Hari Singh's father was a carpenter, but the young boy did not have an interest in this trade. At the age of ten, Hari Singh won a scholarship of two rupees per month which enabled him to attend a night school in Sagar. Later, with the help of another scholarship he went to Jabalpur to undertake further studies. Mathematics was his favorite subject and for this he received a special prize. He passed his Intermediate examination from Hislop College, Nagpur, a free church institution, standing first in the whole province. This successful foundation paved the way for a bright future. Hari Singh was the only student to receive Honours in English and History.

Education

When he was 18 years old, Hari Singh Gour went to the University of Cambridge in England where he took Moral Sciences Tripos and Law Tripos. Unfortunately, the young Hari Singh experienced a great deal of racism as a student and throughout his life. He participated in a mathematics competition, of which the results were not declared. Some years after obtaining his LL.D. he learned that the scholarship which the competition awarded was not given to foreigners, especially "blacks," as Indians were referred to by the British. Since Hari Singh came first in the competition, the scholarship ended up not being awarded to any one. He faced similar treatment in other situations and academic competitions, however he never let this unfair treatment by the British discourage him. Instead, he began to write poetry. In fact, while in England he came to be known in literary circles as a promising poet, becoming acquainted with the likes of George Bernard Shaw. He wrote a book of poetry entitled *Stepping Westward and Other Poems* due to which he became somewhat of a celebrity and was thereby selected a Member of the Royal Society of Literature.

He was admitted as a pensioner at Downing College, Cambridge on June 5, 1889. Gour received his B.A. in 1892; the M.A. in 1896; LL.M. in 1902; and finally the LL.D. in 1908. After his time at Cambridge, he read for the D.Litt. and LL.D. at Trinity College, Dublin. He received an honorary D.Litt. from the University of Delhi, where he served as the institution's first Vice Chancellor.

Career

On his return to India he became a successful lawyer at Raipur. He was called to the Bar, Inner Temple on November 26, 1872. Gour practiced in the High Courts of India, including the Central Provinces, Calcutta, and Allahabad. He wrote two monumental works, *The Law of Transfer in British India* and *The Penal Law of India*. Another book entitled *Hindu Law Code* published later added to his reputation as a great jurist. In the Legislative Assembly in 1921, Dr. Hari Singh Gour denounced the sequestration and suppression of women. He was also a great social reformer and was successful in getting an act passed to enable women to be enrolled as lawyers, while his Civil Marriage Bill of 1923 showed him to be a reformer thinking ahead of his time. Gour was not only a progressive scholar; he demonstrated such forward thinking in his personal life as well. He married Grace Kamalini Chauhan, one of the first female doctors in India. Hari Singh Gour was knighted in 1925.

By his determination and industry combined with a gift of oratory, Sir Hari Singh Gour rose to eminent position in the political scene. He became a Leader of the Opposition and of the Nationalist Party in the Indian Legislative Assembly from 1921 to 1934. He was a Member of the Constituent Assembly that framed India's Constitution, working alongside Mahatma Gandhi and Jawaharlal Nehru. Gour was also President of the High Court Bar Association in Nagpur and President of the Hindu Association. He was an Indian Delegate to the Joint Parliamentary Committee on the Government of India Bill in 1933.

Indian Penal Code

The Indian Penal Code was passed by the Legislative Council of India on October 6, 1860 on which date it received the assent of the Governor-General. Since that time, the Indian Penal Code had come to be the law of the land, with its amendments and modifications. However, the Indian Penal Code retained very severe means of punishment. Sir Hari Singh Gour vehemently opposed such measures, stating:

"No civilized country today imposes such heavy sentences as does the [Indian] Penal Code. Heavy sentences have long gone out of fashion in England and the order of sanctity and perfection attaching to the Penal Code should not deter indigenous legislatures to thoroughly revise the sentences, bringing them into conformity with modern, civilized standards."

The Indian Penal Code was "draconian in its severity with regard to punishment," according to Gour, who firmly believed that solitary confinement as a form of punishment under Section 73 of the Indian Penal Code lacked rational basis. Solitary confinement had been abolished in England and Gour claimed that it would be in keeping with the civilized culture of India to wipe out this kind of punishment—an inhumane mark ironically left by the British colonialists themselves in the Penal Code.

Age of Consent Bill

The 1891 Age of Consent Act had established that the minimum age of consent within marriage for girls should be 12 years. In 1922, Rai Bahadur Bakshi Sohan Lal proposed that the age of consent should be raised from 12 to 14. This motion was defeated. Then in 1924 Sir Hari Singh Gour brought the age of consent issue back into the Legislature with a similar proposal to raise the minimum age from 12 to 14 years for girls. After amendments and the appointment of a select committee, Gour's Bill was passed to raise the age of consent within marriage to 13 for girls in 1925. In March 1928, Gour, who had always been a steadfast proponent of age of consent bills, appealed to the importance of realizing standards of modern clinical psychology and pointed out the emotional problems of early marriage, such as the incidence of polygamy as grooms grew up and decided they desired more compatible partners, possible occurrence of suicide and early death, and generally marital unhappiness for both partners.

Legacy

Besides being a great lawyer and jurist, Dr. Gour was also a great educationist. He organized the University of Delhi as its first Vice Chancellor and was Vice Chancellor of Nagpur University for two successive terms. Of his most important contributions was the founding of the University of Sagar, the oldest university in the state of Madhya Pradesh, in 1946 for which he made a munificent donation. He started the University of Sagar with 20 lakhs and gave about two crores in property as a donation to the University. He became the first Vice Chancellor of the University of Sagar and occupied this position until he died on December 25, 1949. He bequeathed the greater part of his life's savings, a large fortune, to the University of Sagar. The new campus of this University, laid out on the summit of the Patharia Hills with a panoramic view of the town and lake, has been built largely through the benefaction of Dr. Hari Singh Gour and is a fitting memorial to this man of great vision.

He accomplished much, overcoming initial poverty and lasting discrimination. For example, in 1941 Gour was turned away by a hotel in England on account of his race. The Indian Posts and Telegraphs Department issued a commemorative stamp of Dr. Hari Singh Gour on November 26, 1976.

Selected Works

- *The Law of Transfer in British India*, Vol. 1-3 (1902)
- *The Penal Law of India*, Vol. 1-2 (1909)
- *Hindu Code* (1919)
- *India and the New Constitution* (1947)
- *Renaissance of India* (1942)
- *The Spirit of Buddhism* (1929)
- *His only Love* (1929)
- *Random Rhymes* (1892)
- *Facts and Fancies* (1948)
- *Seven Lives* (1944)
- *India and the New Constitution* (1947)
- *Letters from Heaven*
- *Lost Soul*
- *Passing Clouds*

ANOSH IRANI

Anosh Irani (born 1974) is an Indian-Canadian novelist and playwright. An Irani (like Parsi, but of recent Iranian extraction), he was born and raised in Mumbai, although he has indicated that he personally prefers the city's traditional English name, Bombay. After working in advertising in India, he moved to Vancouver in 1998 to study and pursue writing.

His first full-length play, *The Matka King*, premiered in October 2003 at the Arts Club Theatre in Vancouver. His most recent play, *Bombay Black*, won four Dora Awards, including Outstanding New Play. Irani was also featured in *Quill & Quire* as one of a handful of young Canadian "writers to watch."

He published his debut novel, *The Cripple and His Talismans*, in 2004. This dark fable won critical acclaim for its magic realist depiction of the seedy beggars' underworld of India. Irani's second novel, *The Song of Kahunsha*, was chosen as a CBC Book Club One pick, and was selected for the 2007 edition of *Canada Reads*, where it was championed by Donna Morrissey. Kahunsha is a story about the abandoned children of Bombay, struggling for survival and to hold onto hope amidst the violence of the 1993 racial riots.

Education

From 1997 Irani attended the University of British Columbia. He received his Bachelors degree in Creative Writing in 2002.

Works

- *The Matka King* (2003, play)
- *The Cripple and His Talismans* (2004, novel)
- *The Song of Kahunsha* (2006, novel)
- *Bombay Black* (2006, play)

RAJ KAMAL JHA

Raj Kamal Jha (born 1966) is an Indian novelist and journalist. Jha was born in Bihar and was raised in Kolkata, West Bengal, where he went to school at St. Joseph's College.

He then attended the Indian Institute of Technology, Kharagpur where he did his bachelor's in Mechanical Engineering, (but perhaps more significantly, had his first brush with journalism as the editor of the campus magazine, *Alankar*, where his first short fiction appeared). After graduating from IIT, he went to the Graduate School of Journalism at the University of Southern California, where he received his M.A. in 1990.

Jha was an Assistant Editor (News) at *The Statesman* in Kolkata, a Senior Associate Editor at *India Today*, New Delhi, and since 2001 has been working as the Executive Editor of The Indian Express which he joined in 1996 as Deputy Editor. He lives in New Delhi.

The Indian Express has twice won the Vienna-based International Press Institute's award for Excellence in Journalism in 2004 and 2006. Its journalists have won several national and international awards. Jha is the author of three published novels.

His first novel, *The Blue Bedspread* won the 2000 Commonwealth Writers' Prize for Best First Book (Eurasia region) and was a *New York Times* Notable Book of the Year. His second novel *If You Are Afraid of Heights* was a finalist for the Hutch-Crossword Book Award in 2003. He has also been shortlisted for the John Llewellyn Rhys Prize and the Guardian First Book Award.

His third novel, *Fireproof*, debuted in German at the Frankfurt Book Fair in October 2006 (published by Goldmann). It was published to wide critical acclaim by Picador in India in December and in the UK in February 2007. French and Italian editions are due in 2007-8.

Set against the backdrop of the 2002 Gujarat violence, the first attack on innocent Muslim civilians after 9/11, the novel is a chilling, magical tale of a father and his deformed son on a journey across a city where the ghosts of those killed have decided to seek justice.

Jha's fiction is known for its stark simplicity and ability to evoke emotion through attention to detail. John Fowles described *The Blue Bedspread* as the "Coming of age of the

Indian novel." Commenting on his latest book, India Today said: "Here is a chronicle for the 21st century, then, a bildungsroman that tracks the education of the crime-infested soul, completed when the soul cries 'I am guilty' and acknowledges that the burden of this enormous guilt will darken the rest of his life. And that will be his punishment, not the release of the noose or of public abasement in prison."

His fiction is strongly grounded in contemporary Indian themes around change, often taking off from newspaper pages. From domestic violence to the urban-rural divide and, in his latest novel, mass violence and communal tension, Jha's books engage with disturbing subjects unusual in contemporary writing in English but capture those realities of India that escape the mainstream media. His writing, simple as it appears, often calls for a lot of reader participation which evokes sharp, divided reaction. Jha's fiction has been translated into more than a dozen European languages, including French, German, Italian, Dutch, Greek, Hebrew, Turkish, Spanish and Finnish. His short stories have appeared in French and German anthologies as well. His work has been featured in several international literary festivals, including Hay-on-Wye, Munich Writers' Festival, Melbourne Writers' Festival and the Los Angeles Times Book Festival.

Japanese video artist and photographer Noritoshi Hirakawa created four video installations taking scenes from Jha's three novels for an exhibition at the National Gallery of Modern Art in New Delhi in 2007 as part of a special exhibition of contemporary Japanese art called Vanishing Points.

Jha was recently a visiting professor at the graduate school of journalism at the University of California, Berkeley where he taught a course on reporting on India. He was also a fellow at the Yaddo Residency in Saratoga Springs, New York, in 2005.

Works

- 2006-7: *Fireproof*, novel
- 2006: "Zwischen den Welten" Short fiction in a German anthology

- 2003: *If You Are Afraid of Heights*, novel
- 2001: *The Blue Bedspread*, novel

KALKI KRISHNAMURTHY

Kalki was the pen name of Krishnamurthy (September 9, 1899–December 5, 1954), an Indian freedom fighter, novelist, short-story writer, journalist, satirist, travel writer, script-writer, poet, critic, and connoisseur of the arts.

Life

Krishnamurthy was born at Puttamangalam in the Thanjavur district in an orthodox, large Brahmin family with limited means. After primary education in the village, Krishnamurthy joined the National High School at Tiruchi, about 100 kilometres away.

When Mahatma Gandhi launched his non-cooperation movement in 1921, thousands of students gave up their studies to participate; Krishnamurthy was among them. Inspired by Gandhi's speech at a public meeting in Tiruchi, and despite the Secondary School Leaving Certificate examination being just three months away, he left school and joined the Indian National Congress.

In 1922, he was given a one-year prison sentence for participating in the independence struggle. It was during this period that Krishnamurthy came into contact with two people who were to play a major role throughout his life: veteran Congress leader C. Rajagopalachari, and T.Sadasivam, who was to become a life-long friend and partner in journalistic ventures.

Krishnamurthy's first attempt at writing fiction also came during that period. In 1923 he became a sub-editor on *Navasakthi*, a Tamil periodical edited by Tamil scholar and freedom fighter V. Kalyanasundaram, known as "Thiru Vi. Ka". Krishnamurthy's first book was published in 1927.

Leaving Navasakthi in 1928, Krishnamurthy stayed with C. Rajagopalachari at the Gandhi Ashram in Tiruchengode in Salem district and helped him edit *Vimochanam*, a Tamil journal devoted to propagating prohibition. In 1931, he was again imprisoned for six months.

Next year Krishnamurthy joined *Ananda Vikatan*, a weekly edited and published by S.S. Vasan, as its de facto editor. The magazine soon became a household name in middle class families. Krishnamurthy's witty, incisive comments on politics, literature, music and other forms of art were looked forward to with unceasing interest by readers. He wrote under the pen names of "Kalki", "Ra. Ki", "Tamil Theni", "Karnatakam", and so on. Vikatan published many of his short stories and novels (as serials).

The name *Kalki* denotes the impending tenth Avatar of Lord Vishnu in the Hindu religion, who it is said, will bring to an end the Kali Yuga and reinstate Dharma or righteoueness among the worldly beings. He used the name because like the Avatar he wanted to bring about great changes, and also in honour of his mentor Kalyana Sundaram Mudaliar, taking the "Kal" from his name and the "Ki" from his own. He is often referred to as "Kalki Krishnamurthy" or simply "Kalki".

In 1941 he left Ananda Vikatan and rejoined the freedom struggle and courted arrest. On his release after three months he and Sadasivam started the weekly, *Kalki*. He was its editor until his death on December 5, 1954.

Works

Krishnamurthy specialised in the semi-historic genre, where he blended ancient tales, legends and historic facts with fictional escapades to produce epics. The following are his most famous in this category:

- *Ponniyin Selvan*
- *Sivagamiyin Sabadham*
- *Parthiban Kanavu*

He also wrote social novels, which dealt with social awakening, rights and the Indian independence movement. His most famous in this genre were.

- *Alai Osai*

- *Thyaga Bhoomi*

His other novels include:

- *Kalvanin Kaadhali*
- *Poiman Karadu*

His short stories include:

- Kanaiyazhiyin Kanavu

He was also a great patron of Carnatic music. He wrote his criticisms under the pseudonym *Karnatakam*. He also penned many songs and lyrics, most of which were adapted into Carnatic Music.

JASWANT SINGH KANWAL

Jaswant Singh Kanwal was born in Dhudike, Moga District, Punjab, India. He is a short story writer and a novelist with left-leanings. He has published several books. The most notable is Lahoo Di Lo (Dawn of the Blood). This novel is based on the Naxalite movement in Punjab. It was so controversial that during the infamous Emergency days of 1970's, none of the publishers was willing to publish it. Jaswant Singh Kanwal had it published in Singapore and smuggled copies of the novel to India. Only after the emergency was lifted, the novel was published in Punjab. This book has been translated into English.

Sahitya Akademy awarded fellowship to Jaswant Singh Kanwal for his 1996 book Pakhi (Hand Fan) (Short stories). He received the Sahitya Akademy Award for Taushali Di Hanso (Novel) in 1998.

DATTA RAGHUNATH KAVTHEKAR

Datta Raghunath Kavthekar (1901 – 16 August 1979), also known as D. R. Kavthekar, was a renowned Marathi novelist from the 1930s through the late 1970s. He was born in 1901 in a small Wai town on the banks of the Krishna River in Maharashtra state in India. Having lost both parents at an early age, he joined the Indian Army after matriculating. He was a World War I veteran. His first writing at a young age was disposed of by his elder brother, who reprimanded young

Datta for not focusing on his studies. His writing was inspired by his sensitive and observant mind. For depicting the aspects of delicate human relationships in various roles found in common families, his literature appealed to a significant number of readers.

Nagpur University had included his literature in their Master of Arts curriculum.

Kavthekar died on 16 August 1979.

KESAVADEV

P. Kesavadev is a well known novelist and social reformist of modern Kerala. He lived almost 80 years (1904 to 1983) and his entire life was dedicated to the social and cultural development of Kerala state.

He is remembered for his speeches, autobiographies, novels, dramas, short stories, and films. Odayil Ninnu, Nadi, Brandalayam, Ayalkar (Central Academi Award winning novel), Ethirppu (autobiography), Oru Sundariyude Athmakadha etc., are some among his 128 literary works. Kesavadev along with Thakazhi Sivasankara Pillai and Vaikom Muhammad Basheer are considered the exponents of progressive Malayalam Literature. His unfinished novel "Padicha Kallanmar" was recently rewritten and published by his wife Seethalekshmy dev. His only child is a famous diabetologist and a pioneer in telemedicine in diabetes care Jothydev Kesavadev .

The Men

Kesava Dev (His original name was Kesava Pillai). He adopted the name Kesava Dev to get rid of the suffix "Pillai" which signified his caste) was born in a feudal set up. It was a time when caste system was practiced rigorously. A number of retrograde customs and taboos were prevalent. The condition of the toiling section of the community was precarious. Even as a child Kesava Dev was exposed to all the maladies prevailing in the society in general and in the institution of the joint family in particular. A middle school drop out, Kesava Dev, at the age of 13 began his long fight against social evils and every form of injustice. From then on, his life was one of continuous rebellion, and constant revolt against every evil.

The Novels

Kesava Dev emerged as one of the makers of modern Malayalam fiction. He can be referred to as the first writer to usher in the Renaissance in Malayalam literature, by writing the novel "Odayil Ninnu" (From the gutter) (1942) with a rickshaw puller as its hero.

Dev was in the forefront among the writers who employed new norms in the content and characterization in Malayalam fiction. "Odayil Ninnu" came as a shocking revelation that a finest piece of literature can be produced with commonplace themes and unconventional style of prose with ordinary mortals as heroes and heroines. Apart from the fact that the appearance of rickshaw puller was a thrilling experience at that time, the author blazed a new trial in Malayalam literature and many writers followed suit.

"Bhranthalayam" (The Mad House) (1949) is a novel based on the tragedy of partition of the nation. This novel brings out the humanist in Kesava Dev in all its dimensions. "Rowdy", (1958) the novel is based on the story of an orphan abused in every possible manner, resorting to arms in defense against the community. Dev's narrative tinged with humour and sarcasm rips open the shroud of the contemporary society. "Ayalkar" (The Neighbours) (1963) is Kesava Dev's best known work – his masterpiece.

This novel is acclaimed as the chronicle of the evolution of the three leading communities of the State of Kerala-the Nairs, Christians and Ezhavas from the days of feudalism to the post independent era. Writing about the tragedy of the disintegration of the two major tharwads – Mangalassery and Pachazhi-Kesavadev recreates their glorious past and also narrates the trials and tribulations paving the way for their total destruction. The novel on the other hand narrates the history of the state for a period of about fifty years from the times of feudalism to the rise of the new era. This novel won the National Award for literature.

The other major Novels are: Kannadi (1961) Sakhavu Karottu Karanavar (1961) Pankajakshiyude Diary (1963) Swapnam (1967) Adhikaram (1968) SnehikkanVendi (1967) Nadi (1951) Ulakka (1951) Oru Sundariyude Atmakatha (1970) Prema Viddi (1963).

The Short Stories

Kesava Dev was a prolific writer. He has written about 300 short stories. Many of them are superb literary gems. His stories offer a very wide range and variety in theme and technique. One can find finest feelings of tender love, anguish, jealousy, and heroism as well as the trivialities of the ordinary people as the theme is his short stories. In many stories one may find subtle thoughts skilfully brought out by simple words whereas in some others Dev's own anguish fire and zeal find free expression. A few major collections are: Annathe Nadakam (1956) (11 Stories) Thiranjedutha Kathakal 1 (1965) (38 Stories) Thiranjedutha Kathakal 2 (1989) (43 Stories) Katha-Dev (2000) (31 Stories)

Plays

Though Kesava Dev is well known for his contributions as a Novelist and Short Story writer, the full length plays and one act plays he has written were very popular in those days and attracted huge audience when enacted on stages. The plays he has written bring out the powerful social critic in Dev. His works in this field are not many. Plays like Pradhanamanthri (Prime Minister) bring out the pernicious tendencies in politics. Though written way back in 1948, what we see today in our politics is not much different from what Dev has depicted, thereby making the substance of plays relevant even to the present times. Tough many plays were not up the mark in their dramatic content; spicy satire, sharp dialogues and subtle humour made his plays very popular.

The notable Plays are: Pradhanamanthri (1940) Njanippokamunistaavum (1953) Munnottu (1947) Orumuri thenga (1959) Thondukari (1954) Manthriyaakkalle (1949) Mazhayangum Kudayingum (1956)

PRAKASH KONA

Prakash Kona (born July 14, 1967) is an Indian novelist, essayist, poet and theorist who lives in Hyderabad, India. He writes in English, and is the author of six books to date:

- *Words on Lips of a Stranger* [Poetry: 2006, Writers Workshop, Calcutta]
- *Pearls of an Unstrung Necklace* [Fiction: 2005, Fugue State Press, New York]
- *Literary Criticism: A Study of Pluralism (Wittgenstein, Chomsky and Derrida)* [Theory: 2004, Wisdom House Publications, Leeds, England]
- *Streets that Smell of Dying Roses* [Fiction: 2003, Fugue State Press, New York; also Yeti Books, Calicut, India]
- *Poems for Her* (as Kona Prakash Reddy) [Poetry: 1999, Writers Workshop, Calcutta]
- *You and Other Poems* (as Kona Prakash Reddy) [Poetry: 1997, Writers Workshop, Calcutta]

Other works, including essays and fictional vignettes, are published widely on the Internet.

Six poems appeared in November 2007 in Zone Magazine.

His fiction is highly unusual, an experimental combination of free-floating emotion and political theory that can depict, for example, a city or a love relationship in an ambiguous, flowing, non-concrete and yet highly personal and heartfelt manner.

SANDILYAN

Sandilyan is a Tamil author recognised for influencing Tamil literature to a degree comparable to Kalki Krishnamurthy.

He is known for his historical based novels which includes *Kadal Pura, Jeeva Boomi, Cheran Selvi, Kanni Madam, Raja Thilagam, Raja Muthirai, Raja Berikai,Pallava Thilakam*, and *Moukini Vanam*.

The author's other famous novels are *Yavana Rani, KaniMaadam, Vilai Rani* and *Mannan Magal*.

The author is not only well known but also has a rather unusual name. The name 'Sandilyan' is actually derived from the "Sandilya" gothram. He belongs to a clan of Brahmins believed to be the descendants of rishi Sandilya.

Sandilyan's most famous novels were published in *Kumudam*, a weekly Tamil magazine and was instrumental in increasing the circulation to a greater extent. He was one of the very few Tamil writers to get a monthly salary from *Kumudam* for his novels. After leaving *Kumudam*, he unsuccessfully ran a weekly magazine himself by name 'Kamalam'.

SHARAT KUMAR

Sharat Kumar (born July 29, 1937, Meerut, India) is an Indian writer of both fiction and nonfiction. He is best known for his novels "Orange Moon" (2002, English edition) and "Lal Kothi Alvida" ("Farewell Red House") (2004, Hindi). The latter was made into a Hindi television programme of the same name, produced by Balraj Sahni Productions and starring Sahni's son Parikshat Sahni. It began airing in January 2006 on Doordarshan and is still running. Kumar was the original screenwriter for the TV series, adapting his own novel.

Kumar graduated from the National Defence Academy in 1956 and served as an officer in the Indian Navy until 1966. He then pursued a career as a management consultant, authoring books including "Mind Your Management" (2002), which was named Best Management Book of the Year in India. He has served as a director of the Institute of Management Technology in Ghaziabad.

BEM LE HUNTE

Bem Le Hunte, (b. 1964 in Calcutta, India) is an author who has published internationally. She grew up in India and London, studied anthropology at Cambridge University and worked as a lecturer and copywriter before publishing her first work of fiction. Her first great success was *"The Seduction of Silence,"* published by HarperCollins in USA and Australia and by Penguin Group in India. The title was translated into Polish with the new title, *"Kusace Wolanie Ciszy"* by Kameleon. The title follows the story of an Indian family and how it changed through love and loss over a period of about a hundred years, in prose that was described by Geraldine Brooks as 'vivid and arresting,' and as 'ample and fascinating' by Thomas Keneally.

Her second acclaimed title was *"There, Where the Pepper Grows"* that was published by HarperCollins internationally. It is a tale about a Polish Jewish family that ends up in Calcutta whilst in transit to Palestine during the Second World War.

AMULYA MALLADI

Amulya Malladi (born 1974 in Sagar, Madhya Pradesh, India) is an author. She earned her bachelor's degree in electronics engineering from Osmania University, Hyderabad, India and her masters degree in journalism from the University of Memphis, Tennessee, United States.

After graduating from the University of Memphis, she worked as an online editor for a high-tech publishing house in San Francisco and then as a marketing manager for a software company in the Silicon Valley.

After living in the United States for several years, Malladi currently resides in Copenhagen, Denmark with her husband Søren Rasmussen and two sons.

Early Life

Amulya Malladi was born in 1974 in a small town called Sagar, in the central state of Madhya Pradesh in India. Due to Malladi's father's occupation in the Indian Army, Amulya lived all over the country ranging from the Himalayan foothills to the southern city of Madras.

At the age of 11, when she found herself immersed in a world of goblins, pixies and fairies in the works of Enid Blyton, she wrote her first handwritten book of 50 pages. She once said that her affection and affinity towards writing influenced her academic choices. Though she first earned her Bachelor's degree in electrical and electronics engineering from Osmania University, Hyderabad, India, she followed it up with a Master's degree in journalism from University of Memphis, Tennessee. After gaining the journalism degree, she worked as a copy writer and a marketing manager for a software company in Silicon Valley, California. Malladi currently resides in Denmark with her husband and two sons. She has said that "When I first moved to Denmark... Danish sounded to me like the buzzing of bees".

A Breath of Fresh Air

In an interview, she spoke about the influences behind her first book, *A Breath of Fresh Air* (2002). While she was nine years old, her family was living in the Indian city of Bhopal because her father was posted in the Corps of Electrical and Mechanical Engineers.

During that time, on the night of December 3, 1984, methyl isocyanate gas leaked from Bhopal's Union Carbide plant that killed many people. When this gas tragedy occurred, her family and she were staying at the Army Centre which was a few kilometres away from the plant. Due to the wind that blew in a direction opposite to theirs, they remained unaffected by the gas leak. However, she remembered how those affected described the methyl isocyanate gas as chili powder in their lungs. These images stayed with her and took the form of a story, which she wanted to tell but had no idea how to. While living in Utah, the writing process for her first novel began. The San Francisco Weekly wrote in its review about this book:

> *Amulya Malladi's gemlike first novel has a provocative, almost absurd concept. Built on too-familiar notions about womanhood, fidelity, and family...But, the quality of Malladi's writing elevates* Fresh Air *well above standard-issue book-club fodder, and her strong control over plot helps her avoid the overwritten narrative drift that plagues most first novels. The prose ... is economical, more Raymond Carver than Bharati Mukherjee. Plainly told, Malladi's story is a fine study of the tenuous control we have over love and memory.*

A review from the TIME magazine said:

Malladi's subject is...compelling the survivors of the Bhopal tragedy remain neglected and angry after 18 years. [Malladi] was a child in Bhopal when the disaster happened and wasn't affected because her house was upwind of the Carbide factory. The victims of the accident now total 14,000, a number Malladi humanizes by keeping her story intimate.

The Mango Season

As to how Malladi came up with the title and names of the characters from *The Mango Season*, she said in an interview that unless she has a title of the book she is writing, she cannot move on. Same is the case with the names of her characters from her works of literature. Most of the influences on her characters came from her Hyderabad connection, which she corroborated by saying, "I think it's easier to write about a place you've lived in. The research element definitely shrinks and you can write more confidently. I also feel I have an obligation to write about a place I've lived in. I have moved a lot in my life, as a child and even as an adult, and I just feel that it would be such a waste if I wouldn't write about the places I have lived in." She said that writing this book was like taking a trip to Hyderabad.

A review from the Santa Monica Mirror said:

Amulya Malladi lays India out like a living picture before her readers. The smells curl out through the spine of the book, the tastes leave our throats burning with an unknown spice. The heat causes sweat to run down our backs, the curious sounds block the more familiar ones of cars and traffic from our ears.

ODETTE MASCARENHAS

Odette Mascarenhas is a writer from Goa, India, who has authored two books, *Alfie Alphonso*, a kind of Goan version of the Harry Potter story and *Masci: The Man Behind the Legend*, the biography of a humble Goan who went on to become a great chef whose culinary skills were appreciated by maharajahs and more.

ANURAG MATHUR

Anurag Mathur is an Indian author chiefly known for his 1991 novel *The Inscrutable Americans* which described the comical adventures of a young Indian student freshly arrived in the United States.

Anurag did his schooling from The Scindia School, (Gwalior, India). He received his bachelors degree from St. Stephen's College in Delhi, and his masters degree from the University of Tulsa at Tulsa.

He has made a career in journalism and publishing and contributes to various Indian magazines and newspapers. He is also the author of a travel guide called 22 days in India.

VED MEHTA

Ved (Parkash) Mehta (Born March 21, 1934) is a distinguished Indian writer who was born in Lahore, British India (now a Pakistani city) to a Hindu family. He lost his sight at the age of three as the result of a long bout of cerebrospinal meningitis. His father, a doctor, tried to give him an education, like his other children, so that the boy could become a self-supporting citizen of the world.

Mehta has lived in the Western world since 1949; he became an American citizen in 1975. He was educated at Pomona College, at Balliol College, Oxford where he read Modern History, and at Harvard University. His first book was published in 1957. Since then he has written 24 books, as well as hundreds of articles and short stories, for British, Indian and American publications, including the *The New Yorker*, where Mehta worked as a staff writer for 33 years.

He is the recipient of several awards including the Guggenheim Fellowship and the MacArthur Prize. He has been a visiting Fellow at Balliol College, Oxford, held the Rosenkranz Chair in writing at Yale University and taught Literature and History at a number of colleges and universities.

At the age of twenty he was sent to a school for the blind in Arkansas, where he completed his elementary and high school education in three years. From there he went on to Pomona, Oxford and Harvard.

Upon returning to India he felt like a foreigner in his own country and set out to re-discover it. He travelled extensively and met hundreds of people for writing his books "Walking the Indian Streets" and "Portrait of India". Years later he also wrote a book, "Gandhi and his Apostles", because of a profound realization that rich and privileged Indians live in a bubble that bobs up and down on an ocean of poverty, and that Gandhi, like himself, was from that bubble of privilege, for Gandhi too had gone on to study Law in England.

His first book, "Face to Face", a youthful autobiography, was published in 1952, just before he went to Oxford. He dictated it to his first love during his intensely lonely years at Pomona college in California. His blindness prevented him from joining the fast set with their large cars, and he felt like a blind Scherezade telling his story to his amanuensis.

His forays into fiction include "Three Stories from the Raj". Ved Mehta has been writing books for over fifty years, and chose to be a writer over the option he had of being an academician. He writes because he has to, from an inner need and compulsion, and often, as he wryly adds, he "goes on adding to a book long after it has been published."

But notwithstanding his books on India, his forays into fiction, and his long tenure as a staff writer for the New Yorker from 1961 to 1994, his writing appeal is intensely autobiographical. His eleven volume memoir, "Continents of Exile", was completed while working at the same time on other books, over a period of thirty-two years, from 1972 to 2004.

Beginning with the first two volumes, "Daddyji" and "Mummyji", "Continents of Exile" covers the saga of the Mehta and Mehra clans from mid-nineteenth century British India, through Independence and the turmoil of Partition in 1947, as well as his own experiences in a boarding school for the blind at the age of five, as a college student in California and at Oxford in the 1950's, his agonized search for love, his dangerous attempts to live a "normal" life, as though he were not blind, and culminates in "The Red Letters", in which he writes about his father's passionate love affair with a long-lost love who came back into his life as his wife's best friend, and how it affected his mother.

Each of the volumes of "Continents of Exile" can be read independently. They are rich in detail, vivid descriptions, and permeated with his compassion, and his profound insight into himself and his fellow men. At the heart of the series is "Vedi", in which he vividly recalls his experiences at a boarding school for the blind in Bombay in the 1940's. His father had sent him there at the age of five in the mistaken belief that it was a posh, British-type boarding school for blind children. In fact, it was a school and an asylum for destitute blind children, some of them had been beggars. Though little Vedi was given special privileges because of the handsome fee his father paid, like sleeping on a bed with a mattress, instead of wooden planks, and having his meals with the Principal and his family, and was exempted from the class of learning "how to cane chairs", he grew to love his humble classmates.

In "The Ledge between the Streams" he describes the lonely years that followed, as his family did not know how to educate a blind child. He spent much time with the servants in their simple quarters on the grounds of his parents bungalow and learned to feel a profound compassion for their humble but useful lives of loyalty, love and service.

Old photographs of the author's extended family and himself as a child can be seen on his website, as well as Ved Mehta with his wife and children to-day.

Criticism

Mehta was the subject of an unflattering profile by Jennet Conant in the September 1989 issue of Spy magazine. Titled "Slaves of The New Yorker," it documented his reliance on and emotional abuse of a string of editorial assistants, known as "Vedettes." The article and an accompanying sidebar (titled "The Long and the Short of It—But Mostly the Long of It") described Mehta's autobiographical writings as prolix, self-indulgent, and boring.

Publications

- "Face to Face," Atlantic-Little, Brown, Boston, 1957, and Collins, London, 1958. (Secondary Education Annual Book Award, 1958. BBC, serial reading on Light Programme, 1958; dramatization on Home Programme, 1959.)
- "Walking the Indian Streets," Atlantic-Little, Brown, Boston, 1960, and Faber & Faber, London, 1961 (revised edition, Weidenfeld & Nicolson, London, 1971).
- "Fly and the Fly-Bottle," Atlantic-Little, Brown, Boston, and Weidenfeld & Nicolson, London, 1963 (second edition, Columbia University Press, New York, 1983, with introduction by Jasper Griffin).
- "The New Theologian," Harper & Row, New York, and Weidenfeld & Nicolson, London, 1966.
- "Delinquent Chacha" (fiction), Harper & Row, New York, and Collins, London, 1967.
- "Portrait of India," Farrar, Straus & Giroux, New York, and Weidenfeld & Nicolson, London, 1970 (second edition, Yale University Press, New Haven and London, 1993).
- "John Is Easy to Please," Farrar, Straus & Giroux, New York, and Secker & Warburg, London, 1971.
- "Mahatma Gandhi and His Apostles," The Viking Press, New York, and Andre Deutsch, London, 1977 (reissued, Yale University Press, New Haven and London, 1993).
- "The New India," The Viking Press, New York, and Penguin Books, Middlesex, 1978.
- "Photographs of Chachaji," Oxford University Press, New York, 1980, and Oxford University Press, Oxford, 1981.
- "A Family Affair: India Under Three Prime Ministers," Oxford University Press, New York, 1982, and Oxford University Press, Oxford, 1983.
- "Three Stories of the Raj" (fiction), Scolar Press, Berkeley and London, 1986;

- "Rajiv Gandhi and Rama's Kingdom," Yale University Press, New Haven and London, 1995.
- "A Ved Mehta Reader: The Craft of the Essay," Yale University Press, New Haven and London, 1998.
- CONTINENTS OF EXILE (autobiography):
  - "Daddyji," Farrar, Straus & Giroux, New York, and Secker & Warburg, London, 1972
  - "Mamaji," Oxford University Press, New York, 1979, and Oxford University Press, Oxford, 1980
  - "Vedi," Oxford University Press, New York, 1982, and Oxford University Press, Oxford, 1983 (BBC, serial reading on "Book at Bedtime," 1990)
  - "The Ledge Between the Streams," W.W. Norton & Company, New York, and Harvill Press, Collins, London, 1984
  - "Sound-Shadows of the New World," W.W. Norton & Company, New York, and Collins, London, 1986
  - "The Stolen Light," W.W. Norton & Company, New York, and Collins, London, 1989
  - "Up at Oxford," W.W. Norton & Company, New York, and John Murray (Publishers), Ltd., London, 1993
  - "Remembering Mr. Shawn's New Yorker," Overlook Press, Woodstock and New York, 1998 and Sinclair-Stevenson, London, 2005
  - "All For Love," Granta Books, London, and, Thunder's Mouth Press/ Nation Books, New York 2001
  - "Dark Harbor," Thunder's Mouth Press/Nation Books, New York, 2003 and Sinclair-Stevenson, London, 2005
  - "The Red Letters," Thunder's Mouth Press/Nation Books, New York, 2004 and Sinclair-Stevenson, London, 2005 (concluding volume)

MENON MARATH

Sankarankutti Menon Marath, better known as Menon Marath, (born in 1906(?) in Kerala-died January 2, 2003) was an Indo-Anglican novelist who settled in England and spent more than half of his life there.

Menon graduated from Christian College in Madras (now Chennai) and travelled to England in 1934 to pursue postgraduate studies at King's College London. Among a few novels he wrote *The Wound of Spring* (Dennis Dobson,1960) and *The Sale of and Island* (1964) are better known. The third novel is *Janu*.

PANKAJ MISHRA

Pankaj Mishra was born in North India in 1969. He graduated with a bachelor's degree in commerce from Allahabad University before earning his Master of Arts degree in English literature at the Jawaharlal Nehru University in New Delhi. He is the Visiting Fellow for 2007-2008 at the Department of English, University College London, UK.

In 1992, he moved to Mashobra, a Himalayan village, where he began to contribute literary essays and reviews to *The Indian Review of Books, The India Magazine*, and the newspaper *The Pioneer*. His first book was *Butter Chicken in Ludhiana: Travels in Small Town India* (1995), a travelogue that described the social and cultural changes in India in the new context of globalization.

His novel *The Romantics* (2000), an ironic tale of people longing for fulfillment in cultures other than their own, was published in eleven European languages and won the *Los Angeles Times* Art Seidenbaum award for first fiction. His recent book *An End to Suffering: The Buddha in the World* (2004) mixes memoir, history, and philosophy while attempting to explore the Buddha's relevance to contemporary times. *Temptations of the West: How to be Modern in India, Pakistan and Beyond* (2006), describes Mishra's travels through Kashmir, Bollywood, Afghanistan, Tibet, Nepal, and other parts of South and Central Asia.

In 2005, Mishra published an anthology of writing on India, entitled *India in Mind* (Vintage). His writings have been anthologized in *The Picador Book of Journeys* (2000), *The Vintage Book of Modern Indian Literature* (2004), and *Away: The Indian Writer as Expatriate* (Penguin), among other titles. He has introduced new editions of Rudyard Kipling's *Kim* (Modern Library), E. M. Forster's *A Passage to India* (Penguin Classics), and J. G. Farrell's *The Siege of Krishnapur* (NYRB Classics). He has also introduced two volumes of V. S. Naipaul's essays: *The Writer and the World* and *Literary Occasions*.

Mishra writes literary and political essays for *The New York Times*, *The New York Review of Books*, *The Guardian*, and *New Statesman*, among other American, British, and Indian publications.

His work has also appeared in *The Boston Globe*, *Common Knowledge*, the *Financial Times*, *Granta*, *The Independent*, the *London Review of Books*, *n+1*, *The Nation*, *Outlook*, *Poetry*, *Time*, the *The Times Literary Supplement*, *Travel + Leisure*, and *The Washington Post*. He divides his time between London and India, and is presently working on a novel.

His book *Temptations of the West: How to be Modern in India, Pakistan, Tibet and Beyond* was reviewed by *The Economist* (1 July – 7 July 2006 issue).

Mishra's writings regarding Hinduism as a religion and the modern history of nationalist movements among Hindu people in India (he is himself a Hindu of Indian origin) such as the BJP have generated some disquiet among some Hindu circles within India. Responding to critics who allege that he "panders" to "white pro-Muslim audiences in the West", Mishra says that this notion is "optimistic", even before the September 11 attacks.

JAISHREE MISRA

Jaishree Misra is an Indian author, born 1961, whose debut novel *Ancient Promises* was published and sold worldwide by Penguin UK and became a major bestseller in India. Subsequent books include *Accidents Like Love and Marriage*,

Afterwards and *The Little Book of Romance*. A historical novel based on the life of Rani Lakshmibai of Jhansi is published in 2007. She also works full-time as a film classifier at the British Board of Film Classification in London, England. She is a close relative of late Thakazhi Sivasankara Pillai, famous Malayalam writer and Janpith awardee.

PREMENDRA MITRA

Premendra Mitra (1904-1988) was a renowned Bengali poet, novelist and short story writer. He was also an author of thrillers and science fiction.

Life

He was born in Varanasi, India. His father was an employee of the Indian Railways and because of that, he had the opportunity of travelling to many places in India. He was a student of South Suburban School and later at the Scottish Church College in Calcutta. During his initial years, he (unsuccessfully) aspired to be a physician and studied the natural sciences. Later he started out as a school teacher. He even tried to make a career for himself as a businessman, but he was unsuccessful in that venture as well. After trying out the other occupations, in which he met marginal or moderate success, he rediscovered his talents for creativity in writing and eventually became a Bengali language author and poet.

Editor

He edited Bengali journals and news-magazines like *Kollol, Kali Kalam, Banglar Kotha, Bongobani, Songbad*, among others.

Works

His work was first published in the Bengali journal called 'Probasi' (meaning *The Exile*) in 1922. His poems were better known for their sharpness and wit. They also expressed empathy for the sufferings of the proletariat. His short stories were well-structured and innovative, and encompassed the diverse to the divergent in urban Indian society. The themes of poverty, degradation, caste, the intermittent conflict between religion and rationality and themes of the rural-urban divide are a thematically occurring refrain in much of his work. He experimented with the stylistic nuances of Bengali prose and tried to offer alternative linguistic parameters to the high-class elite prosaic Bengali language which has been largely inspired by Tagore and his followers.

He even wrote science fictions and thrillers. As Debjani Sengupta observes in her essay *Sadhanbabu's Friends: Science Fiction in Bengal from 1882-1961*:

> *"...he [Mitra] also wrote brilliant and innovative science fiction. He had himself stated that SF not only talked of utopias, but that the best of them were based on firm scientific temperaments and facts. Two of his most well known stories are* Piprey Puran *("The Story of the Ants") and* Mangalbairi *("The Martian Enemies").* Piprey Puran *begins with a dislocation of time from present reality: "This happened many years ago.*

Everything was strange then... The Earth was beautiful to look at! The ground was covered with soft green grass. Countless varieties of plants sported many hued flowers, and at night the sky was covered with thousands of stars – it was a wonderful sight". This displacement, when our present has become a thing of the past, introduces a comic note in an otherwise sombre story. This future world, now real, is overrun with Ants, huge in size, intelligent and organised.

They have defeated the humans in battle, having taken them completely unawares. When humans were busy fighting each other, the Ants had begun their preparations to take over the planet. Six feet tall, they had emerged from their hideouts in the Andes Mountain and had begun their assault in the year 7757. One by one the cities of Peru, Venezuela and Ecuador came down like blocks of cards. A cavalcade of monstrous Ants had completely surrounded the few remaining humans and had annihilated them.

The only man who escaped unscathed was Don Perito who escaped to Mexico. He was the first human to describe the destruction wrought by the Ants. Within a few years the Ants had taken over Guyana, Brazil, Bolivia and Argentina. The weapon of mass destruction that they used was a powerful bomb attached to the body of an Ant. They also used advanced technological weapons. In the battle that they waged with the humans, the Ants used a kind of searching, powerful light, somewhat green in colour. This light took away human sight in an instant. Under this onslaught all the nations forgot their enmity and came together to fight the common enemy.

This story of the battle of the Ants and Humans is broken into small sub-sections with first-person narrations. The first narrator is the storyteller who begins the story. Soon it is broken by the diary of Asesh Roy, an explorer who had first seen the Ants in 6757. The third narration is by Señor Sabatini, a famous writer of Rio de Janeiro who describes the third deadly attack by the Ants. The fourth and final narration is by Sukhomoy Sarkar, who was imprisoned by the Ants for five years and who gives the most comprehensive details of the social and economic organisation of the Ants.

These breaks in the narrative structure create very interesting fissures in an otherwise continuous story. They not only make the impossible appear possible (because of 'eye-witness' accounts), but give a certain detachment to the narrator so as to emphasize the moral of his tale. This moral is to be found in comparing the Ants with humans, in which the humans are perhaps found wanting. The description by Sukhomoy Sarkar of the society of Ants makes this clear. The Ants live in an advanced democracy where there are no differences in wealth.

What they do have are Ants of differing abilities. The intelligent Ants provide the scientific and technological know-how and are strategists who look after the state. They are highly advanced compared to humans in knowledge and social structures, and have a strict sense of justice. The moral that we see in *Piprey Puran* can also be seen in *Mangalbairi*. When the Earth is attacked by Martians who poison its entire ecosystem by planting a new kind of seed that grows into a deadly flora that spreads like wildfire, all nations are united to fight this common enemy. "In this hour of danger... the one cause of happiness is that... humans have forgotten enmity as if by some magic. The whole world is united today". In both these stories Mitra hints at a time when the very existence of humans will be endangered, when common flowers and trees will be a thing of the past."

Although these are more popular among Bengali-speaking school children and teenagers, they are popular among an older generation of literary aficionados as well. In particular, his creation of the character of Ghanada (meaning *elder brother Ghana*) may be seen from many perspectives: although Ghanada is apparently a disinterested unemployed middle aged male, and who can apparently weave adventures almost at the drop of a hat, the adventures themselves cover themes ranging from crime, human ingenuity, science, history, geography, metaphysics and philosophy.

In terms of facts, they are amazingly accurate. It is obvious that while Ghanada himself has not been involved in any of the adventures he claims to have taken part in, he is certainly a very learned man with an exceptional gift for storytelling. Ghanada may be seen as Mitra's parody or caricature of the Bengali urban middle class celibate intellectual, who is at home in the world of books and knowledge, but has little practical experience whatsoever. It is also interesting to note that like Satyajit Ray's Feluda, the older Ghanada although not abhorring the opposite sex, is not entirely at ease with them either. He stays at an all-male hostel and maintains an almost frugal existence. Ghanada is a self educated person and his education is mostly due to time spent at the local libraries. In a way, it could be argued that these stories also reflect larger patterns of social transformations.

Another masterpice of his creation was the character of "Mejokorta". Mejokarta was a famous "Bhootshikari", meaning ghost-hunter in Bangla. The series of Mejokarta, although not as long as that of Ghanada, has left its prominent mark in the genre of ghost stories in Bangla.

Mitra's literary works were included in the curriculum of school level, secondary, higher secondary and graduation level Bengali literature in Bangladesh.

Poems

- *Prothoma* (First Lady)
- *Somrat* (The Emperor)
- *Ferarri Fouj* (The Lost Army)
- *Sagor Theke Fera* (Returning from the Sea)
- *Horin Cheeta Chil* (Deer, Cheetah and Eagle)
- *Kokhono Megh* (An occasional Cloud)

Novels

- *Paak*(The Turn)
- *Michhil* (The Procession)
- *Uponayon* (The Ceremony)
- *Agamikal* (Tomorrow)
- *Protishod* (Revenge)
- *Kuasha* (Fog)
- *Protidhoni Fere* (Return of Echo)
- *Monudadosh*
- *Piprey Puran* (The Story of the Ants)
- *Mangalbairi* (The Martian Enemies)

(For novels centred around the character of Ghanada, see the article on Ghanada)

Short Story Collections

- *PonchoSor*
- *Benami Bandar* (Unknown Monkey)
- *Putul O Protima* (Doll and Clay Image of Goddess)
- *Mrittika* (Earthen image)
- *Ofuronto* (Endless)
- *Dhuli Dhusor*
- *Mohanagar* (The Great City)
- *Jol Paira* (Water Pigeon)
- *Sreshto Golpo* (Best Stories)
- *Nana Ronge Bona* (Knit with Different Colours)
- *Nirbachita* (Selected)

JAGADISH MOHANTY

Jagadish Mohanty (born 1951) is a renowned Oriya writer, considered as a trendsetter in modern Oriya fiction, has received the prestigious Sarala Award 2003, Orissa Sahitya Akademy Award 1990, Jhankar Award, 1985 Dharitri Award, Prajatantra Award. Born in an iron mines of northern periphery of Orissa, he spent more than 30 years of his life working in the coal mines in western periphery of Orissa. Though he kept himself away from the cultural capital of Orissa, but still his writings highlighted him in the mainstream of Oriya literature and culture.

Indian feminist writer Sarojini Sahoo is his wife and he has two children Anubhav and Sambedana.

Novels

- *Kanishka Kanishka*
- *Nija Nija Panipatha*
- *Uttaradhikar*
- *Durdina*
- *Adrushya Sakala*

Short Stories

- *Ekaki Ashwarohi*
- *Dakshina Duari Ghara*
- *Irsha eka Rutu*
- *Album*
- *Dipahara Dekhinathiba Lokatie*
- *Juddhakshtre Eka*
- *Mephestophelese-ra Pruthibi*
- *Nian O Anyanya Galpa*
- *Suna Ilishi*
- *Sundartam Pap*
- *Saturir Jagadish*
- *Bija Bruxsha Chhaya*

Awards

He has been awarded with prestigious Sarala Award, started by IMFA foundation in 2003 for his short story collection Suna Ilishi Awarded with Orissa Sahitya Akademy, 1990 for his novel *Kanishja Kanishka*. Awarded with Jhankar award for his contribution to Oriya fiction in 1985 Besides this he has been felicated and awarded by Mahanadi Coal fields Limited (a subsidiary of Coal India), M/S J.K.Paper Mills Ltd, Jay Kay Pur, the Daily news paper Dharirti and other various institutions of Orissa.

Editing

He was the editor of a Literary journal "The Sambartaka" from 1980 –82 .the journal has a great significant value in the history of fiction writing in Oriya literature. Documentary Delhi Doordarshan, a National Channel of India has telecast a documentary film on both Jagadish and Sarojini, the couple writer of India under the title of *Literary post card*. Dr. Satti Khanna, of Duke University, Durham directed the documentary.

Translations

His stories have been translated in English, Hindi, Bengali, Malayalam and Telugu. His translated stories have been anthologized in different short story collections of Harper Collins, National Book Trust, Sahitya Academy, and Gyanapitha.

He himself also translated different Oriya prose and poetry into Hindi and has been published in different Hindi literary magazines. He also occasionally writes in Hindi and his first Hindi story was published in Dharmayuga in 1979. Since then he occasionally writes in different Hindi magazines like Samakaleen Bharatiya Sahitya, Dharmayuga, Sarika, Sakshatkar.

DHAN GOPAL MUKERJI

Dhan Gopal Mukerji (July 6, 1890 –July 14, 1936) was the first successful Indian man of letters in the United States. He studied at Duff School (now known as Scottish Church Collegiate School, a constituent unit of Scottish Church College, Calcutta), the University of Calcutta, in India, Tokyo University in Japan and at the University of California, Berkeley and Stanford University in the U.S.

Early Life in India

Dhan Gopal Mukerji was born on 6 July in a village near Calcutta on the edge of a jungle called Kajangal. His father, whom he describes as 'an Olympian who was lost in the world' was a lawyer who gave up his practice due to ill health and studied music instead, while also officiating as priest at the village's temple. Dhan Gopal describes his childhood and adolescence in the first part ('Caste') of his autobiography *Caste and Outcast* (1923). 'Caste' details Dhan Gopal's induction into the Brahminical tradition of his ancestors, and his experiences wandering for a year as an ascetic, as was the custom for boys in strict priestly households. However, disillusioned with the traditional role and impatient of the backward-looking element in strict Hindu society, he left the ascetic life to study at the University of Calcutta. Here, in the circle of his brother Jadugopal Mukherjee's friends, he came in contact with the ideas of the Bengal resistance. Jadu Gopal was subsequently jailed without trial from 1923 to 1927. Dhan Gopal later wrote a memoir about Jadu Gopal, titled *My Brother's Face.*

In Japan: In 1910, hoping to save the younger brother from police action, Dhan Gopal's family sent him to Japan to study industrial machinery. Although he was initially fascinated with the positivistic spirit of industrialization, later he became deeply disillusioned by the assembly line method of production and proclivity towards sheer efficiency which he viewed as dehumanizing, degrading and debasing. He was particularly shocked by how assembly line workers who had suffered fatal accidents were quickly replaced by other workers, without consideration by the factory owners or employers for either their medical recovery, health benefits or adequate compensation. After a short stay in Japan, he boarded a ship for San Francisco.

Experiences in America: Barely out of his teens, Dhan Gopal had absorbed enough revolutionary ideology from his peers to have been well on the way to following in his brother's footsteps, and may not have left India entirely willingly. Dhan Gopal took his ideology with him to America where he fell in with a number of dirt-poor 'anarchists' like himself. His experiences among them, in San Francisco and New York, are detailed in 'Outcast', the second section of his autobiography.

In San Francisco he looked about for a way to support himself and pay for his college education, and soon lit upon writing. Around 1916 he wrote *Rajani or Songs of the Night* a book of poems, and *Laila Majnu* a musical play in three acts, both published by Paul Elder and Co. of San Francisco. At this time, he was a student at the University of California at Berkeley for three years. Financial constraints and his political radicalism made him move on to Stanford University, from where he earned a graduate degree in metaphysics in 1914. He socialized with leftists, anarchists and freethinkers and became aware of the plight of the underclass, the white middle class, Negroes and other East Asian immigrant groups. He married Ethel Ray Dugan, an American artist and painter, in 1918, and they had a son, also called Dhan Gopal.

In the 1920s, Mukerji moved to New York and began his most prolific period of writing, published mainly by E.P. Dutton and Co.. Of his many children's books, *Kari the Elephant* was the first to see publication, in 1922. The most successful such title was *Gay Neck, the Story of a Pigeon* (1927) for which the American Library Association presented him with the Newbery Medal in 1928. This book is about a carrier pigeon ('Gay Neck') and his growing up with the flock owned by the narrator, then his (the pigeon's) drafting as a messenger for the Indian army in France during World War I and finally how the pigeon and his handler return to India and deal with the wounds and memories of war in the seclusion of a lamasery. Mukerji's other children's books include *Ghond, the Hunter* (1928), *The Chief of the Herd* (1929), *Hindu Fables for Little Children* (1929), *Rama, the Hero of India* (1930, produced for the children of Dalton School where his wife taught), and *The Master Monkey* (1932). Many of his works were reworkings of stories he had heard as a child. Others were inspired by his own experiences in India as a child among the jungles of Bengal, or as a yogi in various holy places.

Among Mukerji's writings for adults are *A Son of Mother India Answers* (1928) (partly in response to Katherine Mayo's *Mother India*), *Devotional Passages from the Hindu Bible* and *Visit India with Me* (1929), *Disillusioned India* (1930) and *My Brother's Face* (1932). *The Face of Silence* (1926) is about the late nineteenth and early twentieth century saint and visionary Ramakrishna Paramhansa and is said to have deeply influenced Romain Rolland (See Swami Tathagatananda, 'Dhan Gopal Mukerji and *The Face of Silence*', *Prabuddha Bharati*, January and February 2006 (two part article).)

The details of his later life are hazy, but there is some evidence to believe that relations with his wife entered a difficult phase at the end of his life. In spite of his many friends he felt deeply isolated and marginalized in America, as he could do very little, beyond raising funds and entertaining visiting celebrities, to further the cause of Indian liberty.

The choices he had made in life prevented him from ever returning permanently to India, and it is possible to see his urge to write of the jungles and animals of his native land as a means of compensating for their absence. The unhappiness of his final years drove him further into spirituality, fueled his interest in the spiritual heritage of his motherland and gave urgency to his desire to interpret and explain India to the West. Finally, in 1936, he hanged himself on July 14, shortly after his forty-sixth birthday, in New York City.

Legacy

Dhan Gopal Mukerji is probably the first popular Indian writer in English.

He pre-dates G.V. Desani and Mulk Raj Anand by some ten or twenty years. Krupabai Satthianadhan, the woman who wrote the novels *Kamala* and *Saguna* in the late nineteenth century, was certainly an accomplished writer, but her works did not reach a mass audience until she was rediscovered in the twentieth century. Scattered writings in English by Indians are encountered throughout the nineteenth century, such as the famous *Rajmohan's Wife*, Bankim Chandra Chatterjee's first novel, written in English after the manner of Scott. There was also notable work by figures such as Roquia Sakhawat Hussain, writer of *Sultana's Dream* (1905), the first science fiction piece in English by an Indian, comparable to Charlotte Perkins Gilman's *Herland*. But usually these are byproducts of Indian language work, and Dhan Gopal Mukerji is the first to write seriously and consistently in English.

This was not by choice, but was a product of his unfortunate situation. Dhan Gopal never lost the sense of mission which he shared with his brother, and throughout his life strove to complete the task he had set himself: to emancipate India from foreign rule and win for her culture and philosophy the respect he felt it deserved. In America he associated with fellow exiles like M.N. Roy, the founder of the Communist Party of India, to whom he is said to have suggested the adoption of the pseudonym 'Manabendra'.

Forbidden the more satisfying outlet of activism, he poured his feelings into his writing. Consequently, his language is magical and persuasive, and his observation of animals and their ways is accurate and unsentimental. In his work the Gond hunter and the Brahmin child are equals in their travels in the jungle, and Dhan Gopal Mukerji never (unlike Kipling) anthropomorphises the animals or draws a facile moral from them.

Although he was acutely conscious of his high caste, he saw it more as a responsibility than a privilege, and neither patronized nor denigrated the so-called 'lower' castes and communities.

He was, however, less sound on the subject of women. He writes movingly of child prostitutes in America in the 1910s and 1920s, especially of their plight during the Depression, but he also romanticizes the life of Rangini, a 'tawaif' (courtesan) encountered in *Caste and Outcast*. He also praises his mother's and sisters' strict asceticism, all the more so since his mother is at that time a widow, performing all the hard penances prescribed to Hindu widows of her caste.

BHARATI MUKHERJEE

Bharati Mukherjee (born July 27, 1940) is an award-winning Indian born American writer. She is currently a professor in the department of English at the University of California, Berkeley.

Of Bengali origin, Mukherjee was born in Calcutta (now called Kolkata), West Bengal, India. She later travelled with her parents to Europe after Independence, only returning to Calcutta in the early 1950s. There she attended the Loreto School. She received her B.A. from the University of Calcutta in 1959 and her M.A. from the University of Baroda in 1961. She next travelled to the United States to study at the University of Iowa. She received her M.F.A. from the Iowa Writers' Workshop in 1963 and her Ph.D. in 1969 from the department of Comparative Literature.

Mukherjee married writer Clark Blaise in 1963. Together they have written two works of non-fiction, *Days and Nights in Calcutta* (1977) and *The Sorrow and the Terror: The Haunting Legacy of the Air India Tragedy* (1987). After more than a decade living in Montreal and Toronto in Canada, Mukherjee, Blaise, and their children returned to the United States. She wrote of the decision in "An Invisible Woman," published in a 1981 issue of *Saturday Night.*

Mukherjee has taught at McGill University, Skidmore College, Queens College, and City University of New York.

Works

An early and popular work of fiction is *Jasmine* 1989. In this novel, a young Indian woman becomes an illegal immigrant to the United States and acculturates by taking on a series of different identities.

Mukherjee characters strive to understand the idea of an American identity and whether, in a world of hybridity and multiplicity, such a notion can exist. This is particularly evident in her more recent works *The Holder of the World* (1993), *Leave It to Me* (1997) and *Desirable Daughters* (2002). Her latest novel is *The Tree Bride,* (2004).

Mukerjee is a member of the American Academy of Arts and Sciences.

Bibliography

Novels

- *The Tiger's Daughter* (1971)
- *Wife* (1975)
- *Jasmine* (1989)
- *The Holder of the World* (1993)
- *Leave It to Me* (1997)
- *Desirable Daughters* (2002)
- *The Tree Bride* (2004)

Short Story Collections

- *Darkness* (1985)
- *The Middleman and Other Stories* (1988)

Memoir

- *Days and Nights in Calcutta* (1977, with Clark Blaise)

Non-fiction

- *The Sorrow and the Terror: The Haunting Legacy of the Air India Tragedy* (1987, with Clark Blaise)
- Political Culture and Leadership in India (1991)
- Regionalism in Indian Perspective (1992)

Awards

- 1988: National Book Critics Circle Award (*The Middleman and Other Stories*).

SUROOPA MUKHERJEE

Suroopa Mukherjee is the author of several books for children and young people, including *Bhopal Gas Tragedy: The Worst Industrial Disaster in Human History*, a book about the Bhopal disaster. She teaches English Literature at Delhi University and is the co-ordinator of a student group dedicated to creating youth awareness on issues relating to environmental damage and corporate crime.

Across The Mystic Shore was her debut novel for adults, released by Macmillan New Writing in March 2007.

M. MUKUNDAN

M Mukundan is one of the pioneers of modernity in Malayalam literature. He was born on 10 September 1942 at Mayyazhi in Mahe, a former French territory in Kerala. He is the current President of Kerala Sahitya Akademi.

He is known in Kerala as 'Mayyazhiyude Kadhakaaran' (Story teller of Mayyazhi)-Mayyazhi figures in his early works; 'Mayyazhippuzhayude Theerangalil', 'Daivathinte Vikrithikal', 'Appam Chudunna Kunkiyamma' and 'Lesli Achante Kadangal'.

His first literary work was a short story published in 1961. Mukundan has so far published 11 novels and 10 collections of short stories. Mukundan's latest four novels 'Adithyanum Radhayum Mattu Chilarum', 'Oru Dalit Yuvathiyude Kadanakatha', 'Kesavante Vilapangal' and 'Nirtham ' carries a change in structure and approach.

'Oru Dalit Yuvathiyude Kadanakatha' reveals how Vasundhara, an actress has been insulted in the course of acting due to some unexpected situations. It proclaims the postmodern message that martyrs are created not only through ideologies, but through art also.

'Kesavante Vilapangal' the latest work of Mukundan tells the story of a writer Kesavan who writes a novel on a child named Appukkuttan who grows under the influence of E. M. S. Namboodiripad. 'Daivathinte Vikrithikal' bagged the Kendra Sahithya Academy award and NV Prize. 'Ee Lokam Athiloru Manushyan' bagged the Kerala Sahitya Academy award. Daivathinte Vikrithikal has been translated into English and published By Penguin Books India.

In 2008, Mukundan's magnum opus Mayyazhi Puzhayude Theerangalil fetched him the award for the best novel published in the last 25 years. Three of his novels were made into feature films in Malayalam. Mukundan wrote the script and one of them bagged a state film award. The French government conferred on him the title of Chevalier des Arts et des Lettres in 1998 for his contribution to literature.

ANITA NAIR

Anita Nair is a popular Indian-English writer. She was born at Mundakottakurissi, near Shornur in Kerala State. She was working as the creative director of an advertising agency in Bangalore when she wrote her first book, a collection of short stories called *Satyr of the Subway*, which she sold it to Har-Anand Press. The book won her a fellowship from the Virginia Centre for Creative Arts. Her second book was published by Penguin India, and was the first book by an Indian author to be published by Picador USA. Her books have been published in several languages around the world. She lives in Bangalore.

R. K. NARAYAN

R. K. Narayan (October 10, 1906-May 13, 2001), born Rasipuram Krishnaswami Ayyar Narayanaswami is among the best known and most widely read Indian novelists writing in English.

Most of Narayan's work, starting with his first novel *Swami and Friends* (1935), captures many Indian traits while retaining a unique identity of its own. He was sometimes compared to the American writer William Faulkner, whose novels were also grounded in a compassionate humanism and celebrated the humour and energy of ordinary life.

Narayan lived till age of ninety-four, writing for more than fifty years, and publishing until he was eighty seven. He wrote fourteen novels, five volumes of short stories, a number of travelogues and collections of non-fiction, condensed versions of Indian epics in English, and the memoir *My Days*.

Biography

Birth: R. K. Narayan was born in Madras (now called Chennai), India on October 10, 1906. His father, Rasipuram

Venkatarama Krishnaswami Iyer, was a provincial head-master. He was the third of eight surviving children and an elder brother to popular Indian cartoonist R K Laxman. His full name was Rasipuram Krishnaswami Ayyar Narayanaswami.

Childhood: Narayan's mother, Gnanambal, was quite ill after his birth and enlisted a wet nurse to feed her young son. When she became pregnant again, the two-year-old Narayan was sent to Madras to live with his maternal grandmother, Parvathi, who was called *"Ammani."* He lived with her and one of his uncles, T. N. Seshachalam, until he was a teenager. He only spent a few weeks each summer visiting his parents and siblings. Narayan grew up speaking Tamil and learned English at school.

Education: After completing eight years of education at the Lutheran Mission School near his grandmother's house in Madras, he studied for a short time at the CRC High School. When his father was appointed headmaster of the Maharaja's High School in Mysore, Narayan moved back in with his parents. To his father's consternation, Narayan was an indifferent student and after graduating high school, he failed the college entrance exam in English because he found the primary textbook to be too boring to read. He took the exam again a year later and eventually obtained his bachelor's degree from the University of Mysore.

One of the few Indian-English writers who spent nearly all his time in India, he went abroad to the United States in 1956 at the invitation of the Rockefeller Foundation. Narayan's first published work was the review of a book titled *Development of Maritime Laws of 17th-Century England..* He began his literary career with short stories which appeared in *The Hindu*, and also worked for some time as the Mysore correspondent of *Justice*, a Madras-based newspaper. He also took up teaching at a government school, but left the job within two days.

Writing Career: His writing career began with *Swami and Friends*. At first, he could not get the novel published. Eventually, the draft was shown to Graham Greene by a mutual friend, Purna. Greene liked it so much that he arranged for its publication; Greene was to remain a close friend and admirer of his. After that, he published a continuous stream of novels, all set in Malgudi and each dealing with different characters in that fictional place. Autobiographical content forms a significant part of some of his novels. For example, the events surrounding the death of his young wife and how he coped with the loss form the basis of *The English Teacher*. Mr. Narayan became his own publisher when World War II cut him off from Britain.

Death: R. K. Narayan passed away on May 13, 2001. He was 94. Until his very last days, he remained an avid critic of the changes occurring around his Alwarpet apartment in Chennai, and was also a voracious reader.

Writing Style

Narayan's novels are characterised by Chekhovian simplicity and gentle humour. He told stories of simple folks trying to live their simple lives in a changing world. The characters in his novels were very ordinary, down-to-earth Indians trying to blend tradition with modernisation, often resulting in tragi-comic situations. His writing style was simple, unpretentious and witty with a unique flavour as if he were writing in the native tongue. Many of Narayan's works are rooted in everyday life, though he is not shy of invoking Hindu tales or traditional Indian folklore to emphasize a point. His easy-going outlook on life has sometimes been criticized, though in general he is viewed as an accomplished, sensitive and reasonably prolific writer. His stories are incredibly easy to read because of their simplicity. He almost always writes about India in some way, and usually puts cultural influences about Indian life in his works.

Awards and Recognition

Mr. Narayan won numerous awards and honours for his works. He won the National Prize of the Sahitya Akademi, the Indian literary academy, for *The Guide* in 1958. He was honoured with the Padma Bhushan, a coveted Indian award, for distinguished service to literature in 1964. In 1980, R. K.

Narayan was awarded the AC Benson Medal by the Royal Society of Literature. He was an honorary member of the society. He was elected an honorary member of the American Academy and Institute of Arts and Letters in 1982 and nominated to the Rajya Sabha — the upper house of the Parliament of India — in 1989. In addition, the University of Mysore, Delhi University and the University of Leeds conferred honorary doctorates on him. He was awarded Padma Vibhushan in 2000.

- R.K. Narayan was short listed for the Nobel Prize in Literature several times but never won. Literary circles often joke that the Nobel Committee ignored his works, mistaking them instead for self-help books due to their curious titles (The English Teacher, The Painter of Signs, etc.).
- His works were translated into every European language as well as Hebrew.
- His admirers included Somerset Maugham, John Updike and Graham Greene, who called him the "novelist I admire most in the English language."

Criticism

Though Narayan's writing have been extremely popular amongst the masses, the upper, literary classes never really warmed up to him. It has been said that his writing was pedestrian, with his simple language and stories of village life. One of his most outspoken critics has been Shashi Tharoor. Sandeep Sharma of Himachal Pradesh University, in his M.Phil dissertation entitled : "*The Guide* and *The Vendor of Sweets*: A Structural Study" (2006), has researched on the oedipal as well as homosocial contents in Narayan's narrative. There is nevertheless a respectable body of criticism, some of the best of which is listed below.

- AFZAL-KHAN, Fawsia, *Cultural Imperialism and the Indo-English Novel: Genre and Ideology in R. K. Narayan, Anita Desai, Kamala Markandaya, and Salman Rushdie* (Philadelphia: Pennsylvania State University Press, 1993).

- BEATINA, Mary, *Narayan: A Study in Transcendence* (New York, Washington, D.C./Baltimore, Bern, Frankfurt am Main, Berlin, Brussels, Vienna, & Oxford: Peter Lang Publishing, 1994 [Studies of World Literature in English, vol. 3]).
- BLOOM, Harold, *R. K. Narayan* (New York: Chelsea House Publishing, 1994 [Modern Critical Views Series 2]).
- GOYAL, Bhagwat S., ed., *R. K. Narayan's India: Myth and Reality* (Lahore: South Asia Books, 1993).
- HARIPRASANNA, A., *The World of Malgudi: A Study of R. K. Narayan's Novels* (Lahore: South Asia Books, 1997).
- JHA, Ram, *Gandhian Thought and Indo-anglian novelists: Mulk Raj Anand, Raja Rao, R. K. Narayan, & Bhabani Bhattacharya* (Delhi: Chanakya Publications, 1983).
- KAIN, Geoffrey, ed., *R. K. Narayan: Contemporary Critical Perspectives* (East Lansing: Michigan State University Press, 1998).
- LENNARD, John, 'R. K. Narayan', in Jay Parini, ed., *World Writers in English* (2 vols, New York & London: Charles Scribner's Sons, 2004), II.385–407.
- MISHRA, Pankaj, 'The Great Narayan', in *New York Review of Books*, 22 February 2001 .
- POUSSE, Michel, *R. K. Narayan: A Painter of Modern India* (New York, Washington, D.C./Baltimore, Bern, Frankfurt am Main, Berlin, Brussels, Vienna, & Oxford: Peter Lang Publishing, 1995 [Studies of World Literature in English, vol. 4]).
- PRASAD, V. V. N. Rajendra, *Five Indian Novelists: B. Rajan, Raja Rao, R. K. Narayan, Arun Joshi, Anita Desai* (Lahore: South Asia Books, 1997).
- WALSH, William, *R. K. Narayan* (London: The British Council/Longman, 1971 [Writers & their Work])
- WALSH, William, *R. K. Narayan: A Critical Appreciation* (Chicago: University of Chicago Press, 1983).

Bibliography

Novels

- Swami and Friends (1935)
- The Bachelor of Arts (1937)
- The Dark Room (1938)
- The English Teacher (1945)
- Mr. Sampath-The Printer of Malgudi (1949)
- The Financial Expert (1952)
- Waiting for the Mahatma (1955)
- The Guide (1958)
- The Man-Eater of Malgudi (1961)
- The Vendor of Sweets (1967)
- The Painter of Signs (1976)
- A Tiger for Malgudi (1983)
- Talkative Man (1986)
- The World of Nagaraj (1990)
- A Grandmother's Tale (1994)

Collections

- The World of Malgudi (2000)
- Salt and Sawdust: Stories and Table-Talk

Short Story Collections

An asterisk indicates a collection published only in India.

- Dodu and Other Stories (1943)*
- Cyclone and Other Stories (1945)*
- An Astrologer's Day and Other Short Stories (1947)
- Lawley Road and Other Stories (1956)*
- A Horse and Two Goats (1970)
- Malgudi Days (1982)
- Under the Banyan Tree and Other Stories (1985)
- The Grandmother's Tale and Selected Stories (1993)

- The Watchman
- Fruition at Forty
- Indian Thought(1941)

Non-Fiction

- Next Sunday (1960)
- My Dateless Diary (1964)
- My Days (1974)
- The Emerald Route (1980)
- A Writer's Nightmare (1988)
- Like The Sun

Mythology

- Gods, Demons and Others (1965)
- The Ramayana (1972)
- The Mahabharata (1972)

TV and Movie Adaptations

The Guide was made into a film in both English and Hindi by Dev Anand. It was commercially a most successful venture, but Narayan was not happy with the screen adaptation of his novel. His novel *Mr. Sampath* was made into a film by S.S. Vasan of Gemini Films. Another novel, *The Financial Expert* was made into the Kannada movie *Banker Margayya*. *Swami and Friends*, *The Vendor of Sweets* and some of Narayan's short stories were adapted by the late actor-director Shankar Nag into a television series, *Malgudi Days*. It was shot in the village of Agumbe in Karnataka. This village served as the backdrop for Malgudi, complete with a statue of the British personage. It was serialised and telecast on Doordarshan, the Indian National Television network.

AMPASAYYA NAVEEN

Dr. 'Ampasayya' Naveen is a renowned Telugu novelist and short story writer. He was born in Vavilala, a village in Warangal District of southern Indian state of Andhra Pradesh in 1941. A professor of Economics, his style of thought-provoking narration led him to fictional writing.

He is regarded by many as one of the best writers Andhra Pradesh has ever produced. He rose to literary fame with his novel *Ampasayya* (Bed of Arrows) thirty five years ago. With 28 novels, more than 50 short-stories and several literary essays to his credit, Dr. Naveen has joined the ranks of the most famous Telugu authors such as Vaddera Chandidas, Dr. Keseva Reddy, Ra.Vi Sastri, Vasireddy Sitadevi and Dasarathi Rangacharyulu.

Works

Naveen's novels, *Ampasayya*, *Mullapodalu* (Thorn Bushes) and *Antasravanti* (Inner Stream), (popularly known as the "Ravi Trilogy"), brought the stream of consciousness writing technique to Telugu fiction. *Ampasayya* has gone through seven printings and has been translated into both Hindi (as *Sharshayya*) and English (as *Bed of Thorns*). *Antasravanti* won the Telugu University's best novel award in 1994, which is equal to the state Sahitya Academy Award.

Popular with both his critics and the public, Naveen's explores the dynamics of the human mind and social relations in the context of contemporary issues facing man and society. *Cheekati Rojulu* (Dark Days) graphically depicts the atrocities committed by the state on the citizens of India during the Emergency of 1975-77. It is the first book of its kind to do so in any Indian language. Recently, the novel has been translated into English. *Women's College* and *Vichalitha* (The Disturbed) depict the discrimination and injustice endured by women in India. *Bandhavyalu* focuses on 25 years of socio-economic change in Telangana.

Three collections of short stories, *Life in a College*, *Enimido Adugu* (Eighth step) and *From Anuradha with Love* have all been published by Dr. Naveen. Another short story collection, *Lifescapes* was recently released in English. Apart from winning awards, many of his stories have also been translated into Hindi, English, Tamil, Kannada and Marathi.

Dr. Naveen has also published a large number of critical articles, some of them in English, on Telugu fiction, films and other art forms. He has written a trilogy of novels against the backdrop of the history of Telangana from the early 1940s to the early 1990s as part of the Senior Fellowship awarded to writers of great skill by the Indian department of culture. One of these novels, *Bhandavyalu,* was released on the date of Naveen's Shastipurti, on 24th December 2001. *The second in this trilogy* Kalarekhalu *(Imprints of Time) was released on 24th December 2002, and the third* Chedirina Swapnalu *(Dreams Dispersed) on 24th December 2003.*

Kalarekhalu won the Sahitya Academy Award for Naveen in 2004. Perhaps his greatest achievement though was when Kakatiya University presented him with an honorary Doctorate (Honoris Causa) at their 16th Convocation in 2004.

In 2000, Dr. Naveen had the honour of serving as a member of the Jury appointed by the government of Andhra Pradesh to decide the Nandi Awards for feature films. He has also been nominated to serve as a member of the Academic Senate at Kakatiya University for three years (2006 to 2009).

Recently he visited the USA on an invitation of the ATA (American Telugu Association) and delivered lectures at various locations in Los Angeles, Atlanta, Columbia, Chicago and Detroit.

Awards and Honours

Honorary Doctorate (Honoris causa) awarded by *Kakatiya University* in its 16th Convocation at Warangal in the year 2004.

Prathibha Puraskaram in the category of novel and short story by *Pottisriramulu Telugu University,* Hyderabad for the year 2002.

Raavi shastry award, Hyderabad for the year 2000

Jyesta Literary award, Vishakapatnam in 1999, for his best translation into English of his own short story *Bali* (Sacrifice).

Vishla Sahitya academy award, Jagityala, in 1998, (Lifetime achievement award)

Senior Fellowship for two years (Oct 1997 to Sept. 1999) awarded by the *Department of Culture*, Ministry of HRD, Govt of India, New Delhi, for writing a novel depicting fifty years of socio-economic and political history of telangana from 1944 to 1995.

Best Novel Prize for the year 1994 to *Antasravanthi* (inner Stream) by *Pottisriramulu Telugu University* (State Sahitya Academy Award).

Best Novel Award to *Dagudu Muthalu* (Hide and seek) by *Swathi*(Weekly Magazine) 1978.

Best Short Story to *Chera* (Bondage) by *Andhra Jyothi* (Weekly Magazine) 1987.

Best Short Story to *Thera* (Curtain) by *Andhra Prabha* (Weekly Magazine) 1986.

Best Short Story to *Dhadi* (Attack) by *Pallaki* (Weekly Magazine) 1985.

Best Short Story to *Bali* (Sacrifice) by *Swathi* (Monthly Magazine) 1984.

Best Short Story to *Hatya* (Murder) by *Andhra Jyothi* (Weekly Magazine) 1973.

Naveen Novels : Annotated Bibliography

Ampasayya (Bed of Arrows) depicts the life of University students. The stress is on the psycho economic factors. Narrative technique is stream of consciousness. This novel portrays only 16 hours in the life of a student who stays in a hostel. It has been translated in Hindi, Tamil end English.

Vichelitha (The Disturbed) depicts extra marital relation in a middle class family. If a man commits adultery, society excuses him. If the same is committed by a women, she is severely punished. The novel questions this double standards.

Mullapodalu (Thorn Bushes) is a sequeal of ampasayya. The problem depicted is educated unemployment. Because of unemployment the youth are drawn to different movements like naxalism, separate telangana, etc.

Sowjanya (Name of the Heroine) Narrates the story of unrequited love between Sowjanya and Krishna Rao. Krishna Rao falls in love with Sowjanya, but Sowjanya hates him.

Sankellu (Chains) tells the story of an idealist who loves freedom, but feels that he is in chains. He struggles to liberate himself from bondages like marriage, tradition, etc. Sankellu was made into a teleserial and was telecasted from Gemini TV for 13 weeks in 1999.

Agadhalu (Depths) is the story of a girl who struggles to achieve her life's mission, in the face of heavy odds.

Karuna (Name of the heroine) is the daughter of a police officer who brings her up with strict decipline. Because of this unkind upbringing, karuna becomes a timid girl. When she is faced with a big crisis in her life regarding her marriage, she cannot take a bold decision and therefore ends here life.

Dagudumuthalu (Hide and Seek) depicts the platonic love between chaitanya and vikram who are colleagues in an office. Superficially they quarrel with each other every minute, but in their hearts they worship each other.

Cheekati Rojulu (Dark days) depicts the atrocities committed by the police on an innocent writer during the dark days of emergency of 1975. This novel is written in the form of a diary. This is only telugu novel which highlights state terrorism during the emergency. This novel was translated into Hindi and English.

Mouna Ragalu (Silent tunes) is a story of good number of boys and girls meet during the celebration of a marriage. Most of them are relatives and most cousins. During just a few days they develop deep attachments, but they depress after the marriage, forgetting everything.

Taru Maru (Changes of roles) is the story of childless couple. The husband thinks that his wife has a medical problem. He threatens her that he is going in for a second marriage. But medical examination of both establishes that he himself is unfit for having children. With this revelation their relationship drastically changes. Now the wife begins to dominate the husband.

Anuraga Sravanthi (Stream of Love) :Prabava special novel for December, 1979. yet to be published as book.. This novel depicts the deep love and attachment between a newly married wife and husband.

Pratyusha (Dawn) depicts the miserable life of the teachers in private unaided school. They are paid very meager salaries but are treated by management as bonded labourers.

Andame Vishadam (Bueaty is grief) Swathi (Monthly) special mvoel for May 1981. Yet to appread in book from. Ansame Vishadam shows how sometimes good looks become big curse even for a man.

Theerani daham (Unquenched Thirst) is a novel narrated in the form of letters between a writer and his female admirer. Their relationship is purely platonic.

Chemmagillani kallu (Eyes that don't shed tears) depicts the stormy love affair between a young cricketer and a sales girl.

Cheekati Moosina Ekanthamlo (Lonely in the dark) suggest that it is better to go in for a divorce when a wife and husband realize that it is impossible to live together.

Prayanamulo Pramadalu (Troubles while travelling) is written in the form of a travelogue, Rajeshwar, a lecturer in a women's collage an excursion party of 50 young girls to south India. The travel and tribulations of these girls during the 10 days of going round the places in south India are depicted sensitively .

Anthasravanthi (Inner stream) is the sequeal to ampasayya and mullapodalu. In this novel the married and professional life of the progonist Ravi is depicted. It has won for naveen the prestigious telugu university award which is equivalent to state Sahitya Academy Award, for best novel in 1995. Note: Ampasayya, Mullapodalu and Anthasravanthi have come to be known as the Ravi trilogy in the telugu literary circle. These three depict different days/phases in the life of Ravi. The narrative technique is the stream of consciousness in all the three novels.

Manoranyam (Forest in the mind) is a story of group of friends-3 men and 3 women-meet in a forest to celebrate and welcome the new year. After lot of fun and hilarity they start quarreling with each other under the influence of alcohol.

Women's college is a novel that probes the lives of working women. These women who are employed in a women's college. In spite of earning their own livelihood, suffer many hardships and humiliations at the hands of society.

They have two bosses their employer and the husband. They realize that to rebel and assert their rights is the only solution to their rights is the only solution to their problems.

Drukkonalu (View Points) Published in Andhra Bhoomi (Daily) as daily serial in 1999 in a popular daily. This novel is an experiment in a new narrative technique. As incident takes place (a women is said to have been raped in a dental clinic kept by a quack). The people involved in the incident are : a reporter, a police office, the victim, the quack, etc. giving different versions of the same incident. The truth, however seems to elude observer.

Bandhavyalu (Relationship) depicts changing social and family relationships in telangana region against the background of various movements like the separate Telangana agitation, Naxalite's armed struggle etc., during the last twenty five years. Note: This novel is scheduled to be made into Tele-serial with 260 episodes and approved for telecast by Doordarshan from Jan 2007.

Raktha Kasaram (Pool Of Blood) is the recent novel serialized in "Vijaya Viharam" (Monthly). This novel deals with the contemporary problem of Naxalism in telangana. It depicts the socio-economic reasons for the spread of this movement and how innocent lives are lost in the war between Police and Naxalites. This novel created a stir in literary circles when it was published in the form of a book in March 2006.

Kalarekhalu (Imprints of Time) depicts the social, political and cultural history of Telangana regiond (most backward region of Andhra Pradesh) from 1956 to 1994. This novel won the ventral Sahitya Academy award for year 2004. In its citation, Sahitya Academy said

Kalarekhalu is a socio-autobiographical novel based on the Telangana struggle against the imperialist regime. The novel is unique in its picturization of the struggle of suppressed humanity. The author has successfully captured the sentiments of populace in the threos of liberating themselves. The novel adds magnificently to Indian fiction in telugu

SHARDHA RAM PHILLAURI

Pandit Shardha Ram "Phillauri" (1837 – June 24, 1881) was a Punjabi missionary, social reformer, astrologer, and writer, best remembered for his contributions to Hindi and Punjabi literature. He has been called the "father of modern Punjabi prose."

Shardha Ram was born in 1837 to a Brahmin family in the town of Phillaur, Jalandhar. His father, Jai Dyalu, was an astrologer. At the age of seven, he learned Gurmukhi script. By age ten, he had studied Hindi, Sanskrit, Persian, astrology, and music. Later, he was also a missionary of traditional Hinduism (Sanatana dharma).

In his books, Shardha Ram documented Punjabi culture and language.

Shardha Ram gave forceful lectures on the Mahabharata, and because of this was charged with conducting propaganda against the British government in 1865. As a result, he was exiled temporarily from his home town, Phillaur.

Sharda Ram often visited Amritsar and adjoining Lahore, especially in connection with astrology. During this time, he earned a reputation as an astrologer and wrote several books in Hindi.

Shardha Ram has recently been acknowledged as having written the first novel in Hindi. His novel *Bhagyawati*, believed to have been written mainly in Amritsar, was first published in 1888, after Shardha Ram's death. The novel's portrayal of women and women's rights was progressive for its day.

Shardha Ram died on June 24, 1881 at Lahore.

RAHI MASOOM RAZA

Dr. Rahi Masoom Reza, born in Ghazipur in eastern Uttar Pradesh (India) in a Muslim family, was a famous Urdu shayar. He also wrote in Hindustani and Hindi language. He was also an eminent lyricist of Bollywood.

He wrote the script for a popular TV serial, *Mahabharat.* The TV serial was based on the epic, the Mahabharata. The serial became one of the most popular TV serial of north India, and its peak Television Rating was around 86%.

Several works of Raza vividly depicts the agony and turmoil of the consequences of partition, and its effect on the Hindu-Muslim relationship in the Indian subcontinent, as also the social tension among different social groups of India. For instance, his novel named *Katra Bi Arzoo* (that is, The Lady Desire Street or The Lady Arzoo Street) is set in the city of Allahabad, Katra being a locality of the city.

The novel depicts Hindu-Muslim rivalry. Another novel, named *Topi Shukla* also revolves around the similar sad theme of social tension between the two largest social groups of India, the Hindus and the Muslims.

Some of his stories and literary works also depict the social tension among the social groups belonging to same religious faith but traditionally positioned at different social hierarchical levels. Neem Ka Ped (that is, *A Neem Tree*) vividly depicts the social tension between the landed aristocracy and their serfs.

Works

The following is an illustrative list of his works in different genres of writings:

- Novel
  - *Adha Gaon* (that is, *The Divided Village*)

  * *Dil ek saada kaghaz*
  * *Topi Shukla*
  * *Os ki boond*
  * *Katra Bi arzoo*
- Poetry (books)
  * *Mauz-e-ghul mauz-e-saba* (Urdu)
  * *Ajnabee shahar ajnabee raste* (Urdu)
  * *Main ek Feriwala* (Hindi)
  * *Sheeshe ke Makaan Wale* (Hindi)
- Autobiography
  * *Chotey aadmi ki badee kahaani* (that is, "Big story of a Small man")
- Movie and TV scripts
  * Neem ka Ped-Novel and TV Serial with same name
  * Kissi Se Na Kehna
  * Main Tulsi Tere Aangan Ki
  * Disco Dancer
  * Mahabharat (TV series)
- Movie dialogues
  * Lamhe
  * Karz (film)
  * Aaina
  * Parampara

BALACHANDRA RAJAN

Balachandra Rajan (b. 1920), a scholar of poetry and poetics, focusing particularly on the poetry of John Milton, is Professor Emeritus of English at the University of Western Ontario.

He was Fellow of Trinity College, Cambridge from 1944–1948, but left England to return to his native India, where he served in the Indian Foreign Service until 1961. During that period he served on the Indian Delegation to the United Nations, working extensively with UNESCO and UNICEF. Leaving his diplomatic career to return to academe, Rajan taught at the University of Delhi before emigrating to Canada to take up a position at the University of Western Ontario.

Rajan's scholarly work covers a wide range of English poetry, but has returned frequently to Milton and particularly to Milton's *Paradise Lost.*

He cannot be easily assigned to any critical methodology, but is instead a scholar of poetics in many forms and from many approaches. His 1947 book *Paradise Lost and the Seventeenth Century Reader* is primarily a response to Milton's apparent interest in Arianism, considered a heresy, and argues for a distinction between private and public meaning in Milton's poetry.

The book was influential for William Empson, particularly Empson's critique of strictly theological readings of *Paradise Lost, Milton's God.* Later essays explore what Rajan calls "generic multeity" in *Paradise Lost.* In addition to his work on Milton, Rajan's later criticism addresses issues of meaning, intention, and context in a broad array of writers including Spenser, Yeats, Marvell, Keats, and Macaulay.

Rajan has also written two novels. *The Dark Dancer* is a sobering study of the conflicts of the Partition; *Too Long in the West,* on the other hand, is a more light-hearted satire (perhaps influenced by Tagore's *Farewell, My Friend*) about a girl's return to her home village after an emancipating education in New York.

Critical Works

- *Paradise Lost and the Seventeenth Century Reader.* London: Chatto and Windus, 1947. Reprinted Ann Arbour: University of Michigan Press, 1967.
- *W.B.Yeats: A Critical Introduction.* London: Hutchinson University Library, 1965.
- *The Lofty Rhyme: A Study of Milton's Major Poetry.* London: Routledge, 1970.
- *The Overwhelming Question: A Study of the Poetry of T.S. Eliot.* Toronto: University of Toronto Press, 1976.

- *The Form of the Unfinished: English Poetics from Spenser to Pound*. Princeton: Princeton University Press, 1985.
- *Under Western Eyes: India from Milton to Macaulay*. Durham: Duke University Press, 1999.
- *Milton and the Climate of Reading: Essays*. Toronto: University of Toronto Press, 2006.

Fiction

- *The Dark Dancer*. New York: Simon and Schuster, 1958.
- *Too Long in the West*. New York: Atheneum, 1962.

RAJASHREE

Rajashree is an Indian novelist and film-maker. She has been working in the Bombay film industry after studying film direction at the Film and Television Institute of India. She has written and directed a film, *The Rebel*, which won a National Award and was screened at many film festivals. Her first book, *Trust Me*, has been published by Rupa. It is a best-selling chick lit novel set in the Bombay film industry, Bollywood. She currently lives and works in Bombay, India.

RAJALAKSHMI

T. A. Rajalakshmi (June 2, 1930-January 18, 1965) was a Malayalam writer and poet in India. Born at Cherpulassery, Palakkad, her father was Mararth Achutha Menon and mother was Kutty Malu Amma. As a notable writer she got Kerala Sahithya Academy Award in 1960 for her work "Oru Vazhiyum Kure Nizhalukalum" (A Path and a Few Shadows). It later became a TV serial and will soon be broadcast as a play by All India Radio. Her famous poem is "Ninne Njan Snehikkunnu."

She committed suicide in 1965.

MALAYATTOOR RAMAKRISHNAN

Malayattoor Ramakrishnan (1927-1997) was a prominent Malayali novelist of the 20th century. He is credited with having authored several important works in Malayali literature.

Life

Malayattoor Ramakrishnan was born on May 27, 1927 as K.V.Ramakrishna Iyer in Kalpathi in Palakkad in a family of Kerala Iyers.He was one of six siblings. The family settled down in a small village near the banks of the River Periyar. He studied in Perumbavoor and in Aluva and completed his Bachelor's degree and a Law degree in Thiruvananthapuram.

Even during his student days, he had started writing and cartooning. He became a communist sympathiser and even contested elections in Perumbavoor (he lost). He started his work as a sub-editor in Free Press Journal in Bombay. He was a contributing cartoonist to Shankar's Weekly. He is also credited with the first Malayali translation of Bram Stoker's Dracula apart from translating Sherlock Holmes' novels into Malayalam.

In 1954, he entered the Kerala judicial service and served as a magistrate. That year, he married Krishnaveni (1935-1999). They had two children.

In 1957, Ramakrishnan entered the Indian Administrative Service (IAS). He served as Sub-Collector in Ottapalam, Collector in Kozhikode, and held various positions in the Secretariat of Kerala, including as Member, Board of Revenue and Chairman of the Lalit Kala Akademi. The memoirs of his long career as a bureaucrat are narrated in his work The Service Story.

Malayattoor wrote his best known work-Verukal (Roots) in 1965. It is a semi-autobiographical work which tells the story of a family of Tamil speaking Iyers who settled in Kerala. This won him the Kerala Sahitya Akademi Award.

In 1981, he resigned from the Indian Administrative Service in order to devote his time to writing. It was during the period 1981 to 1997 that his most famous works emerged from his pen. Among his other famous novels are Yakshi, Yantram, Nettoor Mathom and Amritham Thedi. For Yanthram, he was awarded the Vayalar Award.

Malayattoor had also authored scripts for several films. The most famous of these were Yakshi, starring Sathyan and Iyer The Great starring Mammootty. Malayattoor was also a well-known cartoonist and painter. Some of his paintings are displayed in the Kerala Chitra Tirunal Art Gallery.

Malayattoor remained active though his later years and was working on a novel when he died in 1997 at Thiruvanathapuram. He was given a state funeral by the Government of Kerala.

RAJA RAO

Raja Rao (November 8, 1908 – July 8, 2006) was an Indian writer of English language novels and short stories, whose works are deeply rooted in Hinduism. Raja Rao's semi-autobiographical novel, *The Serpent and the Rope* (1960), is a story of a search for spiritual truth in Europe and India. It established him as one of the finest Indian stylists.

Early Life and Career

Raja Rao was born on November 8, 1908 in Hassan, in the state of Mysore (now Karnataka) in South India, into a well-known Brahmin (Hoysala Karnataka) family. He was the eldest of nine siblings-two brothers and seven sisters. His native language was Kannada, but his postgraduate education was in France, and all his publications in book form have been in English. His father taught Kannada at Nizam's College in what was then Hyderabad State. The death of his mother, when he was four, left a lasting impression on the novelist-the absence of a mother and orphanhood are recurring themes in his work. Another influence from early life was his grandfather, with whom he stayed in Hassan and Harihalli.

Rao was educated at Muslim schools, the Madarsa-e-Aliya in Hyderabad and the Aligarh Muslim University. He began learning French at the University. After matriculation in 1927, Rao returned to Hyderabad and studied for his degree at Nizam's College. After graduation from Madras University, having majored in English and History, he won the Asiatic Scholarship of the Government of Hyderabad in 1929, for study abroad.

Rao moved to the University of Montpellier in France. He studied French language and literature, and later at the

Sorbonne in Paris, he explored the Indian influence on Irish literature. He married Camille Mouly, who taught French at Montpellier, in 1931. The marriage lasted until 1939. Later he depicted the breakdown of their marriage in *The Serpent and the Rope*. Rao published his first stories in French and English. During 1931-32 he contributed four articles written in Kannada for *Jaya Karnataka,* an influential journal.

Nationalist Novelist

Returning to India in 1939, he edited with Iqbal Singh, *Changing India,* an anthology of modern Indian thought from Ram Mohan Roy to Jawaharlal Nehru. He participated in the Quit India Movement of 1942. In 1943-1944 he coedited with Ahmed Ali a journal from Bombay called *Tomorrow*. He was the prime mover in the formation of a cultural organization, *Sri Vidya Samiti,* devoted to reviving the values of ancient Indian civilization; this organization failed shortly after inception. In Bombay, he was also associated with *Chetana,* a cultural society for the propagation of Indian thought and values.

Rao's involvement in the nationalist movement is reflected in his first two books. The novel *Kanthapura* (1938) was an account of the impact of Gandhi's teaching on non-violent resistance against the British. The story is seen from the perspective of a small Mysore village in South India. Rao borrows the style and structure from Indian vernacular tales and folk-epic. Rao returned to the theme of Gandhism in the short story collection *The Cow of the Barricades* (1947).

In 1998 he published Gandhi's biography *Great Indian Way: A Life of Mahatma Gandhi.* In 1988 he received the prestigious International Neustadt Prize for Literature. *The Serpent and the Rope* was written after a long silence during which Rao returned to India.

The work dramatized the relationships between Indian and Western culture. The serpent in the title refers to illusion and the rope to reality. *Cat and Shakespeare* (1965) was a metaphysical comedy that answered philosophical questions posed in the earlier novels.

Later Years

Rao relocated to the United States and taught at the University of Texas at Austin from 1966 to 1983, when he retired as Emeritus Professor. Courses he taught included *Marxism to Gandhism, Mahayana Buddhism, Indian philosophy: The Upanishads, Indian philosophy: The Metaphysical Basis of the Male and Female Principle.*

In 1965, he married Katherine Jones, an American stage actress. They have one son, Christopher Rama. In 1986, after his divorce from Katherine, Rao married his third wife, Susan, whom he met when she was a student at the University of Texas in the 1970s.

Rao died on July 8, 2006 at Austin, Texas, at the age of 97.

Notes:

1. Nobel laureate CzesBaw MiBosz published his only poem in the English language for Raja Rao.
2. He was awarded India's third highest civilian award, Padma Bhushan in 1969.
3. A new novel, *Daughter of the Mountain*, is to be published on November 8, 2006, what would have been his 98th birthday.
4. In January 2007, it was announced that Raja Rao has been selected to receive the Padma Vibhushan India's second highest civilian award.

Bibliography

Fiction

- *Kanthapura,* 1938
- *The Cow of the Barricades, and Other Stories,* 1947
- *The Serpent and the Rope,* 1960
- *The Cat and Shakespeare : A Tale of India,* 1965
- *Comrade Kirilov,* 1976
- *The Policeman and the Rose: Stories,* 1978
- *The Chessmaster and His Moves,* 1988

- *On the Ganga Ghat*, 1989
- *The Best of Raja Rao*, 1998

Non-Fiction

- *Changing India: An Anthology* (edited with Iqbal Singh), 1939
- *Whither India?* (edited with Iqbal Singh), 1948
- *The Meaning of India* essays, 1996
- *The Great Indian Way: A Life of Mahatma Gandhi* biography, 1998

Upcoming Work

- *Daughter of the Mountain* (Volume 2 of the *Chessmaster* trilogy) to be published in 2006.
- *A Myrobalan in the Palm of Your Hand* (Volume 3 of the *Chessmaster* trilogy) to be published in 2007.

ANITA RAU BADAMI

Anita Rau Badami (born 24 September 1961) an Indian-Canadian novelist. Born in Rourkela, Orissa, India, she was at the University of Madras and Sophia College in Bombay. She emigrated to Canada in 1991, and earned an M.A. at the University of Calgary. Her first novel, *Tamarind Mem* (1997), grew out of her university thesis. Her critically acclaimed novels deal with the complexities of Indian family life and with the cultural gap that emerges when Indians move to the west.

Badami cites as among her favourite books *Midnight's Children* by Salman Rushdie, *Cat's Eye* and *Surfacing* by Margaret Atwood, *A House for Mr. Biswas* by V. S. Naipaul and *Housekeeping* by Marilynne Robinson .

PRATIBHA RAY

Pratibha Ray is an Indian academic and writer. She was born on 21 January 1943, at Alabol, a remote village in the Balikuda area of Cuttack district, Orissa state. She is one of the famous commercially popular fiction writers in contemporary India. She writes novels and short stories in her mother tongue

Oriya. Her first novel *Barsa Basanta Baishakha*, 1974, proved itself as a best seller for its readability among rural female half literate readers. Later Pratibha developed the tendency to attribute the boldness, the revolt and humanism in her literature to the impact of Vaishnavism, her family religion, which preaches no caste, no class and also due to the influence of her Gandhian teacher-father, Parashuram Das. The search for a "social order based on equality, love, peace and integration", continues, since the novelist and short story writer first wielded her pen at the age of nine. When she wrote for a social order based on equality without class, caste, religion or sex discriminations, some of her critics branded her as a communist and some as feminist. But She says "I am a humanist. Men and women have been created differently for the healthy functioning of society. The specialities women have been endowed with should be nurtured further. As a human being however, woman is equal to man".

She is married to Sri Akshaya Chandra Ray, an Engineer. When her three children, one daughter (Adyasha) and two sons (Anwesh and Ayaskant), arrived in three consecutive years of marriage, she forgot all about being a writer in bringing them up. At the end of five years she wondered whether she would be able to resume her writing and postgraduate studies. But the support she received from her husband and inspiration from her parents helped her to pursue writing and postgraduate studies. She did her Masters in Education and Ph.D. in Educational Psychology, after sending her three children to school. Her post doctoral research was on tribalism and criminology of Bondo Highlander, one of the most primitive tribes of Orissa, India.

Career

She started her professional career as a school teacher and later she taught in various Government Colleges in Orissa for thirty years. She has guided doctoral research and has published many research articles. She took voluntary retirement as a Professor of Education from State Government Service and joined the post of Member, Public Service Commission of Orissa State, a prestigious constitutional post.

Memberships

She is a member of a number of learned societies. She is connected with Indian Council for Cultural Relations, Central Board of Film Certification, Indian Red Cross Society, India International Centre, National Book Trust of India, Central Academy of Letters etc. She has travelled extensively in India and abroad to participate in various Literary & Educational Conferences. She has won a number of National and State awards for her creative writing.

Other Activities

She has active interest in social reform and has fought against social injustice on many occasions. One important incident in her life is protesting against colour (Caste/ religion) discrimination by the high priests of Jagannath Temple at Puri. Now she is fighting a defamation case lodged by the priests against her for her newspaper article in which she wrote against the undesirable behaviour of the priests, titled "The Colour of Religion is Black" (Dharmara Ranga Kala). She works tirelessly in the cyclone-affected areas after the Orissa's Super Cyclone of October, 1999 and she is working for rehabilitation of the orphans and widows of Cyclone affected areas.

Travel

Travelled extensively within India to participate in various National literary and educational conferences. Visited five republics of U.S.S.R in 1986 in a cultural exchange programme sponsored by ISCUS. Had represented India as an Indian Writer in the India fare in Australia " India today 94" sponsored by Indian Council for Cultural Relations, New Delhi in 1994. She gave readings and talks on Indian literature and languages in several Universities of Australia.

She visited USA, U.K and France on speaking tours. She represented India as an Indian writer in the India Festival in Bangladesh in 1996. Attended 7th International Inter-disciplinary Congress on Women in University of Tromsoe, Norway in June 1999 as an Indian delegate. Visited

Norway, Sweden, Finland & Denmark on speaking tour in 1999. Visited Zurich, Switzerland in 2000 to present a paper in the third European Conference on Gender Equality in Higher Education.

Selected Works

Novels

- *Barsa Basanta Baishakha*, 1974
- *Aranya*, 1977
- *Nishidha Prithivi*, 1978
- *Parichya*, 1979
- *Aparichita*, 1979. (A film was made & won best film story award from State Govt. Culture Deptt.)
- *Punyatoya*, 1979. (Tr. To Hindi)
- *Meghamedura*, 1980
- *Adhibari*, 1980
- *Ayamarambha*, 1981
- *Nilatrishna*, 1981. (Tr. to Hindi)
- *Samudrara Swara*, 1982. (Tr. to Hindi)
- *Shilapadma*, 1983. (Orissa Sahitya Akademi Award, 1985; Tr. to Hindi, Marathi, Malayalam, Punjabi and English)
- *Yajnaseni*, 1984 ((Moorti Devi Award,1991 and Sarala Award, 1990. Tr. to English, Hindi, Marathi,A ssamese, Bengali, Gujarati, Hungerian)
- *Dehatit*, 1986
- *Uttarmarg, 1988. (Tr. to Hindi & Punjabi)*
- *Adibhoomi* (Tr. to Hindi & English)
- *Mahamoh*, 1998 (To be published in Hindi, Bengali & Malayalam)
- *Magnamati*, 2004

Travelogue

- Maitri Padapara Shakha Prashakha (USSR), 1990
- Dura Dwividha (UK, France), 1999

- Aparadhira Sweda (Australia), 2000

Short Stories

- SAMANYA KATHANA-1978
- GANGASHIULI 1979
- ASAMAPTA 1980
- AIKATANA 1981
- ANABANA 1983
- HATABAKSA 1983
- GHASA O AKASHA
- CHANDRABHAGA O CHADRAKALA 1984
- Shrestha Galpa 1984
- ABYAKTA (A tele-film has been made on the title story) 1986
- ITIBUT 1987
- HARITPATRA 1989
- Prithak Ishwar 1991
- BHAGABANARA DESHA 1991
- MANUSHYA SWARA 1992
- Swanirvachita Shrestha Galpa 1994
- SASTHASATI 1996
- MOKSHA (A feature film has been made on the title story and has got the best regional film award) 1996
- ULLANGHANA (Sahitya Akademi Award,2000) 1998
- NIVEDANAMIDAM 2000
- GANDHINKA 2002
- JHOTI PAKA KANTHA 2006

ARUNDHATI ROY

Suzanna Arundhati Roy (born November 24, 1961) is an Indian novelist, writer and activist. She won the Booker Prize in 1997 for her first novel, *The God of Small Things* and in 2002, the Lannan Cultural Freedom Prize. Roy was born in Shillong, Meghalaya to a Keralite Syrian Christian mother, the women's rights activist Mary Roy, and a Bengali father, a tea planter by profession. She spent her childhood in Ayemenem or Aymanam in Kerala, and went to school at Corpus Christi, Kottayam, followed by the Lawrence School, Lovedale in the Nilgiris, Tamil Nadu. She then studied architecture at the School of Planning and Architecture, New Delhi, where she met her first husband, architect Gerard DaCunha.

Roy met her second husband, filmmaker Pradip Krishen, in 1984, and became involved in film-making under his influence. She played a village girl in the award-winning movie *Massey Sahib*.

Roy is a cousin of the prominent media personality Prannoy Roy and lives in New Delhi.

Works

Roy first attracted attention when she criticised Shekhar Kapur's film *Bandit Queen*, based on the life of Phoolan Devi, charging Kapur with exploiting Devi and misrepresenting both her life and its meaning.

Roy began writing her first novel, *The God of Small Things*, in 1992, completing it in 1996. The book is semi-autobiographical and a major part captures her childhood experiences in Ayemenem or Aymanam. The book received the 1997 Man Booker Prize for Fiction and was listed as one of the *New York Times* Notable Books of the Year for 1997. The book reached fourth position on the *New York Times* Bestsellers list for Independent Fiction. She received half a million pounds as an advance, and rights to the book were sold in 21 countries.

The God of Small Things received good reviews, including one from John Updike in The New Yorker. However, Carmen Callil, chair of the Booker judges panel in 1996, called *The God of Small Things* "an execrable book" and said it should never have reached the shortlist.

Roy wrote the screenplays for *In Which Annie Gives it Those Ones* (1989) and *Electric Moon* (1992) and a television serial *The Banyan Tree*. She also wrote the documentary *DAM/AGE: A Film with Arundhati Roy* (2002).

In early 2007, Roy announced she would begin work on a second novel.

Activism and Advocacy

The God of Small Things is the only novel written by Roy. She has since devoted herself solely to nonfiction and politics, publishing two more collections of essays, as well as working for social causes. She is a spokesperson of the anti-globalization/ alter-globalization movement and a vehement critic of neo-imperialism and of the global policies of the United States. She also criticizes India's nuclear weapons policies and the approach to industrialization and rapid development as currently being practiced in India, including the Narmada Dam project and the power company Enron's activities in India.

Sardar Sarovar Project

Roy has campaigned along with activist Medha Patkar against the Narmada dam project, saying that the dam will displace half a million people, with little or no compensation, and will not provide the projected irrigation, drinking water and other benefits. Roy donated her Booker prize money as well as royalties from her books on the project to the Narmada Bachao Andolan. Arundhati Roy's opposition to the Narmada Dam project has been criticised as "anti-Gujarat" by Congress and BJP leaders in Gujarat.

In 2002, Roy responded to a contempt notice issued against her by the Indian Supreme Court with an affidavit saying the court's decision to initiate the contempt proceedings based on an unsubstantiated and flawed petition, while refusing to inquire into allegations of corruption in military contracting deals pleading an overload of cases, indicated a "disquieting inclination" by the court to silence criticism and dissent using the power of contempt. The court found Roy's statement, which she refused to disavow or apologize for, constituted criminal contempt and sentenced her to a "symbolic" one day's imprisonment and fined Roy Rs. 2500. Roy served the sentence and opted to pay the fine rather than serve an additional three months' imprisonment for default.

Environmental historian Ramachandra Guha has been critical of Roy's Narmada dam activism. While acknowledging her "courage and commitment" to the cause, Guha writes that her advocacy is hyperbolic and self-indulgent, "Ms. Roy's tendency to exaggerate and simplify, her Manichean view of the world, and her shrill hectoring tone, have given a bad name to environmental analysis". He faults Roy's criticism of Supreme Court judges who were hearing a petition brought by the Narmada Bachao Andolan as careless and irresponsible.

Roy counters that her writing is intentional in its passionate, hysterical tone-"I *am* hysterical. I'm screaming from the bloody rooftops. And he and his smug little club are going 'Shhhh... you'll wake the neighbours!' I *want* to wake the neighbours, that's my whole point. I want everybody to open their eyes".

Gail Omvedt and Roy have had a fierce discussions, in open letters, on Roy's strategy for the Narmada Dam movement. Though the activists disagree on whether to demand stopping the dam building all together (Roy) or searching for intermediate alternatives (Omvedt), the exchange has mostly been, though critical, constructive.

United States Foreign Policy

Roy has strongly criticised the U.S. led invasion of Afghanistan in reaction to the September 11 attacks, decrying its undermining of international law and institutions. She disputes U.S. claims of being a peaceful and freedom-loving nation, listing the numerous armed conflicts the U.S. has been involved in since the second world war as well as its previous support for the Taliban movement and its support for the Northern Alliance (whose "track record is not very different from the Taliban's"). Noting the interests of arms and oil industries in formulating foreign policy, Roy doubts the U.S.'s stated goals of restoring democracy in Afghanistan and argues that its humanitarian efforts there are a cynical public relations exercise. While condemning the 9/11 attacks, she writes that its response has legitimised violence as a political instrument and aided governments around the world in suppressing freedom and civil rights. Her views were criticized by Ian Buruma, who wrote: "The snobbery of her tone alone betrays the lingering, if perhaps unconscious, influence in India of British lefties from the end of the Raj. It is the language of the Bloomsbury drawing room. You could well imagine Bertrand Russell taking this line."

In May 2003 she delivered a speech entitled "Instant-Mix Imperial Democracy" at the Riverside Church in New York City. In it she described the United States as a global empire that reserves the right to bomb any of its subjects at any time, deriving its legitimacy directly from God. The speech was an indictment of the U.S. actions relating to the Iraq War. In June 2005 she took part in the World Tribunal on Iraq. In March 2006, Roy criticized US President George W. Bush's visit to India.

India's Nuclear Weaponisation

In response to India's testing of nuclear weapons in Pokhran, Rajasthan, Roy wrote *The End of Imagination* (1998), a critique of the Indian government's nuclear policies. It was published in her collection *The Cost of Living* (1999), in which she also crusaded against India's massive hydroelectric dam projects in the central and western states of Maharashtra, Madhya Pradesh and Gujarat.

Criticism of Israel

In August 2006, Roy signed a letter written by Professor Steve Trevillion calling Israel's attacks on Lebanon a "war crime" and accused Israel of "state terror".

In 2007, Roy was one of more than 100 artists and writers who signed an open letter initiated by Queers Undermining Israeli Terrorism and the South West Asian, North African Bay Area Queers (SWANABAQ) and calling on the San Francisco International LGBT Film Festival "to honour calls for an international boycott of Israeli political and cultural institutions, by discontinuing Israeli consulate sponsorship of the LGBT film festival and not cosponsoring events with the Israeli consulate."

2001 Indian Parliament Attack

Roy has raised questions about the investigation into the 2001 Indian Parliament attack and the trial of the accused. She has called for the death sentence of Mohammad Afzal to be stayed while a parliamentary enquiry into these questions are conducted and denounced press coverage of the trial. The BJP has criticised Roy for what it alleges is defence of a terrorist that does not lie in the national interest.

The Muthanga 'Incident'

In 2003, the Adivasi Gothra Maha Sabha, a social movement for adivasi land rights in Kerala, organized a major land occupation of a piece of land of a former Eucalyptus plantation in the Muthanga Wildlife Reserve on the border of Kerala and Karnataka. After 48 days, a massive police force was sent into the area to smash the huts that had been built up and brutally evict the people—one participant of the movement and a policeman were killed. The leaders of the movement moreover were badly beaten and arrested. Arundhati Roy immediately travelled to the area, visited the movement's leaders in jail and wrote an open letter to the Chief Minister saying "You have blood on your hands."

Awards

Arundhati Roy was awarded the 1997 Booker Prize for her fiction The God of Small Things. The award carried a prize of about US $30,000 and a citation that noted: 'The book keeps all the promises that it makes.'

In 2002, she won the Lannan Foundation's Cultural Freedom Award for her work "about civil societies that are adversely affected by the world's most powerful governments and corporations" and "to celebrate her life and her ongoing work in the struggle for freedom, justice and cultural diversity."

Roy was awarded the Sydney Peace Prize in May 2004 for her work in social campaigns and her advocacy of non-violence.

In January 2006 she was awarded the Sahitya Akademi award for her collection of essays on contemporary issues, *The Algebra of Infinite Justice*, but she declined to accept it .

Criticisms and Controversies

Economist and prominent free trade advocate Jagdish Bhagwati, on being asked if he'd like his book being reviewed by Roy, said "her conclusions are far more obvious than her arguments and that makes it impossible to function. You don't know where to begin or where to end."

BJP Member of Parliament Balbir Punj criticised Roy's article, titled *Democracy: Who's she when she's at home?*, on the 2002 Gujarat Violence, pointing out a factual error in it and calling the article "dishonest" and a "hate charter against India and the Sangh parivar". Roy acknowledged the factual error and apologised to the family referred to in the erroneous statement but said that such errors do not alter the substance of her own as well as others' accounts of the violence.

In 2003, Arundhati Roy and her husband were found building their house in a protected tribal forest area, in violation of forest law, which bars buying and selling of notified forest land.

List of Writings

Books

- Roy, Arundhati; (1997). *The God of Small Things.* Flamingo.
- Roy, Arundhati; (1999). *The Cost of Living*. It contains the essays *The Greater Common Good* and *The End of Imagination*, which are now included in the book *The Algebra of Infinite Justice*
- Roy, Arundhati; (2002). *The Algebra of Infinite Justice.* Flamingo. (a collection of essays: *The End of Imagination*, *The Greater Common Good*, *Power Politics* [also a book], *The Ladies Have Feelings, So...*, *The Algebra of Infinite Justice*, *War is Peace*, *Democracy*, *War Talk* [also a book] and *Come September*.)
- Foreword to *For Reasons of State* (2003)
- Roy, Arundhati; (2002). *Power Politics.*
- Roy, Arundhati; (2003). *War Talk.* South End Press.

- Roy, Arundhati; (2004). *An Ordinary Person's Guide To Empire*
- Roy, Arundhati; (2004). *Public Power in the Age of Empire*
- Roy, Arundhati; (2004). *The Checkbook and the Cruise Missile: Conversations with Arundhati Roy*. South End Press

Essays, Speeches and Articles

- *Insult and Injury in Afghanistan* (MSNBC, 20 October 2001)
- *War is Peace* (*Outlook*, 29 October 2001)
- *Stop bombing Afghanistan*
- *Instant Democracy* (May 13, 2003)

DILIPKUMAR ROY

Dilipkumar Roy (1897-1980) was a Bengali Indian musician, musicologist, novelist, poet and essayist of a vast culture, endowed as much with intellectual gifts as with an innate devotion.

Cultural Background

Son of Dwijendralal Ray (1863-1913), the famous Bengali poet, playwright, and composer, Dilip and his younger sister Maya lost their mother Surabala Devi in 1903. From his father's side, the family descended from one of the apostles of the medieval Bengali saint Shri Chaitanya. Brilliant as student, since his childhood, Dilip had a fascination for Sanskrit, English, chemistry and mathematics. His passion for music stopped him from securing the highest marks in the Matriculation examination : he stood the twenty-first and, with a scholarship, joined the Presidency College of Kolkata. Here he came close to a future celebrity : Subhas Chandra Bose. With a first class honours in mathematics, he went to Cambridge in 1919 for a tripos. Shortly before this three-year trip to Europe, in his teens he had come under the personal spell of the eminent musicologist Bhatkhande. Dilip had taken advantage of his family background and learnt scores of popular and classical compositions from an unimpeachable source.

This forged his determination to embrace music as a vocation. Therefore, in 1920, in addition to the first part of his tripos, he passed also, brilliantly, the examination in Western music. Along with his lessons in piano, he grew fluent in French, German and Italian, before leaving for Germany and Italy to pursue his studies in music. Inviting Dilip through the International Peace and Freedom Society, Romain Rolland arranged for him a seminar on Indian classical music in Lugano, and got his lectures translated and published in French. At this juncture, Dilip met personalities like Bertrand Russell, Hermann Hesse, Georges Duhamel.

From Vienna, invited by president Masaryk, Dilip visited Prague, on his way to Budapest, Rome, Florence and Naples, to discover the heart of the tradition of European music. The ancient modes like Ionian, Lydian, Mixolydian, Dorian, Aeolian, and Phyrgian, reminded him, respectively, of the Indian *that* or *melakarta* ("parent scales") like Bilâval, Iman, Khamâj, Kâfi, Asâvari, and Bhaïravi.

Romain Rolland and Dilipkumar

In his diary, *Inde*, Romain Rolland speaks of Dilip frequently. He records Dilip's first visit on 23 August 1920: "...His is no ordinary intelligence... A young man, tall and well-built, (...) in his complexion the orange-brown of a Creole features, except for the lips..." Talking about his songs, Rolland mentions, "Especially a religious song by Tansen... I find there some affinity with Gregorian melodies and, furthermore, with the Greek hymns that had been at the very source (...)" And Rolland goes on: "By listening to the popular melodies one is better able to grasp the pure and natural genius of the Hindu race.

Dilipkumar Roy sings some of them, so charmingly, delicately, cheerfully, poetically, exhibiting such a mastery of rhythm-that they could just as well be popular songs of our own (...) One realizes-how popular art admits far fewer boundaries than sophisticated art."

And about Dilip's voice: "He sings with nasal intonations and his voice reaches quite high, with a singular suppleness in the ceaseless blossoming of vocal improvisations and ornaments..." On 24 October 1927, Romain Rolland describes another visit from Dilip: "He belongs to a type which is the best of aristocratic India." On listening to an old hymn to the goddess Kali sung by Dilip, Rolland mentions: "It is simply captivating, an overflow of passion that implores, laments, reaches fever pitch, subsides, from soprano to bass notes (...) and begins again, with doubled and exacting ecstasy..."

Experiments in Music

While in Europe, Dilip realised "the greatness and the deficiency" of Indian classical music as practised by his contemporaries. Instead of mediocre word-supports to elaborate melodic and rhythmic compositions, Dilip was convinced that the modern Indian languages-the daughters of Sanskrit could provide more adequate lyrics for the classical models (as demonstrated by composers like his own father or Tagore, among others). Back in India, he joined Bhatkhande and, following the latter's methodology, he set to travelling widely, collecting and publishing serial notes on raga-variants from regional masters, with notations of specific compositions.

He went further in having lessons from stalwarts like Abdul Karim, Faiyaz Khan, Chandan Chaube, Gaurishankar Mishra, Surendranath Majumdar, Hafiz Ali Khan. In his famous works, *bhramyaman* ('Globe-trotting'), *sangitiki* ('About Music'), *gitashri* ('Song as an Art') etc., he recorded in details his experiences, illustrated by notations. Perhaps nobody in India has left such numerous and precise notations. Like Bhatkhande and his pupil Ratanjankar, Dilip wrote and demonstrated how Indian classical music could be taught on a purely academic basis, with a syllabus, somewhat demystifying the shrouded master-to-disciple secrecy. As an outspoken music critic, he attained considerable fame, especially in his audacious analysis of the sacrosanct Gurus. His first-hand experience, enhanced by his deep investigation and reflections, opened a new horizon in the domain of thinking, practising and teaching music.

Embracing the Cosmic Soul

Whereas the very ancient Indian tradition of lieder-like lyrics, passing through the 9th century *carya-pada* songs, admitted and encouraged the *tana* (improvised musical phrases), Tagore, who had composed more than 2000 lyrics, wanted to individualise his compositions in the European way and protect their execution according to an authorised notation. A peerless expert of the *tana* and phrase-variations, Dilip had argued and obtained-exceptionally-Tagore's permission to interpret the latter's songs as he wished. Composing songs in Sanskrit, Bengali, Hindi and English, keeping intact some popular or classical melodies even from Russian, German, Italian or French music, he had the rare facility of passing from one language to another, while interpreting them.

Among the paramount contributions of Dilip, we find compositions of an Indian type of opera, based on the traditional model of the *kirtana*: this involves an emotional catharsis through a succession of modal and rhythmic patterns, compatible with the classical schools of Indian dance. Though on this experimental form, too, Tagore has left the stamp of his genius, much was yet to come. After a long discussion with Tagore on the subtleties of Bengali prosody, Dilip saw the aged poet dedicating him the former's study on the subject, *chhanda*. Requested by the University of Kolkata, Dilip himself also wrote a treatise on the subject, *chhandasiki*.

In one of his letters to Dilip, the poet admitted : "I have a sincere affection for you. My heart is attracted by your unmixed truthfulness and frankness." Attaining popularity for the force, the sweetness, and the range of his voice, Dilip was admired by listeners like Sri Aurobindo, Tagore, and Gandhi. In the 1940s, a hit film in Hindi flooded the country with the songs of Mîrâ Bâi, that princess-saint of medieval India. Though they were sung by the golden-voiced M.S. Subbulakshmi, they had all been collected or composed by Dilipkumar. In homage to her teacher, Subbulakshmi has written that when Dilip "sings (...), it is an outpouring of the individual soul, yearning to be embraced by the cosmic soul."

Dilip created his own style of fiction, involved in a constant psychological analysis. Most of his characters are mystic or spiritual in their essence, situated at a meeting point between the East and the West. As a poet, instead of following the melodic lyrical style developed by Tagore and innate to the Bengali genius, Dilip followed the harmonic structure created by Madhusudan Datta and brought up to-date by his own father Dwijendralal Roy.

Last Phase

After a second visit to Europe, in 1928 Dilip settled at the Ashram of Sri Aurobindo in Pondicherry. His imposing correspondence with Sri Aurobindo reveals a hitherto unknown aspect of the Master who declared cherishing him "like a friend and a son". In the early 50s, two patriotic songs composed by Dilip ("ham bharatke" and "nishan uncha, kadam badha") appealed to the General Kariappa, who wanted to include them in the official list of marching songs for the Indian Army. In 1953, on returning from a world tour, accompanied by his disciple Indira Devi, he founded the Hari Krishna Mandir in 1959 at Pune. Dilip co-authored an autobiographical book titled Pilgrims of the Stars with Indira Devi.

A spiritual classic, Pilgrims of the Stars offers the reader an inspiring and humorous glimpse into the daily struggles and victories of two great souls. East West Journal stated that the book was, "... as remarkable as it is rewarding for the reader." Honoured by the Sanskrit Academy of Kolkata as the 'Source of the Nectar of Melody' (*sura-sudhâkara*), Dilip was elected member of the Indian State Academy of Fine Arts. Author of more than 50 records (several of them still reprinted by the HMV-India); 8 volumes of songs with notation; 21 volumes in English and 46 in Bengali containing novels, poems, plays, epistles, reminiscences and essays. Dilip's was a luminous personality, graced by a cheerful affection and an eagerness to share-with all those who approached him-whatever wealth he had accumulated over the years. He reminded the old adage: "The heavier the branches grow with fruits, the lower they stoop." He was on the look out for young talents and he was generous in his attempt to help them asserting themselves. The firework of melodic improvisations during his youthful years had something of the elan vital depicted, for instance, by Van Gogh. When Dilipkumar Roy was fiftyish, these had yielded considerably to other crafts, expressing deeper intonations of a spiritual attainment. Dilip passed away in Hari Krishna Mandir, Pune in 1980.

NAYANTARA SAHGAL

Nayantara Sahgal (born 10 May 1927) is an Indian writer in English. Her fiction deals with India's elite responding to the crises engendered by political change; she was one of the first female Indo-Anglian writers to receive wide recognition. She is a member of the Nehru-Gandhi family, the second of the three daughters born to Jawaharlal Nehru's sister, Vijaya Lakshmi Pandit.

Her father was a successful barrister and classical scholar who translated the Kashmiri epic history Raj Tarangini into English from Sanskrit. He died in Lucknow prison jail in 1944, leaving behind his wife and their three daughters Chandralekha Mehta, Nayantara Sehgal and Rita Dar.

Sahgal attended a number of schools as a girl, given the turmoil in the Nehru-Gandhi family during the last years (1935-47) of the Indian freedom struggle, wherein her father would die in prison while Nayantara and her sister Chandralekha were overseas attending college. Her uncle Jawaharlal Nehru too was in and out of prison, as a political prisoner, in the 1930s and 1940s.

Ultimately, she graduated from Woodstock School in the Himalayan hill station of Landour in 1943 and later from Wellesley College (B.A., 1947), which she attended along with her sister Chandralekha, who graduated 2 years earlier in 1945. She has made her home for decades in Dehradun, a town close to Landour where she had been in boarding school (at Woodstock).

Sahgal, who has been married twice, was latterly married to E.N. Mangat Rai, a Punjabi Christian who was a distinguished

Indian Civil Service officer. Rai died aged 87 in 2003 in Dehradun, where Sahgal and he had lived for several decades, in the house once owned by her mother.

Though part of the Nehru-Gandhi family, Sahgal developed a reputation for maintaining her independent critical sense. Her independent tone, and her mother's, would lead to both falling out with her cousin Indira Gandhi during the most autocratic phases of Mrs. Gandhi's time in office in the late 1960s and throughout the 1970s. Indira Gandhi canceled Sahgal's scheduled appointment as India's Ambassador to Italy within days of her return to power. Not one to be intimidated, Sahgal would (in 1982) write a scathing, insightful account of Gandhi's rise to power.

Books

- "A voice for freedom".
- *Prison and Chocolate Cake* (memoir; 1954)
- *From Fear Set Free* (novel; 1963)
- *Time To Be Happy* (novel; 1963)
- *This Time of Morning* (novel; 1965)
- *Storm in Chandigarh* (novel; 1969)
- *Sunlight Surrounds You* (novel; 1970) (with Chandralekha Mehta and Rita Dar *i.e.* her two sisters; this was the daughters' tribute to their mother)
- *The Day in Shadow* (novel; 1971)
- *Indira Gandhi: Her Road to Power* (novel; 1982)
- *Plans for Departure* (novel; 1985)
- *Rich Like Us* (novel; 1985)
- *Mistaken Identity* (novel; 1988)
- *A Situation in New Delhi (novel; 1989)*
- *Lesser Breeds* (novel; 2003)

SAROJINI SAHOO

Sarojini Sahoo (born 1956) is an Indian feminist writer who has received the Orissa Sahitya Academy Award, 1993, the Jhankar Award, 1992, the Bhubaneswar Book Fair Award and the Prajatantra Award.

Born in a small town of Dhenkanal in Orissa (India), Sarojini has MA and PhD degrees in Oriya Literature and a Bachelor of Law from Utkal University.

She now teaches at a degree college in Belpahar, Jharsuguda, Orissa.

She is the second daughter of Ishwar Chandra Sahoo and (late) Nalini Devi and is married to Jagadish Mohanty, a veteran writer of Orissa, and has a son and a daughter.

Short Stories

She has published eight anthologies of short stories.

Her other Oriya anthologies of short stories are:

- *Sukhara Muhanmuhin* (1981)
- *NijaGahirareNije* (1989)
- *Amrutara Pratikshare* (1992)
- *Chowkath* (1994)
- *Tarali Jauthiba Durga* (1995)
- *Deshantari* (1999)
- *Dukha Apramita* (2006)
- *Sarojini Sahoo short stories* (2006) (ISBN 81-89040-26-X

The most recent selected short stories were translated into English from Oriya and published by Grassroots (Kolkata).

She has been conferred with Orissa Sahitya Akademi Award and Bhubaneswar Book Fair award for her short stories collection *Amrutara Pratikshare.*

Novels

Seven novels are published so far:

- *Upanibesh* (1998)
- *Pratibandi* (1999)
- *Swapna Khojali Mane* (2000)
- *Mahajatra* (2001)

- *Gambhiri Ghara* (2005)
- *Bishad Ishwari* (2006)
- "Pakshibasa" (2008)

Her novel *Gambhiri Ghara* proved to be a bestseller in Oriya literature. Her novels have gained a reputation for the frankness about sexuality and of feminist outlook. This novel has been translated in to Bengali (Bangladesh) under the title of "Mithya Gerosthali" and has been published by Anupam prakashani, Dhaka, Bangladesh in 2007 .

Awards

She has been conferred with:

- Orissa Sahitya Academy Award, 1993,
- the Jhankar Award, 1992,
- the Bhubaneswar Book Fair Award (1993), and
- the Prajatantra Award (1981,1993),

Feminism

Sarojini Sahoo is a prime figure and trendsetter of feminism in contemporary Oriya literature. For her, feminism is not a "gender problem" or any confrontational attack on male hegemony. So, it is quite different from that of Virginia Woolf or Judith Butler. She accepts feminism as a total entity of femalehood which is completely separate from the man's world. She writes with a greater consciousness of women bodies, which would create a more honest and appropriate style of openness, fragmentation and non-linearity... Her fictions always project a feminine sensibility from puberty to menopause. The feminine feelings like restrictions in adolescence, pregnancy, the fear factors like being raped or being condemned by society and the concept of a bad girl, etc, always have thematic exposure in her novels and short stories.

Her feminism is always linked with the sexual politics of a woman. She denies patriarchy limits of sexual expression for a woman and she identifies women's sexual liberation as the real motive behind the women's movement.. For her, orgasm is the body's natural call to feminist politics: if being a woman is this good, women must be worth something. Her novels like *Upanibesh*, *Pratibandi* and *Gambhiri Ghara* cover a myriad of areas from sexuality to philosophy, from the politics of the home to politics of the world.

Sexuality

Sexuality is something that can be related to a lot of other aspects of culture, tightly linked with an individual life, or into the evolution of a culture. Anyone's class or ethnic or geographic identity could be closely associated to his/her sexuality, or any one's sense of art or literature. Sexuality is not just an entity in itself. But still, either in west or in east, there is a reluctant outlook towards sexuality, and society has always tried to hide it from any open forum. The censorship on speech, and adding decorum to dress and declaring the sexual organs.

But neither the society, nor the legislature, even the judiciary, also do not stand by the side of sexuality to support it. In the West, James Joyce's *Ulysses* or even Radclyffe Hall's *Loneliness in the Well* or Virginia Woolf's *Orlando* are some examples which have to suffer a lot for describing sexuality in literature. In the west, sexuality in literature grew with feminism. Simone De Beauvoir in her book *The Second Sex*, first elaborately described the gender role and problem away from the biological differences. In Oriya literature, Sarojini is considered as a prime person to discuss sexuality in her fiction with a sincere effort to express her feminist ideas..

The novel *Upanibesh* was the first attempt in Oriya Literature to focus the sexuality as a part of social revolt by any woman.

Medha, the protagonist of Sarojini's novel, was a bohemian. In her pre-marital stage, she was thinking that it was boring to live with a man life-long. Perhaps she wanted a chain free life, where there would be only love, only sex and wouldn't be any monotony. But she had to marry Bhaskar. Can Indian society imagine a lady with bohemianism?

In her novel *Pratibandi*,. Sarojini has also described the thematic development of sexuality in a woman. Priyanka, the protagonist of the novel has to encounter the loneliness in the exile of Saragpali, a remote village of India. This lonliness develops into a sexual urge and soon Priyanka finds herself sexually attached with a former Member of Parliament. Though there is an age gap between them, his intelligence impresses her and she discovers a hidden archaeologist in him. Sarojini has painted successfully the difference of sensibility towards sexuality among male and female. Sarojini has her own credibility for the frankness to deals with the sensitive matters either it may be in politics or in sexuality. She has gained a reputation and has her own place in the history of Oriya fiction.

Her novel *Gambhiri Ghara* she describes an unusual relationship between two people, a Hindu house wife of India and a Muslim artist of Pakistan. It is a net oriented novel. A woman meets a very sexually experienced man. One day he asks if she had any such experience. The woman, Kuki, scolds him and insults him by calling him a caterpillar. She said without love lust is like hunger of a caterpillar. Gradually they become involved with love, lust and spiritually. That man considers her as his daughter, lover, mother, and above all these as a Goddess.

They both madly love each other, through the internet and on the phone. They use obscene language; they kiss each other online. Kuki does not lead a happy conjugal life though she has a love marriage with Aniket. The novel is not limited to only a love story. It has a greater aspect. It deals with the relationship between State and individual. Safique, who is not a Muslim by temperament, and as a historian, thinks the Pakistan of today has separated itself from its roots and looks towards Arabian legends for his history.

He protests that the syllabus of history for the school would start from seventh century AD, not from the Mahenjodaro and Harappa. This broad Safique was once arrested after the bomb blast of London for allegation of being associated with the terrorist. But is it a true fact? Later Kuki came to know that Safiques is trapped by a military junta. The ex-lover of Tabassum had revenged on Safique by arresting him with an allegation of terrorism.

Here Sarojini deals with the question of terrorism. There is often discussion about terrorism caused by an individual or by a group. Society rarely discusses terrorism caused by a state. What is a state? Is it a group of people that resides within a political and geographical boundaries? Are a state's identity, mood and wishes separate from its ruler? Is the wish of George W. Bush not considered as the wish of America? Has it reflected the mood and wish of the people of America? So, every time, the state's arranged anarchism or terrorism is merely a reflection of a terrorism caused by an individual. The great truth lies beneath Safique, as a terrorist develops from the mind of a military man.

Thus from sexuality to politics, Sarojini's frank view always stir the readers..

SULEKHA SANYAL

Sulekha Sanyal, (1928–1962) was a Bengali woman writer and activist.

She grew up in Korkandi, now in Bangladesh, in a decaying zamindar family that had once been indigo planters, and was to become a member of the Communist Party of India. An early influence on her was the Brahmo philosopher and reformer, Ramtanu Lahiri, who was related to her mother. She was married, briefly and unsuccessfully, from 1948 to 1956.

Her chief work is Nabankur (The Seedling) 1956, translated by Gouranga P. Chattopadhyay and published by Stree in 2001. Its heroine, Chhobi, is a young girl from a rural zamindar family in Bengal of the 1930s, and the book follows her as she learns to fight injustice, protest against the privileges denied her but granted to her brothers, and the restrictions of the patriarchal society around her. World War II breaks out, cutting short Chhobi's education in the city. She returns to the village, gets involved with relief work and witnesses the Bengal Famine of 1942.

Much of the story mirrors Sanyal's own life, for she was born into a similar family, educated briefly in Chittagong, then got involved in politics during the Bengal Famine. Her first stories were accepted by the radical newspaper *Jugantar*. Late in life she was awarded a degree in Bengali literature by Bardhaman University.

Sulekha Sanyal also wrote a collection of short stories, *Sindure Megh* (Clouds Tinged with Red). Her *Dewal Padma* (Wallflowers) was published in 1964, after her early death from leukaemia.

KRUPABAI SATTHIANADHAN

Krupabai Satthianadhan (1862-1894) was one of the first Indian women to write in English, and certainly the first woman novelist in English from India.

Krupabai was born to Haripunt and Radhabai Khisty, Hindu converts to Christianity, in Ahmednagar, then in the Bombay Presidency. Her father died when she was still a child, and she was brought up by her mother and elder brother, Bhasker. Bhasker, who was much older, had a strong influence on her and endeavoured to awaken her intellect by lending her books and discussing many issues with her. However he too died young, and Krupabai immortalised him in her semi-autobiographical novel *Saguna: A Story of Native Christian Life*. Her mother, though formally a Christian, still followed many Hindu practices.

Krupabai was deeply wounded by Bhasker's death, and two European missionary ladies took charge of her and her education. This was her first encounter with the British at close quarters, and as *Saguna* shows it was a mixed experience. Later on she went to boarding school in the city of Bombay. She met an American woman doctor there who got her interested in medicine. Krupabai had absorbed her father's missionary ideals early in life and decided that by becoming a doctor she could help other women, especially those in purdah. By this time her health was already showing signs of deterioration, so although she won a scholarship to go to England and study medicine, she was not allowed to go. However, the Madras Medical College agreed to admit her in 1878, and she became a boarder at the house of the Reverend W.T. Satthianadhan, an extremely well known Christian missionary. Her academic performance was brilliant from the start, but due to strain and overwork she had her first breakdown in health a year later, and had to return to her sister in Pune to convalesce in 1879.

A year later she was back at Madras, where she met and developed a friendship with Samuel Satthianadhan, the Reverend's son. In 1881 Samuel and Krupabai married. Soon after Samuel got a job as Headmaster of Breeks Memorial School in Ootacamund. In Ootacamund Krupabai was able to start a school for Muslim girls with help from the Church MIssionary Society, and she also taught in a number of other girls schools as well.

Ootacamund was a hill station renowned for its salubrious climate and Krupabai's health stayed fair. She was able to find the time and energy to write, and published articles under the byline 'An Indian Lady' in leading periodicals. Three years later the couple moved to Rajamundry, and Krupabai became ill again, so they relocated to Kumbakonam. In spite of the changeableness of her health this was a very productive period for her, and by the time they returned permanently to Madras in 1886 she was ready to begin a fullscale novel. *Saguna* was serialised between 1877 and 1878 in the prestigious *Madras Christian College Magazine*.

However, during this time her only child died before reaching its first birthday and she was plunged into depression for which she required streatment. Her tuberculosis was diagnosed in Bombay but was certified beyond cure. Knowing that she had little time to live, she began work on *Kamala*. She worked continuously on the book till her death, breaking off only to write a memoir of her father-in-law and an unfinished one of her mother-in-law.

Her death came as a great blow to her admirers and just a few months afterwards a scholarship for women was set up in her memory at the Madras Medical College, and a memorial medal at the University of Madras for the best female Matriculation candidate in English. Her novels were published as books and translated into Tamil.

GEETANJALI SHREE

Geetanjali Shree (born 1957) is a Hindi novelist and short story writer based in New Delhi, India. She is the author of several short stories and three novels: Private Life, The Roof Beneath My Feet, and Mai. Mai was short listed for the Crossword Book Award in 2001. She has also written a critical work on Premchand.

Her first story, Bel Patra (1987) was published in the literary magazine Hans and was followed by *Anugoonj* (1991), an anthology of short stories. The English translation of Mai by Nita Kumar catapulted her into fame. The novel is about three generations of women and the men around them, in a North Indian middle class family. Mai is being translated into Russian and Korean.

Geetanjali Shree is the recipient of Indu Sharma award and has been a fellow of Ministry of Culture, India, and Japan Foundation. She also participates in theater and works with Vivadi, a theater group comprising writers, artists, dancers, and painters.

VIKRAM SETH

Vikram Seth, born June 20, 1952 is an Indian poet, novelist, travel writer, librettist, children's writer, biographer and memoirist. An unusually forthcoming writer whose published material is replete with un-or thinly-disguised details as to the personal lives of himself and his intimates related in a highly engaging narrative voice.

Vikram Seth was born in Calcutta (now Kolkata); his family lived in a number of cities including the Bata Shoe Company town of Batanagar, near Calcutta, Patna and London, though never in Calcutta proper during his childhood, and he spent extended periods away at boarding school from the age of five.

His father, Prem, was an executive of the Bata India Limited shoe company who migrated to post-Partition India from West Punjab in Pakistan; he had unsuccessfully courted a Sikh girl before meeting Seth's mother, Leila; she had a chaste premarital dalliance with an unsuitable Christian boy and was the first woman judge on the Delhi High Court as well as the first woman to become Chief Justice of a state High Court, at Simla. She studied law in London while pregnant with Seth's younger brother and came first in her Bar examinations conducted only weeks after she delivered her second child.

That child, Vikram Seth's younger brother, Shantum, leads Buddhist meditational tours; his younger sister, Aradhana, is a film-maker married to an Austrian diplomat. She worked on Deepa Mehta's *Earth* and *Fire*. (Compare the characters Haresh, Lata, Savita and two of the Chatterji siblings in *A Suitable Boy*: Seth has been candid in acknowledging that many of his fictional personnel are drawn from life; he has said that only the dog Cuddles in *A Suitable Boy* has his real name — "Because he can't sue". Justice Leila Seth has said in her memoir *On Balance* that other characters in *A Suitable Boy* are composites but Haresh is a portrait of her husband Prem.)

Having lived in London for many years, Seth now maintains residences near Salisbury, England, where he is a notable participant in local literary and cultural events, having bought in 1996 and renovated the house of the seventeenth century Anglican divine and metaphysical poet George Herbert, and in Delhi, where he lives with his parents and keeps his extensive library and papers.

Education

He attended St Michael's High School in Patna, Welham Boys' School in Dehra Dun and later joined The Doon School, also in Dehradun, and told a Doon Founder's Day gathering in 1992 of his "terrible feeling of loneliness and isolation" while studying at the prestigious institution. Seth said:

> *Sometimes, at lights out, I wished I would never wake up to hear the chhota hazri bell. For days after I left I thought of school as a kind of jungle, and looked back on it with a shudder. I was teased and bullied by my classmates and my seniors because of my interest in studies and reading, because of my lack of interest in*

games, because of my unwillingness to join gangs and groups.

The experience—intensified to outright sexual abuse at the hands of older boys—is given to Tapan, the younger brother of Amit Chatterjee, the character bearing numerous similarities to Seth himself in *A Suitable Boy* (Amit takes charge of withdrawing the boy from the school and enrolling him in a day school). The widely-quoted comments themselves, however, and the fact that he made them, perhaps should not be relied upon entirely to characterise either his schooldays or Seth the man; in his speech to the Doon students he also spoke of the advantages the school conferred on him and offered words of encouragement and inspiration.

And in an interview with the Australian Broadcasting Corporation's Margaret Throsby, his slightly younger contemporary at Doon, the anthropologist and novelist Amitav Ghosh, expressed surprise at the report of how Seth had characterised his school days: in his own recollection Seth had been deservedly lionised by both students and staff, his winning personality and brilliant intellect having been well in evidence even then.

He completed his A-levels at Tonbridge School in Kent, England, and read Philosophy, Politics and Economics (PPE) at Corpus Christi College, Oxford. He undertook doctoral studies at Stanford University where he has stated that he spent "11 years (from 1975 to 1986) not getting an economics Ph.D." While formally engaged in postgraduate economics courses at Stanford he also undertook poetics studies—he was Wallace Stegner Fellow in Creative Writing in 1977-1978—with the poet Timothy Steele, whose traditionally structured verse with formal rhyme and metre (together with that of Robert Frost and Philip Larkin) inspired Seth to adopt a similar formal discipline in his own poetry. "I wanted to have some contact with the writing programme," Seth recalled in 2003 interview. "So I went to this office and asked if there was anyone who could help with poetry. There were two poets there and the one nearest the door was Timothy Steele, who writes with rhyme and metre. If the other fellow had been closer, I'd probably have turned out a poet of free verse." He also enrolled in Mandarin language courses at Stanford that later helped him gain fluency in the language during his stint in China.

In 1980-82 Seth did extensive field work in China gathering data for his intended doctoral dissertation on Chinese population planning; he was attached to Nanjing University while in China and became fluent in Mandarin within six months, later translating Chinese as well as Hindi poetry into English. He took advantage of his Chinese language fluency to return home to Delhi overland via Xinjiang and Tibet, resulting in *From Heaven Lake: Travels Through Sinkiang and Tibet* (1983), a combination travel narrative and personal memoir written at the suggestion of his father.

Personal Life

Avocations: A famous polymath, Seth detailed in an interview (in the year 2005) in the Australian magazine *Good Weekend* that he has studied several languages, including Welsh, German and, later, French in addition to the oft-noted Mandarin, English (which he describes as "my instrument" in answer to Indians who query his not writing in his native Hindi), Urdu (so useful to him during the travels in Sinkiang and Tibet detailed in *From Heaven Lake*), which he reads and writes in Nasta'liq script, and Hindi, which he reads and writes in the Devangar+ script. He plays the Indian flute and the cello and sings German lieder, especially Schubert.

Business Acumen

Seth is famously astute as a businessman. His late literary agent Giles Gordon recalled being interviewed by Seth for the position: Vikram sat at one end of a long table and he began to grill us. It was absolutely incredible. He wanted to know our literary tastes, our views on poetry, our views on plays, which novelists we liked.

But notwithstanding the acute commercial savvy Seth has become renowned for, he later explained to Gordon that he had passed the interview not because of commercial considerations, but because unlike the others he was the only agent who seemed as interested in his poetry as in his other writing. That being said, Seth followed what he has described as "the ludicrous advance for that book" (£200,000 for *A Suitable Boy*) with £500,000 for *An Equal Music* and £1.4 million for *Two Lives*. He prepared an acrostic poem for his address at Gordon's 2005 memorial service:

Gone though you have, I heard your voice today.

I tried to make out what the words might mean,

Like something seen half-clearly on a screen:

Each savoured reference, each laughing bark,

Sage comment, bad pun, indiscreet remark.

Gone since you have, grief too in time will go,

Or share space with old joy; it must be so.

Rest then in peace, but spare us some elation.

Death cannot put down every conversation.

Over and out, as you once used to say?

Not on your life. You're on this line to stay.

Gay and Bisexual Themes

In each of Seth's novels and in much of his poetry, there have been central or peripheral gay or bisexual themes and characters; in particular one of the central relationships in *The Golden Gate* and the association between Maan and Firoz in *A Suitable Boy*. Seth has been discreet but not secretive about his personal life, occasionally citing his early poem "Dubious" without further comment:

Some men like Jack and some like Jill

I'm glad I like them both but still

I wonder if this freewheeling

Really is an enlightened thing,

Or is its greater scope a sign

Of deviance from some party line?

In the strict ranks of Gay and Straight

What is my status: Stray? Or Great?

Seth has said that "the 'I' in my poems is almost always me," so one might well early have concluded from his citation of this poem alone that he identified as bisexual; also, *Mappings* and Seth's other books of poetry contain love poems addressed to both male and female objects. However, Seth's mother, Justice Leila Seth, laid the issue to rest. She wrote in her memoir *On Balance*,

At the time [of a dispute with Seth over sleeping arrangements for a visiting friend] I didn't realise that Vikram was bisexual. This understanding came to me much later and I found it hard to come to terms with his homosexuality. Premo found it even harder....But we loved him and accepted it without understanding it.

Beyond the dedication in *An Equal Music*, Seth has expressly acknowledged his ten-year relationship with his former partner, Philippe Honore. Indian-born San Francisco journalist Sandip Roy reports that Seth discussed the issue of his sexuality candidly in a television programme with his sister Aradhana. In a book tour radio interview, Roy probed further: Seth said that this was not something he'd ever hidden, but that he just didn't wish to be defined by it. On the other hand, he said that he was conscious of the fact that being open about his sexuality might help other bisexual or gay people, and that he had given leave to his mother to write about it partially for that reason.

Seth has been increasingly forthright in recent years on the issue of gay rights in his native India. In an interview on CNN-IBN aired 21 January 2006, Seth talked about the law in India relating to homosexuality. He called section 377 of the Indian *Penal Code* barbaric and archaic. He advocated its removal, saying that the British who introduced this have removed it in their own country. He gave three reasons for it being removed: (1) it is silly (as India is following something outdated); (2) it is cruel (as it causes intolerable pain and self-doubt); and (3) it is harmful (as it promotes underground activities which pose a health problem). He wished that young Indians would not have to worry about their sexuality. He suggested that the government was afraid of losing votes and it was fear that drove its indisposition to amend the current draconian criminal sanctions against homosexuality. Continuing with the theme, Seth said in an interview with Sheela Reddy published in Outlook India on 2 October 2006,

I don't particularly like talking about these matters myself. I am a private person and I don't feel my friends' lives and my own should be part of the public's right to know. But in a case like this where so much is at stake, where the happiness, at a conservative estimate, of 50 million people and their right not to be fearful or lonely and to be with the people whom they love is at issue, and the happiness of their families as well, then it really is incumbent on us to speak out.

Writing

Poetry: Seth is now best known for his novels, though he has characterised himself as a poet first and novelist second. He has published five volumes of poetry. His first, *Mappings* (1980), was originally privately published; it attracted little attention and indeed Philip Larkin, to whom he sent it for comment, referred to it rather scornfully among his intimates, though he offered Seth encouragement. Whether or not Seth's poetry is expressly influenced by Larkin, it contains similar elements: a highly colloquial vocabulary and syntax with enjambement and rhyme; closely structured form but without rigidity.

Travel Writing: From Heaven Lake: Travels Through Sinkiang and Tibet

His travel book *From Heaven Lake: Travels Through Sinkiang and Tibet* (1983) was his first popular success — even here he makes frequent asides in verse — and won the Thomas Cook award for travel writing. Among its considerable charms for Seth's admirers is the extensive insight it affords as to Seth as a person, who is for once candid about the reality and effect of living abroad — though not in particular of being in Diaspora— a theme which arises in his poetry but nowhere in his fiction:

Increasingly of late, and particularly when I drink, I find my thoughts drawn into the past rather than

impelled into the future. I recall drinking sherry in California and dreaming of my earlier student days in England, where I ate dalmoth and dreamed of Delhi. What is the purpose, I wonder, of all this restlessness? I sometimes seem to myself to wander around the world merely accumulating material for future nostalgias. (p.35)

Hybrid: The "novel in verse" The Golden Gate

The first of his novels, *The Golden Gate* (1986), is indeed a novel in verse about the lives of a number of young professionals in San Francisco. The novel is written entirely in rhyming tetrameter sonnets after the style of Charles Johnston's 1977 translation of Alcksandr Pushkin's *Eugene Onegin* (although *Eugene Onegin*, both in the original Russian and in Johnston's translation, are in the Onegin stanza of iambic tetrameter). He had encountered it in a Stanford second-hand bookstore and it changed the direction of his career, shifting his focus from academic to literary work. The likelihood of commercial success seemed highly doubtful — and the scepticism of friends as to the novel's viability is facetiously quoted within the novel; but the verse novel received wide acclaim (Gore Vidal dubbed it "The Great California Novel") and achieved healthy sales. The novel contains a strong element of affectionate satire, something occasionally missed by Seth's more earnest critics, as with his subsequent novel, *A Suitable Boy*. In the text of "The Golden Gate", Seth rhymes his own surname with the word "away", indicating that the English pronunciation of his name is similar to "Say".

Novels in Prose

A Suitable Boy: After the success of *The Golden Gate*, Seth took up residence in his parents' house back in Delhi to work on his second novel, *A Suitable Boy* (1993). Though initially conceived as a short piece detailing the domestic drama of an Indian mother's search for an appropriate husband for her marriageable Indian daughter against the background of the formative years of India after Independence, the novel grew and Seth was to labour over it for almost a decade.

The 1471-page novel is a four-family saga set in post-independence, post-Partition India, and alternatively satirically and earnestly examines issues of national politics in the period leading up to the first post-Independence national election of 1952, inter-sectarian animosity, the status of lower caste peoples such as the jatav, land reform and the eclipse of the feudal princes and landlords, academic affairs, inter-and intra-family relations and a range of further issues of importance to the characters. The Indian journalist and novelist Khushwant Singh has said of the novel that, "I lived through that period and I couldn't find a flaw. It really is an authentic picture of Nehru's India." The novel was, despite its formidable length, a bestseller, and propelled Seth into the public spotlight and assured his reputation. English critics greeted *A Suitable Boy* with almost universal enthusiasm (notwithstanding its somewhat controversial passing-over for the Booker Prize shortlist), though it received mixed reviews from some American critics.

An Equal Music: Seth's third novel, *An Equal Music* (1999), set in contemporary Europe, focuses on the lives of classical musicians and their music: so integral to the novel is the discussion by the characters of their performance repertoire (some of it very slightly obscure) that Seth successfully marketed a companion double CD containing performances of all the music referred to.

Readers and critics without musical knowledge occasionally complained that Michael, the protagonist, was simply not a likeable (or unlikeable) enough character to sustain interest throughout a substantial novel and that the focus on the music for its own sake can be trying for the uninitiated. Musically knowledgeable readers, especially those who perform, were with rare exceptions unstinting in their enthusiasm and praise. Paolo Isotta, one of Italy's most significant music critics, wrote in the influential newspaper *Il Corriere della Sera* of the Italian translation that no European writer had ever shown such a knowledge of European classical music, nor had any European novel before managed to convey the psychology, the technical abilities, even the human potentialities of those who practise music for a living

Seth credits his then-partner, the French violinist Philippe Honore, as inspiring him with the idea for *An Equal Music* in an acrostic sonnet on Honore's name which is the epigraph to *An Equal Music*:

Perhaps this could have stayed unstated.
Had our words turned to other things
In the grey park, the rain abated,
Life would have quickened other strings.
I list your gifts in this creation:
Pen, paper, ink and inspiration,
Peace to the heart with touch or word,
Ease to the soul with note and chord.
How did that walk, those winter hours,
Occasion this? No lightning came;
Nor did I sense, when touched by flame,
Our story lit with borrowed powers-
Rather, by what our spirits burned,
Embered in words, to us returned.

Seth together with Philippe Honore marketed a double CD of the music mentioned in *An Equal Music*, performed by Honore.

Biography/Memoir: Two Lives

His most recent book, *Two Lives*, is a non-fiction family memoir written at the suggestion of his mother, and published in October, 2005.

It focuses on the lives of his great uncle (Shanti Behari Seth) and German-Jewish great aunt (Henny Caro) who met in Berlin in the early 1930s while Shanti was a student there and with whom Seth stayed extensively on going to England at age 17 for school at Tonbridge and then to attend Oxford. As with *From Heaven Lake*, *Two Lives* contains much autobiography and this is a considerable part of its appeal.

Range

Seth's range is demonstrated by the historical accuracy of *A Suitable Boy*, with the nuanced cultivated-Indian English of the narrative voice and the entirely in-character voices of the principals of the story; the correspondingly accurate depiction of northern California yuppies of the 1980s in *The Golden Gate*; and his portrait of the world of western classical musicians in *An Equal Music*. He has continued to produce volumes of poetry at intervals alongside his publications in a range of other forms, including translations from Chinese poets. Despite his erudition in a wide range of disciplines, both his prose and poetry are characterised by their accessibility and he has said that he works to ensure this.

In most of Seth's writing (apart from *An Equal Music*, narrated in the first person by its central character), there is a strong, engaging narrative persona — sometimes, as in *From Heaven Lake*, obviously Seth himself; at other times, in his novels and poems, intermittently so. He has complained about some of his readers assuming on book tours a degree of intimacy with him that they have not earned.

A film of *A Suitable Boy* is slated to go into production in 2007, an earlier attempt at a television serialisation having been abandoned.

Published Works

Novels

- *The Golden Gate* (1986)
- *A Suitable Boy*, (1993)
- *An Equal Music*, (1999)

Poetry

- *Mappings* (1980)
- *The Humble Administrator's Garden* (1985)
- *All You Who Sleep Tonight* (1990)
- *Beastly Tales* (1991)
- *Three Chinese Poets* (1992)

- *The Frog and the nightingale*

Children's Book

- *Beastly Tales* (1991)

Libretto

- *Arion and the Dolphin* (1994) for the English National Opera

Non-fiction

- *From Heaven Lake*, (1983)
- *Two Lives*, (2005)

Prizes and Awards

- 1983 Thomas Cook Travel Book Award *From Heaven Lake: Travels Through Sinkiang and Tibet*
- 1985 Commonwealth Poetry Prize (Asia) *The Humble Administrator's Garden*
- 1993 Irish Times International Fiction Prize (shortlist) *A Suitable Boy*
- 1994 Commonwealth Writers Prize (Overall Winner, Best Book) *A Suitable Boy*
- 1994 WH Smith Literary Award *A Suitable Boy*
- 2001 EMMA (BT Ethnic and Multicultural Media Award) for Best Book/Novel *An Equal Music*
- 2005 Pravasi Bharatiya Samman
- 2007 Padma Shri award.

GITHA HARIHARAN

Githa Hariharan (b. 1954) is an Indian author and editor.

Githa Hariharan is an Indian writer based in New Delhi. She was born in Coimbatore, Tamilnadu and grew up in Bombay. Her first novel 'The Thousand Faces of Night' won the Commonwealth Writers Prize in 1993.

Author of:

- *The Winning Team* (2004)
- *In Times of Siege* (2003)

- *When Dreams Travel* (1999)
- *The Ghosts of Vasu Master* (1994)
- *The Art of Dying* (1993)
- *The Thousand Faces of Night* (1992)

Editor of:

- *A Southern Harvest*
- *Sorry, Best Friend!*

Awards and Nominations

1993-Commonwealth Writers Prize-Best First Book (*The Thousand Faces of Night*)

AKHIL SHARMA

Akhil Sharma (born July 22, 1971 in Delhi) is an investment banker and fiction writer.

Born in Delhi, India, he migrated to the United States when he was eight, and grew up in Edison, New Jersey. Sharma studied at Princeton University, where he earned his B.A. in public policy at the Woodrow Wilson School. While there, he also studied under a succession of notable writers, including Russell Banks, Toni Morrison, Joyce Carol Oates, Paul Auster, John McPhee, and Tony Kushner. He then won a Stegner Fellowship to the writing programme at Stanford, where he won several O. Henry Prizes. He then attempted to become a screenwriter, but, disappointed with his fortunes, left to attend Harvard Law School.

Sharma is the author of one novel, *An Obedient Father,* for which he won the 2000 PEN/Hemingway Award and the 2001 Whiting Writers' Award. He has also published stories in *The New Yorker, The Atlantic Monthly, The Quarterly, Fiction,* the *Best American Short Stories* anthology, and the *O. Henry Award Winners* anthology.

Works

- Sharma, Akhil. 2000. An Obedient Father. Farrar, Strauss, and Giroux.

- 1995 (May). "If You Sing Like That for Me"— A Short Story. The Atlantic Monthly. 275(5):70-88.
- "Cosmopolitan," *Children Playing Before a Statue of Hercules*

PARTAP SHARMA

Partap Sharma (born December 12, 1939) is an Indian playwright, novelist, author of books for children, commentator, actor and documentary film-maker. Sharma was born in Lahore, which was then part of India, and is the oldest son of Dr. Baij Nath Sharma and Dayawati (Pandit) Sharma. Sharma's father was a civil engineer who served as Technical Advisor to governments in Ceylon (now Sri Lanka), Tanganyika and Libya and later retired to their ancestral property in Punjab as a farmer. This colourful Punjabi village forms much of the backdrop of Sharma's novel, *Days of the Turban.*

Sharma's early education was in Trinity College, Kandy, Ceylon, and Bishop Cotton School, Shimla. Sharma received a triple promotion and completed school at 14 before going to study at St. Xavier's College, Bombay; all other universities in India required a minimum age of 16. He is married to Susan Amanda Pick and they have two daughters: Namrita and Tara.

Sharma's association with the Indian National Theatre, Mumbai, began in 1961 with the production by it of his first full-length play "Bars Invisible" and continued until the production of the banned "A Touch of Brightness." While working on his writing, Sharma freelanced as a narrator for short films and newsreels and directed a few documentaries for the Government of India. Sharma has voiced many national and international award-winning documentaries and short films. He is known as the golden voice of India, and was honoured with the Dadasaheb Phalke Award as 'The Voice of India'. He is the voice on most of the Son et lumière shows produced in India, including the one still running forty years later, at the Delhi Fort, in Delhi. Sharma was the TV host of the popular programme "What's the Good Word?" produced by Television Centre, Mumbai.

Writings

Books

The Surangini Tales: The Surangini Tales (1973) is a children's book, about Surangini, daughter of the village zamindar. She is the most beautiful maiden anyone has ever seen. Kalu, the poor weaver, loves her, but only the wealthiest of eligible young men can ask for her hand in marriage. Unless, Kalu with his deft hands, quick wit and unselfish love can produce something like a miracle, unexpected and amazing, on the day she is to choose her bridegroom....!

Dog Detective Ranjha: Dog Detective Ranjha (1978) is a story book about Sharma's Alsatian dog Ranjha. Sharma dedicates the book to animal lovers the world over, and particularly in India where some of the world's earliest animal stories were written. Even today the streets in India are open not only to traffic and human beings but also the friendly cows and bulls who wander freely as they please, sometimes absentmindedly standing in a bus queue or staring in with curiosity from the doorstep of a shop. There are even festivals for the less loved creatures, like snakes. Birds, of course, are often fed little morsels even by those who can hardly afford a daily meal for themselves. In the great epic, Mahabharata, it is said that when the legendary hero, Yuddhister went to heaven he insisted that his dog should be allowed to accompany him. 'Sharma has written a good, old-fashioned adventure story book, its rather solid virtues enlivened by the amusing device of having events narrated by the dog.'-Rosemary Stones, Children's Book Bulletin (UK).

The Little Master of the Elephant: The Little Master of the Elephant (1984) tells the story of a parched land, where people are dying or leaving. Chintu and his elephant Vivek go in search of water to save a dying uncle. They come back with a retinue of people and animals and a river of water instead of first a bucketful. This is just the beginning of their adventures together and their search for the meaning of life. In a part Chintu finds love and is promised to be king and find the meaning of what he is looking for.

Top Dog: Top Dog (1985) has more stories about Ranjha, the dog detective. They live in Mumbai and Ranjha has been so skilfully trained in the art of tracking that he has become famous for the crimes he has solved. All the stories in this book are based on real cases and Ranjha tells us, in his own words, about some of the most puzzling he has helped to solve. He tracked down a local thief, he got involved in a particularly unpleasant case of what seemed to be ritual murder, he got to the bottom of a series of thefts from a warehouse that had reduced the owner of the goods to despair. He helped to find and return to her family a little girl, who had been kidnapped.

Days of the Turban: Sharma's novel *Days of the Turban* (1986) presents a picture of Indian Society from the inside. It shows a country in transition, where old values are under attack from new ideas but where, in the end, the traditions and ways of life still have their place.

It tells the story of Balbir, the youngest member of a wealthy Punjabi family, the descendant of a great Brahmin warrior dynasty. In the Punjab the family counts for everything. Over-educated and bored with life in a Punjabi village, Balbir wants only to escape, to get away from the demands of ever-present family. Most of all he would like to follow his glamorous elder brother Raskaan, who has escaped to Europe and become westernised and rich, a businessman in Berlin.

Searching for adventure and trying to raise the money to finance his escape, Balbir becomes entangled with local gunrunners. Venturing into the golden Temple at Amritsar with a message for the Sikh extremists who have fortified it, he is held hostage to ensure that his cousin Satyavan will provide the arms the movement needs. The book provides an insight into the mind of extremists. It shows how extremism builds on fear and then has to reach further into terrorism, not necessarily to further its aim, but for its leadership to keep ahead of its supporters and rivals. The descent from revolutionary to terrorist can be jagged and rapid.

A Touch of Brightness: Invited to tour four theatres in Britain for a commercial run and selected for the first

Commonwealth Arts Festival, the play was banned in Mumbai in 1965 on the grounds that it was set in the infamous redlight area of the city and therefore 'dealt with subjects which should not be depicted on stage'.

To prevent the Indian National Theatre's troupe of actors from going abroad to present the work, fifteen passports were impounded overnight. Seven years later, in 1972, the Mumbai High Court decreed that the censoring authority had 'exceeded its jurisdiction' and the ban was revoked.

Meanwhile, the play was studied at various universities (including one or two in India) and produced on stage and published abroad. Eventually, it was again produced by the Indian National Theatre in Mumbai in 1973. The play has also been produced and published in at least five countries in various languages. In 2006 it was selected by Sahitya Akademi (India's National Academy of Letters) to launch a series of contemporary plays by Indian writers in English.

It was broadcast for the first time over radio by the BBC Third Programme on 3 Nov. 1967 with a cast that included Academy Award winner Dame Judi Dench, and music specially composed for it by the famous sitar player, Pandit Ravi Shankar. Well known literary critic Walter Allen wrote of this play when it was first broadcast "the most imaginatively satisfying" experience in his recent listening. It was rebroadcast on BBC 7 on Saturday 6 October 2007 at 9am with a repeat on Sunday October at 3am.

In 1999, Geeta Citygirl staged the American premiere of *A TOUCH OF BRIGHTNESS* at Aaron Davis Hall in Harlem, NY. Partap Sharma was present for the opening night performance.

Zen Katha: The Zen Katha of Bodhidharma is a historical play about the founder of zen who was also a master of martial arts. Revered in China, Okinawa and Japan, the Indian monk Bodhidharma was, till the writing, performance and publication of this play, almost forgotten in his homeland India.

It tells the story of how Bodhidharma, born a prince in South India in the fifth century, had to discover ways to excel at unarmed combat because the royal Pallavas prided themselves on their wrestling skills. The Prince became a monk and fled from the demands of a throne to China, but could not so easily escape the woman who loved him.

Sammy!: The irrepressible 'Mahatma' in Gandhi is the Inner Voice he could not ignore. This intricately crafted play portrays Gandhi's journey from a tongue-tied lawyer to a shrewd politician and finally the Mahatma (Great Soul). Set against the dramatic background of India's struggle for freedom, this outstanding play surprises our expectation at every turn of the story. Full of humour and style, the play makes past events seem like present gossip and the audience is transported deeper within themselves.

The play brings alive Gandhi's philosophy, pragmatism, and sense of humour. Partap Sharma's play unwinds Gandhi's concepts and his techniques for non-violent struggle. The play is captivating as we realise that Gandhi's struggle has no enemy, no arms, no hate nor revenge, but only the inner strength of millions of ordinary men, women and children.

The play has won the 2006 META awards in India for Best Original Script, Best Director, Best Actor and Best Costumes. It is playing to great acclaim in India, and S.E Asia and after the European Premiere in Brussels in October 2006, travelled to the US, UK in 2007. It then travelled to New Zealand and Australia where it received standing ovations.

Begum Sumroo: Set in the late eighteenth century *The Rebel Courtesan, Begum Sumroo* (she is also known as Begum Samru), traces the picaresque adventures of a legendary historical figure from British India, Begum (Queen) Sumroo. Farzana is a peerless courtesan who morphs into a powerful ruler, known for her political accomplishments as well as her amorous liaisons. After seducing Walter Reinhardt Sombre, a Swiss German mercenary, she acquires the kingdom of Sardhana from Emperor Shah Alam, and commands a fierce brigade of 3000 European and Indian soldiers.

It is said that tourists who visited British India were advised to see the Taj Mahal, and to pay their respects to the

Begum! The story is of an amazing Indian woman who was ahead of her time and ours.

Staged Plays

- Brothers Under The Skin, (1956)
- Bars Invisible (1961)
- A Touch Of Brightness (1965)
- The Word (1966)
- The Professor Has A Warcry (1970)
- Queen Bee (1976)
- Power Play (1991)
- Begum Sumroo (1997),
- Zen Katha (2004)
- SAMMY! (2005)

Documentaries and Films

Partap Sharma has directed some outstanding documentaries, as independent producer and for the Government of India's Films Division, and Channel Four Television, U.K. His film credits include:

- The Framework of Famine, 1967, an investigation of how nature's devastation is compounded by human corruption and inefficiency; banned for it's "ruthless candour" then released after other documentary-makers protested.
- The Flickering Flame, 1974, a study of the mismanagement of the energy crisis and its effect on the suburban housewife; banned and never released.
- Kamli, 1976, a short film depicting the status of women in rural Indian society.
- The Empty Hand, 1982, (co-directed) a prize-winning audiovisual about the art of karate.
- Viewpoint Amritsar, 1984, co-directed a film about the Golden Temple and environs in the aftermath of Operation Bluestar.

- The British Raj Through Indian Eyes, 1992, a documentary series telecast in 1992 by Channel Four Television UK. Part I: The Uprising of 1857. Part II: The Massacre at Jallianwallah Bagh 1919.

The British Empire and Commonwealth Museum in Bristol, UK, now has a permanent section entitled 'The Sharma Archive' consisting of 30 video and 67 audio tapes made by Partap Sharma. Interviews and footage of Indian nationalists, freedom fighters and writers. Indian perspectives on the Raj. Some transcripts available (CDs, Videos and Cassettes).

- Sailing Around The World And Discover America Yachting Rally, two video programmes directed by Sandhya Divecha and produced by Sharma's Indofocus Films Pvt. Ltd.
- British Raj Hindustani Nazron Se, 1995-98, A Hindi TV Serial.

Children's Film

The Case Of The Hidden Ear-Ring, 1983

Feature Films

As an actor Sharma played a role in the Merchant-Ivory film "Shakespeare Wallah". Other films include the lead role in the following Hindi films:

- Phir Bhi (1971)
- Andolan (1975)
- Tyaag Patra (1980)
- Pehla Kadam (1980)
- Nehru – The Jewel of India (1989)
- The Bandung Sonata (2002) Filmed in China, Sharma played Nehru in this international film which was subsequently re-titled for release in China as *Chou-en-Lai in Bandung*.

Awards & Honours

Sharma won numerous first prizes in school & university in debating, elocution & acting including first prize at the All

India Inter-University Youth Festival, Delhi, in 1958. 1971 National Award for the lead role in the feature film "Phir Bhi" which also won the National Award for the best Hindi film of the year.

Cleo Award U.S.A for best voice.

1976 RAPA First Prize for best voice in radio spots.

1992 the "Hamid Sayani" Trophy for a lifetime of all-round excellence in radio and television.

2000 Ad Club of Mumbai Award for Lifetime Contribution to Advertising.

2003" Dadasaheb Phalke Award"

2006 "Meta Award" for Best Original Script for SAMMY!

2007 "Yuva Thespo 9 Lifetime Achievement Award "

Trivia

Bollywood actress Tara Sharma is Partap Sharma's daughter.

ACHARYA SHIVPUJAN SAHAY

Acharya Shivpujan Sahay is a Hindi a novelist (Dehati Duniya 1926), a short story writer (Vibhuti 1935), editor and prose writer.

Sahay was born in a middle class Kayastha land-owning family in the Unwans village near Buxar on 9 August 1893. After his early education and a short stint as a Hindi language teacher at Ara (1903-1921) he went to Kolkata and joined *Matwala* as an editor in 1923. He went to Lucknow in 1924 to join the editorial department of *Madhuri* where he worked with Hindi author Premchand and edited his *Rangbhumi* and some of his other stories. After a year he returned to Calcutta and continued editing short-lived journals such as *Samanway, Mauji, Golmal, Upanyas Tarang.*

Finally Sahay moved to Varanasi (K[i) to work as a freelance editor. For a short period in 1931, he went to Sultanganj near Bhagalpur to edit *Ganga*, but returned to Varanasi where he was commissioned to edit *Jagaran*, a literary fortnightly brought out by Jayashankar Prasad and his circle of friends in 1932. He once again found himself working beside Premchand. He also went on to become a prominent member of the Nagari Pracharini Sabha and similar literary circles in Varanasi.

In 1935 he moved to Laheria Sarai (Darbhanga) to work as editor of *Balak* and other publications of Pustak Bhandar owned by Ramlochan Sharan. In 1939 he joined Rajendra College, Chapra as Professor of Hindi Language. In 1946, on a year's leave, he moved to Patna to edit *Himalaya*, a literary monthly.

In 1949 Sahay finally came to Patna to work as Secretary of Bihar Rashtra Bhasha Parished, a government academy where he edited and published more than 50 volumes of Hindi reference works. Later he became Director of the Parishad and compiled and edited "Hindi Sahitya Aur Bihar' a literary history.

His own works were compiled and published in 4 volumes of *Shipujan Rachanavali* (1956-59). Shivpujan Sahay is also remembered for his editing of several literary commemoration volumes, chiefly *Dwivedi Abhinandan Granth* (1933), *Rajendra Abhinandan Granth* (1950) and *Jayanti Smarak Granth* (1942). He also edited Dr Rajendra Prasad's *Atmakatha*.

He died in Patna on 21 January 1963. His posthumously published books are *Wey Din Wey Log* (1965), *Mera Jeevan* (1985), *Smritishesh* (1994), *Hindi Bhasha Aur Sahitya* (1996), and *Gram Sudhar* (2007). He was awarded Padmabhushan award in 1960.

JASPREET SINGH

Jaspreet Singh is a Canadian writer.

He grew up in India and moved to Canada in 1990. He is the author of *Seventeen Tomatoes: Tales from Kashmir*. He holds a PhD in chemical engineering from McGill University. His play, *Speak, Oppenheimer*, written for Montreal's Infinite Theatre, involves three physicists, including J. Robert Oppenheimer.

From August 2006 until June 2007, Singh was a resident in the Markin-Flanagan Distinguished Writers Programme at the University of Calgary.

KHUSHWANT SINGH

Khushwant Singh (born 2 February 1915 in Hadali, British India, now in Punjab, Pakistan) is a prominent Indian novelist and journalist. Singh's weekly column, "With Malice towards One and All", carried by several Indian newspapers, is among the most widely-read columns in the country.

An important Indo-Anglian novelist, Singh is best known for his trenchant secularism, his humour, and an abiding love of poetry. His comparisons of social and behavioural characteristics of Westerners and Indians are laced with acid wit. He served as editor of several well-known literary and news magazines, as well as two major broadsheet newspapers, through the 1970s and 1980s.

Life and Career

Singh was educated at Government College, Lahore and St. Stephen's College in Delhi before reading for the Bar at King's College London. His father, Sir Sobha Singh, was a prominent builder in Lutyens' Delhi.

In August 1947, days before the partition of India and Pakistan, Singh, then a lawyer practicing in the High Court in Lahore, drove to his family's summer cottage at Kasauli in the foothills of the Himalayas. Continuing on to Delhi along 200 miles of strangely vacant road, he came upon a Jeep full of armed Sikhs who boasted that they had just massacred a village of Muslims. Such experiences were to be powerfully distilled in Singh's 1956 novel *Train to Pakistan*. (The 2006 edition of Train to Pakistan, published by Roli Books in New Delhi, also contains 66 photographs by Margaret Bourke-White that capture the partition's violent aftermath.)

Singh has edited *Yojana*, an Indian government journal; *The Illustrated Weekly of India*, a newsweekly; and two major Indian newspapers, *The National Herald* and the *Hindustan*

Times. During his tenure, *The Illustrated Weekly* became India's pre-eminent newsweekly. After Singh's departure, it suffered a huge drop in readership .

From 1980 through 1986, Singh was a member of Rajya Sabha, the upper house of the Indian parliament. Awarded the Padma Bhushan in 1974 for service to his country, in 1984 he returned the award in protest against the siege of the Golden Temple by the Indian Army. Undeterred, in 2007 the Indian government awarded Singh an even more prestigious honour, the Padma Vibhushan.

A self-proclaimed agnostic, lover of fine scotch whiskey and admirer of female beauty, he nonetheless leads a very disciplined life, waking up at 4 am each day and continuing to write his columns by hand. His works range from political commentary and contemporary satire to outstanding translations of Sikh religious texts and Urdu poetry. Despite the name, his column "With Malice Towards One and All" regularly contains secular exhortations and messages of peace, brotherhood and tolerance. In addition, he is one of the last remaining writers to have personally known most of the stalwart writers and poets of Urdu and Punjabi languages, and profiles his recently deceased contemporaries in his column. One of the most striking aspects of his weekly writings is his outright honesty; he will openly admit to his weaknesses and mistakes, along with an acceptance of his declining health and physical abilities in more recent times.

As a public figure, Singh has been accused of favouring the ruling Congress party, especially during the reign of Indira Gandhi. He is better viewed as an establishment liberal. Singh's faith in secular forces has been shaken by events such as anti-Sikh riots that followed Indira Gandhi's assassination, in which major Congress politicians were alleged to be involved. But he has remained resolutely positive on the promise of Indian democracy .

Honours and Awards

- Padma Bhushan, Government of India (1974)
- *Honest Man of the Year*, Sulabh International (2000)

- Punjab Rattan Award, The Government of Punjab (2006)
- Padma Vibhushan, Government of India (2007)

Bibliography

- *The Mark of Vishnu and Other Stories*, 1950
- *The History of Sikhs*, 1953
- *Train to Pakistan*, 1956
- *The Voice of God and Other Stories*, 1957
- *I Shall Not Hear the Nightingale*, 1959
- *The Sikhs Today*, 1959
- *The Fall of the Kingdom of the Punjab*, 1962
- *A History of the Sikhs*, 1963
- *Ranjit Singh: The Maharajah of the Punjab*, 1963
- *Ghadar 1915: India's first armed revolution*, 1966
- *A Bride for the Sahib and Other Stories*, 1967
- *Black Jasmine*, 1971
- *Tragedy of Punjab*, 1984
- *Delhi: A Novel*, 1990
- *Sex, Scotch and Scholarship: Selected Writings*, 1992
- *Not a Nice Man to Know: The Best of Khushwant Singh*, 1993
- *We Indians*, 1993
- *Women and Men in My Life*, 1995
- *Uncertain Liaisons; Sex, Strife and Togetherness in Urban India*, 1995
- *The Company of Women*, 1999
- *Truth, Love and a Little Malice* (an autobiography), 2002
- *With Malice towards One and All*
- *The End of India*, 2003
- *Burial at the Sea*, 2004
- *Paradise and Other Stories*, 2004
- *Death at My Doorstep*, 2005
- *The Illustrated History of the Sikhs*, 2006

NANAK SINGH

Nanak Singh (born Hans Raj, July 4, 1897 — 1971) was a poet, songwriter and novelist in the Punjabi language. His writing in support of India's independence movement forced the British to arrest him. He published several novels which won him literary acclaim.

Early Life

He was born as Hans Raj to a poor Punjabi Hindu family in the Jhelum district (now in Pakistan) and changed his name to Nanak Singh after adopting Sikhism. Due to poverty, he did not receive a formal education. He started his writing career at an early age, writing verses on historical events. Later, Nanak Singh started to write devotional songs, encouraging Sikhs to join the Gurdwara Reform Movement. In 1918, he published his first book containing hymns in praise of the Sikh Gurus, which is considered his first commercial success.

Role in Freedom Struggle

On April 13, 1919, British troops shot and killed 379 peaceful rally participants in what became known as the Jallianwala Bagh massacre on Baisakhi (Punjabi New Year) day in Amritsar.

Nanak Singh was present at the rally in which two of his friends were killed. This incident impelled Nanak Singh to write Khooni Visakhi-*Bloody Baisakhi (Punjabi New Year)*, an epic poem that mocked and targeted colonial rule. The British Government became extremely concerned about his provocative writing and banned the book.

Nanak Singh also participated in India's independence struggle by joining the Akali movement. He began editing Akali papers. This also was noticed by the British Government. Singh was charged with participation in unlawful political activities and was sent to Borstal Jail, Lahore. He described the savagery and oppression of the British on peaceful Sikhs during the Guru Ka Bagh Morcha demonstration in his second book of poetry, 'Zakhmi Dil'. It was published in January 1923 and was banned within two weeks. Nanak Singh wrote novels while in jail. He wrote over 40,000 pages in long hand Gurmukhi (Punjabi) script. He was recognized with many awards, including Punjab's highest literary award in 1960. His great historical novel, Ik Mian Do Talwaran (One Sheath and Two Swords, 1959) won him India's highest literary honour, the Sahitya Akademi Award in 1962.

Prolific Writer

He wrote the novel *Pavitar Paapi* (*Saintly Sinner*) in 1942. The novel became immensely popular and won him literary acclaim. It was translated into Hindi and several other Indian languages and was adapted into a film in 1968. Currently, the novel is in its 28th reprint in Punjabi. His grandson, Navdeep Singh Suri, translated the book into English.

Quoting the Tribune, "Nanak Singh was the best selling novelist in India for thirty to forty years. He wrote over 50 books including novels and collection of short stories. He made significant contributions to various literary genres. For him character was the determination of incident and incident the illustration of character. His greatest contribution to Punjabi fiction is its secularisation. He depicted excerpts from contemporary life, cloaked with a veil of romantic idealism."

In his novel *Chitta Lahu* (White Blood), Nanak Singh writes, "It seems to imply that in the lifeblood of our society, red corpuscles have disappeared." Natasha Tolstoy, granddaughter of novelist Leo Tolstoy, translated Nanak Singh's novel *Chitta Lahu* into Russian. She visited Nanak Singh in Amritsar to present the first copy of the translated novel to him.

Bibliography

1. Gagan Damama Bajia
2. Sarapia Roohan
3. Koi Hariya Boota Rahio Ree
4. Ek Myaan Wich Do Talwaran
5. Chalawa

6. Pujari
7. Banjar
8. Sangam
9. Aastak Naastak
10. Nasoor
11. Adamkhor
12. Majhdhar
13. Dhindale Parchawe
14. Garid Di Duniya
15. Pyaar Di Duniya
16. Meri Duniya
17. Chitrakaar
18. Suman Kanta
19. Kati Hoyi Patang
20. Aug Di Khed
21. Tuti Veena
22. Gangajali Di Sharaab
23. Khoon De Sohile
24. Pavitar Papi
25. Chitta Lahoo
26. Pholadi Phul
27. Love Marriage
28. Jeevan Sangram
29. Door Kinara
30. Adh Khirya Phul
31. Pathar Kamba
32. Kagachan Di Berhi
33. Prashchit
34. Kaal Chakar
35. Matreyi Maan
36. Paap Di Khatti
37. Soolan Di Sejh

38. Patchar De Panchi
39. Sadran Di Haar
40. Hanjhooyan De Haar
41. Supneyan Di Kabar
42. Var Nahin Saraap
43. Anseetey Jakham
44. Pathar De Khumb
45. Mitha Mahura
46. Prem Sangeet
47. France Da Daakoo
48. Rajni
49. Sunheri Jild
50. Thandian Chawan
51. Midhe Hoye Phul
52. Tasveer De Doven Paase
53. B.A. Paas
54. Meriya Kahaniyaan
55. Mere Naatak
56. Taash Di Aadat
57. Lumba Penda
58. Vishwaas Ghaat
59. Rab Apne Asli Roop Wich

Trivia

Indian President Giani Zail Singh brought a copy of *Khooni Visakhi* to India from a museum in England. His centenary was celebrated in 1997. In Singh's honour, India's Prime Minister Inder Kumar Gujral released a postal stamp in 1998.

INDRA SINHA

Indra Sinha (born in 1950 in Colaba, which is part of Mumbai in the state of Maharashtra, India) is an Anglo-Indian /Indian English novelist and translator. Formerly a copywriter for Collett Dickenson Pearce & Partners, Sinha has the distinction of having been voted one of the top ten British copywriters of all time.

Indra Sinha's books, in addition to his translations of ancient Sanskrit texts into English, include a non-fiction memoir of the pre-internet generation *(Cybergypsies),* and novels based on the case of K. M. Nanavati vs. State of Maharashtra *(The Death of Mr. Love),* and the Bhopal disaster *(Animal's People). Animal's People,* his most recent book, was a 2007 Man Booker Prize nominee.

Sinha is the son of an Indian naval officer and an English writer. He was educated at Mayo College, Ajmer, Rajasthan in India, where he studied Hindi and Sanskrit; Oakham School, Rutland, England and Pembroke College, Cambridge in England, where he studied English literature. After living in England for four decades, he and his wife currently live in southern France. They have three grown-up children.

> *"I was invited by a publisher to write the text for* Tantra. *Having done some research, what fascinated me was the evidence that many 'tantric' ideas actually came to India from the Mediterranean. It is rather a dry read and debunks reports of orgies and sexual mischief — sorry to disappoint." – Indra Sinha,* Interview.

Books

- 1980. *The Love Teachings of Kama Sutra: With extracts from Koka Shastra, Ananga Ranga and other famous Indian works on love.* Translations from Sanskrit and commentary. London: Hamlyn. Hardcover first edition: ISBN 0-60034-158-5. First North American edition 1997, New York: Marlowe & Co. Paperback: ISBN 1-56924-779-X.
- 1993. *Tantra: The Search for Ecstasy* (also known with the subtitle "The Cult of Ecstasy"). London: Hamlyn. ISBN 0-60057-699-X.
- 1993. *The Great Book of Tantra: Translations and Images from the Classic Indian Text.* Rochester: Inner

Traditions-Bear & Company. ISBN 0-89281-487-X. London: Hamlyn paperback edition: ISBN 0600599981.

- 1999. *The Cybergypsies: a True Tale of Lust, War, and Betrayal on the Electronic Frontier*. New York: Viking Press, hardcover first edition. ISBN 0-67088-630-0. New York: Simon & Schuster paperback edition: ISBN 0-68481-929-5.
- 2002. *The Death of Mr Love*. New York: Scribner (Simon & Schuster). ISBN 0-74320-698-3. (See also: K. M. Nanavati vs. State of Maharashtra.)
- 2007. *Animal's People*. New York: Simon & Schuster. ISBN 0-74325-920-3. (See also: Bhopal disaster.)

SIVASANKARI

Sivasankari (born October 14, 1942) is a popular Tamil writer and activist. She is one of the four Tamil writers asked by the United States Library of Congress to record their voice as part of the South Asian Literary Recordings Project. She has over 30 novels, 150 short stories, 13 travelogues and 2 biographies to her credit.

She is working on her ambitious *Knit India Through Literature* project whose goal according to her is "learn more about the culture, history and literature of the people of each State and introduce them to their fellow Indians through the works of a few writers selected from each of these languages".

Started in 1993, the project's plan is to publish the analysis in four volumes.

She is also the founder of Awakened Group for National Integration (AGNI).

Awards and Accolades

- Kasturi Srinivasan Award in 1983
- Bharatiya Bhasha Parishad Award in 1990
- Raja Sir Annamalai Chettiyar Award in 1988
- Tamil Annai Award

INDIRA SOUNDARAJAN

Indira Soundarajan is a well known Tamil author who is famously known by the TV serial "Marma Desam". His works include short stories, novels. He has penned screenplays and dialogue for Television serials. He lives in Madurai.

He is famous for bringing the little-known world of "Sithars" to the attention of the common man. Even otherwise, his works are mystical and involve ghosts and fantastical spells.

His collection of stories for the serials in the name "Marma Desam" includes the following: 1) Ragasiyamai Oru Ragasiyam 2) Vidathu Karuppu-A novel in the name "Vittu Vidu Karuppa" which was later made as a serial. 3) Sorna Regai 4) Iyandira Paravai and 5) Vaanathu Manidhargal.

His well known works include:

- Marmadesam (Mysterious Land)
- Ruthra Veena (Ruthra means Sivan and Veena is a Musical Instrument)

He has also written the screenplay for the Tamil movie 'Sringaram', a first for him.

C P SURENDRAN

C. P. Surendran is a Resident Editor for Pune with *The Times of India* and English poet and novelist.

His first novel *An Iron Harvest* about the Naxalite uprising, was published by Roli Books. He has also published three collection of poetry. He currently lives in Mumbai.

Bibliography

Novels

- *An Iron Harvest* (Roli Books)

Poetry

- *Gemini II* (Penguin Viking)
- *Posthumous Poems* (Penguin Viking)
- *Canaries On The Moon* (Yeti Press)

TV VARKEY

T. V. Varkey is a Kerala-born Indian-writer, who writes novels and short stories both in Malayalam (his mother tongue) and English. He lives in Tripunithura, very close to Kochi.

Born: April 2, 1938 Mevelloor, Kottayam, Kerala, India

Occupation: Novelist, Short Story Writer, Professor and Literary Activist

Influences: Franz Kafka, Albert Camus, Dostoevsky, Garcia Márquez, Gunter Grass

Life

T.V. Varkey was born on April 2, 1938 into a middle-class family (Thazhakuzhy), at Mevelloor, in Kottayam district. His father, Mathew Varkey (1912-1998), was of Kunnathur family and mother, Thressiamma (1916-1978) was of Vembenil family. He had his primary and high school education at Government L.P. S., Velloor, and St. Paul's, Veliyanad (Tripunithura), respectively. He did his degree at Sacred Heart College, Thevara, and Master's at St. Berchman's, Changanacherry, both in language and literature. Varkey, a gold medallist of the University of Kerala for literary debate, used to publish articles, poems and stories in periodicals, and had won many prizes in various competitions, at an early age itself.

Teaching was his primary calling and he joined S. B College as lecturer in 1964. Two years later he had short stint as a journalist at Deepika, a daily published from Kottayam. Afterwards he worked at Kuriakose Elias College, Mannanam, near Kottayam as a Lecturer and Professor until 1993. During this period he penned his major novels and short stories, besides being a literary activist.

Important Works

In his first novel, Vazhiyum Niazhalum (The Road and The shadow), Varkey has employed the stream-of-consciousness technique in telling the love story of a widow. It was a daring experiment in Malayalam when new trends were not very much in vogue. Reviewer, Dr. Radhakrishnan, writes about one of his other novels, Sooryante Maranam (The Death of the Sun), in the Indian Express: "...depicts both Promethean defiance and Sisyphean despair." Dr. K. M. Tharakan, renowned critic praises Mulmaram (The Thorny Tree), his next important novel, as the "story of a man, a village and an epoch in the history of Kerala." "Chhaya" (The Shadow), Varkey's award winning novel is the tale of a human being whose inner self is tragically split into pieces like shattered glass, expounding the unique features of abnormal psychology, in particular the multiple personality...." writes senior critic Dr. M. Leelavathy. Manjupokunna Thalamurakal (The Vanishing Generations) is Varkey's magnum opus. It is a compelling family saga of a hundred and twenty-five years, which is well integrated with the history of the Syrian Catholic Church of Kerala. The novel, Thrikalam (The Three Seasons) is an analysis of modern ideal personality against the backdrop of fascinating three sets of people living in different families in the same colony. Death becomes a plaything for a heroic personality here.

T. V. Varkey's three scores of short stories have a unique place in Malayalam literature. Njan Verum Njan (I'm mere I) received much praise as the best story of 1986 and the Vice-chancellor is an award winning story. Veedum Kozhikoovunnu (Again the Cock Crows) was the chosen story of 1984, and Aviswasi (The Unbeliever), Gandhi Sishayan (Gandhi's Disciple) are noted for their ironical and sarcastic narration. Style and vision: T. V. Varkey's literary creations are in-depth analysis of his characters, which reflect different shades of his views. His style of writing is personal and sardonic. Most of his writings are serious comedies, although their tone and fictional strategies may "muffle" things.

Awards:

- Gold medal (University of Kerala) for Debate – 1962
- 'Vipula' National Short Story Award – 1988
- 'Sachethana' Award for novel—1989

Films:

- Sooriyante Maranam. Directed by award winning director Rajeev Nath, and won a state award.

- Njan Sivan Pillai (under the title Keli), directed by Bharathan, an artistic, experimental film maker. The film was commercially too successful.

Titles

Novels : Vazhiyum Niazhalum (The Road and The shadow), Vilakku (The Lamp), Sooriyante Maranam (The Death of the Sun), Nam Chithalukal (We're Termites), Mulmaram (The Thorny Tree), Njan Sivan Pillai, (I am Sivan Pillai), Chhaya, (The Shadow), Manjupokunna Thalamurakal (The Vanishing Generations), Thrikalam (The Three Seasons)

Short Stories : Aviswasi (The Unbeliever), The Vice-Chancellor,, Veedum Kozhikoovunnu (Again the Cock Crows), Gandhi Sishayan (Gandhi's Disciple),Njan Verum Njan (I'm mere I) etc

SHASHI THAROOR

Shashi Tharoor (born 9 March 1956 in London) is an Indian diplomat at the United Nations (UN). In 2006, he was the official candidate of India for the succession to United Nations Secretary-General Kofi Annan, and came second out of seven official candidates in the race. Tharoor served as the UN Under-Secretary General for Communications and Public Information between June 2002 and February 2007. He is an author, journalist, and fellow of the USC Centre on Public Diplomacy. Tharoor is an Indian national, from the state of Kerala.

Education

In India Tharoor studied at Montfort School in Yercaud, Bombay Scottish School and Campion School in Mumbai, attended High School at St. Xavier's Collegiate School in Kolkata and graduated with a Bachelor of Arts degree in history from St. Stephen's College, Delhi. While at St. Stephen's Tharoor was actively involved in the Debating Society, which is where he cultivated his Received Pronunciation accent, Quiz Club, and Students' Union, of which he was the elected President. He then completed a Ph.D at The Fletcher School of Law and

Diplomacy at Tufts University, Massachusetts, where he also earned two Master's degrees.

- Since 1978, Tharoor has been working for the United Nations, serving with the UN High Commissioner for Refugees, whose Singapore office he headed during the "boat people" crisis.
- Since October 1989, he has been a senior official at the United Nations headquarters in New York, where, until late 1996, he was responsible for peacekeeping operations in the former Yugoslavia.
- From January 1997 to July 1998, he was executive assistant to UN Secretary General Kofi Annan.
- In July 1998, he was appointed director of communications and special projects in the office of the Secretary-General.
- In January 2001, he was appointed by the Secretary-General as interim head of the Department of Public Information.
- On 1 June 2002, he was confirmed as the Under Secretary General for Communications and Public Information. In this capacity, he is responsible for the communication strategy, enhancing the image and effectiveness of the UN.
- In 2003, the Secretary-General appointed him United Nations Coordinator for Multilingualism.
- Resigned from the post of Under Secretary General on the 9th of February 2007.

Candidacy for the Post of Secretary-General

On June 15, 2006, the Government of India announced its backing for Tharoor's candidacy as Kofi Annan's successor for the post of UN Secretary General.

Tharoor came second (behind Ban Ki-moon) in each of the four straw polls conducted by the UN Security Council on 24 July, 14 September, 28 September and 2 October. In the fourth poll, Ban emerged as the only candidate with the support of all five permanent members, each of whom has the power to veto candidates. After the vote, Tharoor withdrew his candidacy, telling reporters he was "confident that Ban will win."

Post-UN Career

In February 2007, it was reported in the Indian press that Tharoor might be inducted into council of ministers of Prime Minister Manmohan Singh as Minister of State for External Affairs.

In the same month, it was reported in an American gossip blog that Tharoor was a finalist for the position of dean of the USC Annenberg School for Communication in Los Angeles. Dr. Tharoor—in addition to a variety of other activities in his private life—is Chairman of Dubai-based Afras Ventures. He is additionally the Joint Chairman of UNSICAD (United Nations Simulation International Conference at Abu Dhabi and Dubai)—the World Summit to be held in the United Arab Emirates in June 2008.

Literary Career

Tharoor has written numerous books in English. Most of his literary creations are centred on Indian themes and they are markedly "Indo-nostalgic." Perhaps his most famous work is *The Great Indian Novel*, published in 1989, in which he uses the narrative and theme of the famous Indian epic Mahabharata to weave a satirical story of Indian life in a non-linear mode with the characters drawn from the Indian Independence Movement. His novel *Show Business* (1992) was made into the film *Bollywood* (1994). The late Ismail Merchant had announced his wish to make a film of Tharoor's novel *Riot* shortly before Merchant's death in 2005.

Tharoor has written a fortnightly column for *The Hindu* newspaper since 2001 and a weekly column, "Shashi on Sunday," in the *Times of India* since January 2007. Previously he was a columnist for the *Gentleman* magazine and the *Indian Express* newspaper, as well as a frequent contributor to *Newsweek International* and the *International Herald Tribune*. His op-eds and book reviews have appeared in the *Washington Post*, the

New York Times and the *Los Angeles Times*, amongst other papers. Tharoor began writing at the age of 6 and his first published story appeared in the "Bharat Jyoti" in Mumbai at age 10. His World War-II adventure novel *Operation Bellows*, inspired by the Biggles books, was serialized in the Junior Statesman starting a week before his 11th birthday.

Works

Fiction

- *Riot* (2001)
- *Show Business* (1992)
- *The Five Dollar Smile and Other Stories* (1990)
- *The Great Indian Novel* (1989)

Non-fiction

- *The Elephant, the Tiger and the Cell Phone: India—The Emerging 21st Century Power* (2007)
- *Bookless in Baghdad* (2005)
- *Nehru: The Invention of India* (2003)
- *Kerala: God's own country* (2002)
- *India: From Midnight to the Millennium* (1997)
- *Reasons of State* (1982)

Awards and Recognition

- In 1976, at age 20, he won the Rajika Kripalani Young Journalist Award for the Best Indian Journalist under 30.
- In 1990, he won the Federation of Indian Publishers-Hindustan Times Literary Award for the Best Book of the Year for *The Great Indian Novel*, which also won a Commonwealth Writers' Prize in 1991 for the Best Book of the Year in the Eurasian Region.
- In 1998, Tharoor was awarded the Excelsior Award for excellence in literature by the Association of Indians in America (AIA) and the Network of Indian Professionals (NetIP).

- He received the honorary degree of Doctor of Letters in International Affairs from the University of Puget Sound in May 2000.
- In January 1998, he was named by the World Economic Forum in Davos, Switzerland, as a "Global Leader of Tomorrow."
- In 2004, he was awarded the prestigious Pravasi Bharatiya Samman, India's highest honour for non-resident Indians, but did not accept it owing to UN rules prohibiting acceptance of governmental honours.
- In 2007 he accepted the Pravasi Bharatiya Samman award, India's highest honour for non-resident Indians which he had been unable to accept four years earlier due to UN rules .

Personal

He married Tilottama Tharoor, a journalist and scholar, at the age of 21, from whom he is now divorced. He is the father of twin sons, Ishaan and Kanishk, who have recently graduated from Yale. One of the twins, Ishaan lives in Hong Kong and works for *Time* magazine and the other brother, Kanishk, is a resident of London working for openDemocracy. Recently he got remarried to Christa Giles, a Canadian who is Deputy Secretary of the United Nations Disarmament Commission.

Tharoor is known for his passionate interest in cricket, especially Indian cricket, about which he has written in such publications as *The Cricketer International*, *The Illustrated Weekly of India* and *The Hindu*. An outstanding actor and debater in school and college, Tharoor won numerous prizes at inter-collegiate "winter festivals" and similar competitions. He played Antony to Mira Nair's Cleopatra in a 1974 production of *Antony and Cleopatra*. At St. Stephen's in the early 1970s he founded the Quiz Club, which is still in existence; he also revived the Wodehouse Society, which is no longer in existence. Upon election as President of the College Union (campaign slogan: "Shashi Tharoor *jeetega zaroor*") he relinquished the editorship of the campus humour magazine "Kooler Talk." He was invited by St. Stephen's College to deliver the college's

125th Anniversary Jubilee Lecture in 2005. He is an elected Fellow of the New York Institute for the Humanities and a member of the Advisory Board of the Indo-American Arts Council. He also serves on the Board of Directors of Breakthrough, an international human rights organization.

At the Fletcher School of Law and Diplomacy in 1976, he founded and was the first chair of the editorial board of the Fletcher Forum of International Affairs, a journal examining issues in international relations .

HARILAL UPADHYAY

Shri Harilal Upadhyay (January 22, 1916(1916-01-22)-January 15, 1994) was a Gujarati author. He is considered as one of the all-time great Gujarati authors. He wrote more than a hundred books in Gujarati. His works include historical novels, social novels, short story collections, biographies, the great Mahabharat series, children's literature, poems and Plays. He was used to writing columns and articles in news papers and magazines like Kismat, Lok Tantra, Lok Gurjari (Lok Gurjaree), Jyotir Vignan (Jyotir Vigyan) and others, on regular and occassional bases. He was also an award winner Astrologer (Astrologist).

Historical Novels

Suryavansh/Rajasthan: His work includes books on Suryavansh and Rajasthan like:

- *Shaurya Pratapi Maharana Pratap*
- *Desh Gaurav Bhamashah*
- *Jay Chittod*
- *Chittod Ni Rangarjana : Roop Rani Padmini*
- *Mevad Ni Tejchhaya*
- *Mevad Na Maharathi : Nari Ratna Panna Dai*
- *Mevad No Kesri*

Chandravansh/Gujarat: Historical works include books with Gujarat as background and/or Chandravansh:

- *Shaurya Pratapi Chandravansh*

- *Rudhir Nu Rajtilak*
- *Raj Satta Na Rang*
- *Lakho Fulani*
- *Ran Medan*
- *Ek Bhalo Saput*
- *Tati Talvar*
- *Navanagar Na Narbanka*
- *Managal Fera*
- *Rajsatta Na Rang*
- *Nayan Ughadyu Ne Phool Kharyu*
- *Kachchh Bhoomi Na Kesri*
- *Padata Gadh Na Padchhaya (Part 1 and 2)*

Modh Brahmins

- *Otrada Vayara Utho Utho*
- *Sonavarani* (The history of Modh Brahmins)

Socio-Historical: Social tales based on historical background

- *Kalank Ane Kirtirekha*
- *Vijay Vardaan*
- *Bhagya devata*
- *Roshani*
- *Aparajita*

The Mahabharata: He also wrote *The Mahabharata* series, which contains seven parts:

- *Bhishma Pratigna*
- *Dharma Pratigna*
- *Kurukshetra*
- *Bhishma No Shantibodh*
- *Dharma Vijay*
- *Mahaprasthaan*
- *Yog Viyog*

Social Novels

- *Ramkali (Roop Mangala)*
- *Rahi Gai Man Ni Man Ma*
- *Gauri*
- *Tan Bhukhya Koi Dhan Bhukhya*
- *Preete Parovaya*
- *Dharati Lal Gulal*
- *Nathi Sukaya Neer*
- *Sukh Savaya Thay*
- *Kundan Chadyu Kante*
- *Savazada Senjal Pie*
- *Man Dubya Mrugjal Ma*
- *Kesar Bhino Kanth*
- *Varso Re Ur na Amee*
- *Amrut Bhini Ankhaladi*
- *Tej Chhavai Raat*
- *Haiye Madhaya Het*
- *Nisha Sunave Naad*
- *Alka*
- *Man Pankhi Na Mala*
- *Kanchan Lage Na Kaat*
- *Antar Khole Ankh*
- *Nari Hati Ek Namani*
- *Paras Sparshe Ek J War*
- *Ugyo Chandra Amase*
- *Dhabakatu Dhan*
- *Rajpur Ni Lachhu*
- *Van Man Khili Vasant*
- *Gori To Gunial Bhali*
- *Dharm Ane Rajkaran*
- *Andhkaar Chhaya*

- *Saheli*
- *Sukhlalsa*
- *Man Ne Lagi Maya*
- *Pagla Padya Kankuvarna*
- *Chhanydee*
- *Roshnee*

Short Story Collections

- *Saurashtra No Vartaras*
- *Saurashtra Ni Rasgatha (2 parts)*
- *Saurashtra Ni Veergathao (5 parts)*
- *Sorthi Lokvato*
- *Jeevanchhaya*
- *Pushp Mangal (Baal Vartao-Kids Literature)*

Biographies

- *Harsiddhi Ane Hinglaj*
- *Sant Dada Mekan*
- *Sant Dharamshi Bhagat*
- *Mast Avdhoot Moondiya Swami*
- *Naag Mahima*
- *Chhelnami Saurashtra*
- *Karma Prabhaav*
- *Shakti Parichay (about Mahadevi Hinglajmata, Mahadevi Harsiddhi And Mahadevi Khodiyar)*

His Achievements

- *Jyotirvigyan Sanshodhan Award*
- *Kanaiyalal Munshi Award*

V. BALAKUMARAN

Balakumaran (b. 5th July 1946) is a famous Tamil writer, author of over 150 novels, 100 short stories, and dialogue/screenplay writer for over 14 films. He has also contributed to

Tamil periodicals such as Ananda Vikatan and Kumudam. His writings are noted for a distinct philosophical and religious tone. He presently resides at Mylapore, Chennai. Fondly called as Ezhuthu Sithar by his fans.

Novels Written

- Mercury pookkal
- Irumbhu kudhiraigal
- Thayumanavan
- Agalya
- Endrenrum anbudan
- Udayar
- Shenbagathottam
- Pani vizhum malar vanam
- Kadal neelam
- Naan enna solli vittaen
- Kadarpaalam
- Pey Karumbu
- Nigumbalai
- Kadalora Kuruvigal
- Karaiyora Muthalaihal
- Payanihal Kavanikkavum
- Thunai
- Meettatha Veenai
- Vetrilai Kodi
- Manja Kaani
- Karnanin Kathai
- Shakthi
- Guru
- Katru Kondal Kutramillai
- En Manathu Thamaraipu
- Kalyana Murungai
- Peria Purana Kathaigal

- Kannaadi Koburangal
- Katigai
- Ammavum 10 Katturaigalum, etc.

Contribution to Films

Balakumaran's contribution to films has largely been in the field of screenplay making and dialogue writing. His skills in crafting the dialogue for any conceivable character are notorious in Kollywood. List of the films to which Balakumaran contributed:

- Nayakan
- Guna
- Shenbagathottam
- Gentleman
- Kadhalan
- Kizhakku Malai
- Madangal Aezhu
- Ragasiya Police
- Baasha
- Sivasakthi
- Ullasam
- Velai
- Jeans

Current Literary Works

- Epic on Rajendra Cholan
- Monthly Novels on various themes
- bn

Awards

- Literary Awards won :
  * Irumbu Kudhiraigal – Raja Sir Annamalai Chettiyar Trust Award
  * Mercury Pookal–Illakkiya Sindhanai Awards

  * Kadarpalam–State Award (II Prize) (Short Story Collection)
  * Sugajeevanam – State Award (I Prize) (short story collection)
- Cinema Awards Won :
  * Guna – Cinema Express Award
  * Kaadalan – State Award (Best dialogue Writer)
- Other Awards : Honoured with "Sindhanai Chemmal" title (From Lions Club Madras)

ARDASHIR VAKIL

Ardashir Vakil is an author whose first novel, *Beach Boy*, won a Betty Trask Award in 1997 and was shortlisted for the Whitbread First Novel Award. His second novel, "One Day" was short-listed for the Encore Award.

Born in Bombay and educated at The Doon School, he now lives in London with his wife and two daughters. He teaches Creative Writing at Goldsmiths and University of East Anglia.

SHREEKUMAR VARMA

Shreekumar Varma is an Indian author, newspaper columnist and poet, known for the novels *Lament of Mohini* (Penguin, 2000) and *Devil's Garden: Tales Of Pappudom* (Puffin, 2006) and the historical book for children, *The Royal Rebel* (Macmillan, 1997). He is the great grandson of the artist Raja Ravi Varma and grandson of Regent Maharani Sethu Lakshmi Bayi, the last ruling Maharani of Travancore.

He was born in 1955 in Satelmond Palace, Poojapura, Thiruvananthapuram. His parents left Kerala and settled down in Madras when he was four. He studied in the Good Shepherd Convent, the Madras Christian College High School and the Madras Christian College, from where he completed his MA and M.Phil in English Literature. Later he taught briefly at the college. He also did a course in Journalism from the Bhavan's College of Journalism and Mass Communication. He took part in plays in school and college, and also participated in and devised programmes for All India Radio. He worked for the Indian Express and the Film Industry Journal (renamed Cinema Today) in Bombay. Back in Madras, he was associated with a printing press, as well as a publishing and creative training unit. He lives in Chennai, and is a full-time writer and adjunct professor at the Chennai Mathematical Institute. He is married to Geeta and has two sons, Vinayak and Karthik.

His two award-winning plays, *The Dark Lord* and *Bow Of Rama,* were staged by The British Council and The Madras Players respectively. His play, *Platform*, was staged by The Madras Players, the oldest running English language theatre group in India, in January 2005 to launch their golden jubilee celebrations.

He has written regular columns for The New Indian Express, The Economic Times Madras Plus, Ritz Magazine, Fiji Times and the Deccan Herald.

He has contributed poetry, fiction and non-fiction to several anthologies, including Poetry Society of India volumes, Aesthetica Quarterly Review, Pulse Berlin Magazine, A Hudson View Poetry Digest, Where The Rain Is Born: Writings from Kerala, The Puffin Book of Poetry for Children, the Puffin Book of Funny Stories, The Tenth Rasa: An Anthology of Indian Nonsense (Penguin), A Cup Of Chai & Other Stories (Unisun Publications) and Favourite Stories for Boys (Puffin).

His new novel *Maria's Room* was Longlisted for the inaugural Man Asia Literary Prize (2007).

His poetry was used as text for the dance recitals Vamshi and Monsoon by noted Bharatanatyam exponent Indira Kadambi.

He was awarded the Charles Wallace Fellowship for the year 2004, and was Writer-in-Residence at Stirling University, Scotland.

YANDAMURI VEERENDRANATH

Yandamoori Veerendranath is a Telugu author; people recognize him easily by his surname Yandamoori.

Born on 14 November 1948 at rajolu, East Godavari Dist, Andhra Pradesh as son of Mr. Yandamoori Chakrapani (worked as Income Tax employee) and Mrs. Yandamoori Narasamaamba.

He did his schooling at Kakinada, Rajahmundry, Jammalamadugu, Anantapuram and Hyderabad. And he has studied B.Com at Kakinada. Later at 1972 he finished his Chartered Accountancy at ICAI and has become a Chartered Accountant.

Veerendranath is a man who believes dignity of labour. During his schooldays, he used to conduct tuitions. And while doing B.Com, he has worked in accounts department of a company where he has to write the cash flow statements.

After finishing Chartered Accountancy, he has worked for 5 years in State Financial Corporation and for 10 years as Chief officer in Andhra Bank Small Scale Industries dept. He has resigned his job to concentrate more on literature.

Yandamoori Veerendranath has got married to Anugeetha on 10 March 1974. Their son Mr. Praneeth Yandamoori, an MBA graduate from INSEAD of France and is now working as a Business Planning and Control Executive with a multinational company.

Mr. Veerendranath is a multi-faceted character, being a playwright, novelist, movie director, personality development motivator and a Sahitya Academy award winner.

In Telugu literature, there has been dark days for male writers as female writers like Yaddanapoodi Sulochana Rani were ruling the hearts of people with all necessary sentimental stuff. Many writers used to write stories novels with female pen names. Yandamoori is such a writer who has breaked these mental blocks of readers as well as fellow writers and has come up with his story *TULASI DALAM* without using any pen names. He wrote about 50 novels including *Vennello Aadapilla*, *Antarmukham*. His works are translated into Tamil, Kannada, Malayalam, English, Hindi, and Marathi.

His personality development book *Vijayaniki 5 metlu* (Success in Five Steps) has broken the all time record of Telugu literature, by crossing a turnover of Rupees Two Crores. He has started Saraswati Vidya Peetham at Kakinada, a one-crore project, to educate Tribal and poor students the importance of education and personality development.

Yandamuri Veerendranath is one of the best-known contemporary novelists writing in the Telugu language. He is a native of Andhra Pradesh, India.

Many of his novels have been made into motion pictures in Telugu.

His works include both fiction and non-fiction :

Fiction:

- Stuvartpuram Police Station
- Akhari Poratam
- Rakta Sindhooram
- Oka Radha iddaru krishnulu
- Radha-Kunthi
- Nissabdam neeku naaku madhya
- Kshaminchu Supriya
- Rushi
- Yugaantham
- Duppatlo minnaagu
- Swara Bhetalam
- Bharya Gunavati Shatru
- Agni pravesam
- Chengalva poodanda
- Nallanchu tella cheera
- Abhilasha
- 13-14-15
- Manchu parvatam
- Vennello Godaari
- Parnasala
- Praarthana

- Maro Hiroshima
- Ankitam
- Siggestondi
- Atadu Ame Priyudu
- Thriller
- Cheekatlo Suryudu
- Ladies Hostel
- Atade Ame Sainyam
- Anaitikam
- Dhyeyam
- Prema
- Rakshasudu
- Marana Mrudangam
- The Dairy of Mrs.Sarada
- Priyuralu Piliche
- Ashtavakra
- Tulasi
- Tulasidalam
- Dabbu Minus Dabbu
- Casanova 99
- Dabbu to the power of Dabbu
- Antarmukham
- Anando brahma
- Vennello Adapilla
- Rendu Gundela Chappudu
- Oka Varshakalapu Sayantram
- Best of Yandamoori Veerendranath

Non-fiction :

- Popular rachanalu cheyatam ela?
- Manchi Muthyalu
- Padamati Koyila Pallavi

- Graphology
- Mimmalni mee pillalu preminchalante
- Meeru manchi ammayi kaadu
- Mimmalni meeru gelavagalaru
- Vijayam vaipu payanam
- Pillala perla prapancham
- Chaduvu-Ekagratha
- Vijayamlo bhagaswamyam
- Mind Power-No.1 avatam ela?
- Vijayaniki 5 Metlu
- Vijayaniki Aro Mettu
- Tappu cheddaam randi
- Vijaya rahasyaalu
- Manchu poola varsham

His Hobbies are :

- Reading
- Writing
- Collecting Pens
- Gardening
- Cooking

He first film as a dialogue writer, won best regional award from President of India. His films include 'Abhilasha', 'Marana Mrudangam', 'Challenge', 'Jagadeka Veerudu – Athiloka Sundari'. His TV Serials won two Golden Nandi award. He also directed a film with Mega-Star Chiranjeevi.

Awards:

- Sahitya Academy Award for Raghupati raghava rajaram in 1982.
- Nandi Award as Best Director for Vennello Adapilla serial in 1996.
- Nandi Award as Best Socially Relevant Film Director for Vijayam vaipu payanam in 2002 and many more.

DEVAKI NANDAN KHATRI

Devaki Nandan Khatri (1861-1913) was the first author of mystery novels in Hindi. He wrote *Chandrakanta, Chandrakanta Santati, Kajar ki Kothari, Narendra-Mohini, Kusum Kumari, Virendra Veer, Gupt Godna* and *Bhootnath*. He is also known as Babu Devakinandan Khatri. *Bhootnath* was incomplete and completed by his son, Durga Prasad Khatri, who also wrote the concluding volumes of *Bhootnath saga* as *Rohtasmath*

Babu Devaki Nandan Khatri was born at Samastipur, Bihar. After his earlier education he moved to Tekari Estate in Gaya. He became an employee of the Raja of Benares. He started a printing press called "Lahari" and started a Hindi monthly, "Sudarshan", in 1898. There is also a book shop with the name *Lahari Book Depot*. Lahari Press is situated at Ram Katora Road, Near Ram Katora Crossing, Varanasi, India. Durga Prasad Khatri's son, Kamlapati Khatri, and grandson "Sonny". The various works of au Devakinandan Khatri and Durga Prasad Khatri are still published by Lahari Press.

Babu Devaki Nandan Khatri made a strong contribution to the learning of the Hindi language by the people of the times. People were so mesmerised by the works *Chandrakanta, Chandrakanta Santiti* and *Bhootnath* that they started to learn Hindi just to be able to read the works. Babu Devaki Nandan Khatri did not write any work at one go and then publish the same. He used to write "bayaans"-chapters-on the run from the British and these were published and distributed widely. People would enthusiastically await the new "bayaans" and congregate around those who could read Hindi to hear the latest exploits in the continuing saga. The works "Chandrakanta" and "Bhootnath" have been made into television serials.

ACHARYA CHATURSEN

Acharya Chatursen Shastri was an eminent writer of Hindi, and he wrote many historical fictions. A number of his works gave themes to many Hindi movies of the Bollywood, and he also exclusively wrote scripts for many Hindi movies.

Career

His books are very historic and detailed in life in the ancient India. These books can be seen as a logical binding of history and philosophy and are worth recommending to anyone who is looking to know more about India before the advent of Islam and who also wants to see Hinduism in positive light.

He was a friend of Jawaharlal Nehru, India's first Prime Minister, but he opposed Nehru's proposition of secular India. Nehru tried to ban his books after Congress came to power and accused Acharya Chatursen of fuelling tensions between Hindus and Muslims.

Writings

His works include:

- Vayam Rakshamah
- Vaishali ki Nagarvadhu (1948)
- Goli
- Dharamputra
- Sona aur Khoon
- Neelmani
- Narmedh
- Somnath Mahalay
- Bharat mein Islam
- Achchi Aadatein
- Aparajita
- Aadarsh Bhojan
- Nirog Jivan

MANOHAR SHYAM JOSHI

Manohar Shyam Joshi (1933-2006) was an Hindi writer, journalist, and scriptwriter, most known as the writer of Indian television's first soap opera, Hum Log (1982) and its early hits Buniyaad (1987) and Kakaji Kahin, a political satire .

Biography

Manohar Shyam Joshi was born on August 9, 1933 at Ajmer in Rajasthan, and belonged to a Kumaoni Brahmin family from Almora, now in the state of Uttarakhand.

Career

Television: He is often called "the Father of Indian Soap Operas" being the writer of India's first Television soap opera, Hum Log. Made in 1982, when television was still a luxury item for majority of Indians, the serial dealt with the everyday struggles of the middle-class India,, making it an instant hit, especial because every Indian could identify with it. His another popular creation was Buniyaad (1987-1988), directed by Ramesh Sippy, a serial based around the life a family displaced by the Partition of India in 1947; both went on to deeply influence an entire generation of Indians as well as the Indian television industry. In the following years he wrote many more long running serials like, 'Mungeri Lal Ke Hasin Sapney', 'Kakaji Kahin', 'Hamrahi', 'Zameen Aasman' and 'Gatha'.

Films: He had a penchant for subtle comedy and satire alike, this allowed him to write for cinema based on a variety of subjects, like 'Hey Ram', 'Appu Raja', 'Papa Kahte Hain' and 'Brashtachar'. He was also dubbing artiste of repute, and dubbed for films like Appu Raja and Hey Ram .

Novels: Manohar Shyam Joshi is also known for his novels which have dealt with varied topics ranging from (Kasap), described as one of the greatest love stories in Hindi, to devastating political satire like Netaji Kahin.

He was a prominent post-modernist authors in modern Hindi literature, as amiably demostrated by his cult novel *Kuru kuru Swaahaa* and his novella *Hariya Hercules ki Hairaani*. He was awarded the prestigious Sahitya Akademi Award in 2005 for Hindi, for his novel *Kyap*, an allegory of modern India, known for its sensitive portrayal of the Kumaoni traditions of his home-state Uttarakhand.

Journalism: He had a long stint as a journalist, both in the broadcast and the print media. He worked with All India

Radio, New Delhi, in the Hindi News section and then with the Films Division of India in Mumbai, where he wrote the scripts for many documentaries. This is when he started writing his famous landmark interviews with ordinary folks, which were serialised in the Sarika magazine. It was not long before he was handpicked by Sachidananda Vatsayan Agyeya for a new Hindi news magazine 'Dinaman', being brought out by the Times of India group. Agyeya was to be the editor and Joshi the Assistant Editor. In late 70s he remained the editor of the Morning Echo weekly brought out by the Hindustan Times.

Later, he moved on as the editor of the leading Hindi magazine Saptahik Hindustan and the English Weekend Review. His journalistic writings have covered a wide range of topics from popular science to political intrigues. Until his death, he wrote an opinion column for Outlook Saptahik, Hindi magazine from Outlook India .

Manohar Shyam Joshi, passed away on March 30, 2006, at the age of 73, in Delhi, India. He is survived by his wife and three sons. Upon his death, Prime minister, Manmohan Singh called him, "..one of the most influential writers and commentators in Hindi in recent times" .

Literary Works

- Kasap
- Netaji Kahin
- Kuru Kuru Swaahaa
- Hariya Hercules Ki Hairani, Rajkamal & Sons, 1999.
- Baaton-baaton mein
- Prabhu Tum Kaise Kissago (Short Stories)
- Mandir Ghaat ki Pauriyaan (Short Stories)
- Us Desh Ka Yaron Kya Kahna
- Baton Baton Mein (Interviews)
- Kaise Kissago
- Ek Durlabh Vyaktitva
- Ta Ta Professor

- Kyaap
- Hamzad, Rajkamal & Sons, 1999.
- Main Kaun Hoon?

Television Serials

- Hum Log (1982)
- Buniyaad (1987)
- Kakaji Kahin
- Mungeri Lal ke Haseen Sapne
- Hamrahi
- Zameen Aasman (1995)
- Gatha (1997) .

Filmography

- Manzil (1979)-Screenplay
- Bhrashtachar (1989)-Screenplay
- Papa Kahte Hain
- Appu Raja
- Limited Manuski (1995)-Screenplay
- Hey Ram (2000)-Dialogue

Awards

- MP Sahitya Parishad Samman
- Sharad Joshi Samman
- Shikhar Samman
- Delhi Hindi Academy Award
- Onida and Uptron Award for TV writing
- 2005 Sahitya Akademi Award

KAMLESHWAR

Kamleshwar (January 6, 1932-January 27, 2007), was a prominent Hindi writer of the 20th century, and a script and dialogue writer in Hindi films and television. He most famous works, have been films like Aandhi, Mausam, Chhoti Si Baat, and Rang Birangi. Considered, a part of the league of Hindi writers, like Mohan Rakesh, Nirmal Verma and Bhisham Sahni, who left the old pre-independence, literary preoccupations and presented the new sensibilities, that reflected new moorings of a post-independence India, thus launching, the Hindi literature's 'Nayi Kahani' (New Story) movement in the 1950s,, he was awarded the 2003 Sahitya Akademi Award for his cult Hindi novel, 'Kitne Pakistan', and also the Padma Bhushan in 2005.

Biography

Early Life and Education: Kamleshwar Prasad Saxena was born in the Mainpuri district of Uttar Pradesh, India, where he spent his early years. Kamleshwar's first story 'Comrade' was published in 1948 .

Later he did his graduation and followed by a Master's degree in Hindi literature from Allahabad University. His first novel 'Badnam Gali (Cursed lane) was published while he was still a student, he later started his literary career in Allahabad itself.

Career

Early Career and Literary Career: In his early days, he worked as a proof reader, growing up to become, the editor of 'Vihan', literary magazine in late 50's.

This was followed by editorship of many Hindi magazines, like 'Nayi Kahaniyan' (1963-66), 'Sarika' (1967-78), 'Katha Yatra' (1978-79), 'Ganga' (1984-88) and weeklies, 'lngit' (1961-63) and 'Shree Varsha' (1979-80), besides this, he also remained the editor of Hindi dailies, 'Dainik Jagaran' (1990-1992), and 'Dainik Bhaskar' (1996-2002), and helped revive the Hindi magazine, 'Sarika', as its editor by bringing focus on new and emerging voices of modern India, an effort which reflected his encouragement to Marathi Dalit writers and Bohra Muslim litterateurs, thus opening new vistas for Hindi readers.

Kamleshwar became famous for his short stories, and some other works, which depicted the contemporary life in a vivid style of presentation. With the publication of his story,

'Raja Narbansiya' (1957), he was immediately placed in league of leading writers of his times.

In his prolific career, spanning four decades, he wrote over three hundred stories, including, Maans Ka Dariya, 'Neeli Jheel' and 'Kasbe Ka Aadmi', published over ten collections of short stories, ten novels most prominent among them being, Ek Sadak Sattawan Galiyan, Laute Huye Musajir, Kaali Aandhi, Aagami Ateet, Registan and Kitne Pakistan, apart from 35 other literary works in different genres ranging from literary criticism, travelogue, memoirs, to socio-cultural commentary .

Films

He move to Bombay in the 70s and started writing scripts and dialogues for Hindi films, in the next decade or so, he worked for over 75 feature films, which include films like Gulzar's Aandhi, based on his novel Kaali Aandhi, Mausam; Basu Chatterjee's Rajnigandha, Chhoti Si Baat and Rang Birangi and Ravi Chopra's triller, The Burning Train. In fact, reminiscing his worksd noted poet-director, Gulzar said, "..in 'Kitne Pakistan'... there is a description where a handkerchief falls off the bridge; I always used to tell him that I could write a complete short story on this one line only." .

Television

By late 70s, he had made his first short TV film the "Jamuna Bazar", near river Yamuna in Delhi, and soon switched to television scriptwriting, and eventually became the 'Additional Director General' of Doordarshan, India's national television channel, (1980-82), during his tenure, in a matter of 24 months, the entire nation was connected with television network .

Over the years, he wrote stories in ten TV serials including, Chandrakanta, Aakash Ganga,· Yug and Betal Pachisi, and popular serials based on literary works, Darpan and Ek Kahani, hosted a popular talk show on Doordarshan, 'Parikrama', started a weekly literary show, 'Patrika', and also produced and directed several TV Programes and investigative documentaries on social and political issues for Doordarshan .

Later Years

He was awarded the 2003 Sahitya Akademi Award, for his novel based on the Partition of India in 1947, 'Kitne Pakistan' (How Many Pakistans), which explored the way, nations fracture, through an allegorical court trial, wherein historical and political figures are present as witnesses, and the *Padma Bhushan* in 2005.

He died, on January 27, 2007 at Faridabad following a heart attack, after being in poor health for several years.

A collection of his short stories in English translation, "Not Flowers of Henna", was released in 2007 .

Literary Works

- Jo Maine Jiya (Part 1)
- Yadon Ke Chirag (Part 2)
- Jalti Hui Nadi (Part 3)
- Meri Priya Kahaniyan
- Kamleshwar Kee Shreshtha Kahaniyan
- Samagra Kahaniyan
- Ek Sarak Sattavan Galiyan
- The Street with Fifty-Seven Lanes (Translation)
- Teesra Aadmi
- George Pancham Ki Naak
- Mehfil
- Bharatmata Gramvasini
- Hindustan Hamara
- Ankho Dekha Pakistan
- Tumhara Kamleshwar
- Parikrama
- Chandrakanta (Espcially re-written by him for the Popluar TV serial)
- Samagra Upanyas (All of his 10 novels in one collection)
- Atmakatha (3 Parts)

- Samudra Mein Khoya Aadmi
- Subah Dopahar Sham
- Dak Bangla
- Registan
- Kali Aandhi
- Katha Prasthan
- Kohra
- Anbita Vyatit
- Aagami Atit
- Raja Nirbansiya
- Mere Hamsafar
- Vahi Baat
- Hindustani Gazalein
- Swatantryottar Hindi Kahaniyan
- Maans Ka Dariya
- Mati Ho Gai Sona
- Bayaan
- Pati Patni Aur Vah
- Des-Pardes
- Gulmohar Phir Khilega
- Khoyi Hui Dishayein
- Kahani Ki Teesri Duniya
- Kasbe Ka Aadmi
- Kashmir Rat Ke Baad
- Amma
- Aaj Ke Prasiddh Shayar-Shaharyar
- Aazadi Mubarak

Bibliography

- Kitne Pakistan, Rajpal & Sons, 2004.
- Partitions. (Translation of Kitne Pakistan), Penguin Books, 2006.

Filmography

- Sara Akash (1969) (dialogue)
- Aandhi (1975) (story)
- Mausam (1975) (story)
- Amanush (1975) (dialogue)
- Chhoti Si Baat (1975) (dialogue & screenplay)
- Ram Balram (1980) (dialogue & screenplay)
- Saajan Ki Saheli (1981) (dialogue & screenplay)
- The Burning Train (1980) (dialogue & screenplay)
- Souten (1983) (dialogue)
- Rang Birangi (1983) (story)
- Yeh Desh (1984) (dialogue)
- Laila (1984) (dialogue & screenplay)
- Preeti (1986) (dialogue & screenplay)
- Souten Ki Beti (1989) (dialogue)

NARENDRA KOHLI

Narendra Kohli (born January 6, 1940, Sialkot) is one of the most prominent Hindi language author of modern times. Leader of cultural renissance in hindi literature in modern times, his legendary works include all time greats like "Abhyudaya", "Mahasamar", "Vasudeva" and "Todo, Kara Todo". In recognition of his great literary presence, the post 1985 period is termed as 'Kohli Yuga'. His contribution to Hindi literature is often compared to the legendary writer Premchand.

With his writings began the cultural renissance of Modern Hindi Literature. He is credited with synthesizing the essential elements of Indian philosophy and culture in his epic writings, which include his best known classic, Mahasamar. His epic writings effertlessly engross the reader in the story, and by the virtue of his art, this master story-teller elucidates the complicated concepts of Indian Philosophy like Law of Karma with such an ease and grace the reader can imbibe the complete theory via situational examples, without even an inkling that he is being taught.

His works also assert the timeless nature of Human mind and behaviour. In the world literature, he occupies the same place as count Leo Tolstoy. It is only a matter of time when his writings, translated in many languages, can spread the timeless message of India throughout the world.

Early Life

Narendra Kohli was born to Parmananda Kohli and Vidyavanti in Punjab province of Undivided India. His first school was the Dev Samaj High School in Lahore. Then he attended the Ganda Singh High School in Sialkot for a few months. In 1947, after the partition of India, the family moved to Jamshedpur (Bihar). He resumed his schooling in third grade at Dhatkidih Lower Primary school. He spent fourth to seventh grade (1949-53) at New Middle English school. Urdu was the medium of instruction for all subjects except English, which was limited to reading and writing. From eighth to eleventh grade, he attended KMPM High School in Jamshedpur. He selected the science stream in high school. The medium of instruction was Urdu till this point.

For higher education, he joined the Jamshedpur Co-operative College. He took the IA exams in 1959 from Bihar University with Compulsory English, Compulsory Hindi, Psychology, Logic, and special Hindi as his subjects. He completed his BA (Hons.) in 1961 from Jamshedpur Co-operative College (Ranchi University) in Hindi. He completed his MA in 1963 at Ramjas College (University of Delhi). Later, in 1970, he did his Ph. D. from the University of Delhi.

Literature

Narendra Kohli is a novelist, short story writer, playwright, and satirist. His first story was in sixth grade for the handwritten class magazine. In eighth grade, his Urdu story *Hindostan: Jannat Nishan* was published in the school's printed magazine. As a child author, some of his first Hindi stories were published by *Kishore* (Patna), *Avaaz* (Dhanbad) etc. During his IA years, *Sarita* (Delhi) published his story *Paani ka Jug, Gilas aur Ketli* in its *Nae Ankur* ("New Sprouts") column.

But it was only after February 1960 that his works started getting published regularly. He considers *Do Haath* published by *Kahani* (Allahabad) as his first published work. He turned to satire around 1965. Later, he wrote a huge 1800 page novel *Abhyudaya* (in four parts) which was based on *Ram Katha*. He also wrote *Abhigyaan*, a novel based on *Krishna Katha* and *Mahasamar*, based on Mahabharata.

After this, he wrote a new series of novels. Among these were *Toro Kara Toro*, based on life of Swami Vivekananda.

HARISHANKAR PARSAI

Harishankar Parsai (1924 – 1995) was a Hindi writer. He was born in Jamnia village near by Itarsi of Hoshangabad district in Madhya Pradesh. He completed his M.A. in English from Nagpur University. After pursuing writing along with his service for some time, he quit his job and took writing as a full-time career. He settled in Jabalpur (M.P) and started a literature magazine called *Vasudha*. He had to stop the magazine after the publication suffered economic losses. {Date of birth 22 August 1924, per Manas Publishing, in Inspector Matateen on The Moon}

Major Works

- Story Collections:
- Hanste Hai Rote Hai
- Jaise Unke Din Fire

Essays:

- Vaishnav ki Fislan
- Tirchchi Rekhayein
- Thithurta hua Garnatantra
- Viklaang Shraddha ka Daur
- Pagdandiyon ka zamana
- Shikayat mujhe bhi hai
- Bhoot ke paano peeche
- Apni-Apni Beemari

- Awara Bheed Ke Khatrey
- Aisa Bhi Socha Jata Hai
- Kag Bhagoda
- Tat Ki Khoj
- Do Nak Waley Log
- Premchand Ke Phatey Jootey
- Mati Kahe Kumhar Se
- Sadachar Ka Taveez

Memoirs:

- Hum ek umr se waaqif hain
- Jaane-pechane log

Novels:

- Rani Nagfani ki kahani
- Jwala Aur Jal

He won Sahitya Academy Award for "Viklaang Shraddha ka daur".

Writing Style

His writing had elements of sarcasm and humour. Corruption and exploitation are two major issues his writings address.

PHANISHWAR NATH 'RENU'

Phanishwar Nath 'Renu' (March 4, 1921-April 11, 1977) was one of the greatest writers of modern Hindi literature in the post-Premchand era. He is the author of Maila Anchal', which after Premchand's Godan, is regarded as the most significant Hindi novel. Phanishwar Nath 'Renu' is most known for promoting the voice of the contemporary rural India through the genre of 'Aanchalik Upanyas' (Regional Story), and is placed amongst the pioneering Hindi writers who brought regional voices into the mainstream Hindi literature.

His short story *Maare Gaye Gulfam* was adapted into a film Teesri Kasam by Basu Bhattacharya (produced by the poet-lyricist Shailendra) in 1966 for which he also wrote the dialogues. Later his short story 'Panchlight' (Patromax) was made into a TV short film.

Biography

Phanishwar Nath 'Renu' was born on 4th March 1921, at village Aurahi Hingna near Forbesganj, in Araria district (then Purnea district), Bihar .

His primary education was held in Araria and Forbesganj. He did his Matriculation from Viratnagar Adarsh Vidyalaya(school), Viratnagar, Nepal while staying with Koirala Family. After Passing out IA from Kashi Hindu Vishvavidyalay (university) in 1942 he took part in the Indian Freedom Struggle. Later he participated in the Nepali revolutionary movement in 1950 which resulted in the establishment of democracy in Nepal. He ushered in 'Anchlik Kata' (Regional Story) of Hindi writing. He had a very close friendship with Sachchidananda Hirananda Vatsyayana Agyey-his contemporary poet.

Writing Style

The intimacy in writing brought to the reader with use of local flavor of Hindi in contrast to *Khari Boli Hindi* was entirely new literary experience.

His very first novel which is also considered his masterpiece, *Maila Anchal* (The Soiled Linen, 1954), was a social novel that depicted the life of rural Bihar and its people, especially the backward and the deprived. He was subsequently awarded one of India's highest civilian honours, the Padma Sri.

Later during Jayaprakash Narayan Andolan, he gave up his award in solidarity. His short story *Panchlight* (Petromax) is beautiful in its depiction of human behaviour. One can find many parallels between his and Premchand's writings.

Curiously Katihar railway station figures in many of his writings.

He wrote descriptive prose with rapid character building. He would then sets about reflecting on his characters and backgrounds from every angle. *Ek Aadim Ratri Ki Mehak* which is straight forward story with touchy ending, is one example his unending need for exploring pristine emotions of his characters.

Literary Works

Novels

- Maila Anchal
- Parti Parikatha
- Juloos
- Deerghtapa
- Kitne Chaurahe
- Paltu Babu Road

Stories

- Maare Gaye Gulfam (Teesri Kasam)
- Lal Pan Ki Begum
- Panchlight
- Thes
- Samvadiya
- Tabe Ekla Chalo Re
- Lakshmi

Story Collections (Katha-Sangrah)

- Thumri
- Agnikhor
- Acche Aadmi
- Ek Adim Ratri Ki Mehak
- Ek Shravani duphari

Memoirs

- Rindjal Dhanjal
- Van Talsi ki gandh
- Shrut Ashrut Purva

Reportage

- Hrin Jal-Dhan Jal

- Nepali Kranti Katha
- Van tulsi ki gandh
- Shruth Asruth purve
- Pahli kranti katha

JAISHANKAR PRASAD

Jaishankar Prasad (January 30, 1889-January 14, 1937) was one of the most famous figures in modern Hindi literature. He was a dramatist, novelist, poet and story-writer. Prasad belonged to the *Chhayavaadi* school of Hindi poetry. His most famous work is *Kamayani*.

Biography

He was born in an elite family in Varanasi, Uttar Pradesh, India. His father Babu Devki Prasad, also known as Sunghani Sahu, was a tobacco dealer. He lost his father at an early age. He had to encounter some family problems at a relatively young age. However, he remained interested in literature, language, and history from his childhood days. He had a special inclination towards the Vedas. These interest are reflected in many of his own works. He was also interested in study of ancient relics. Apart from being a poet, he was also a philosopher, historian and a sculptor. In later years he made himself aloof from worldly matters, and adapted a nearly ascetic life. Though, some of his interests such as chess, gardening, shashtrarth and poetry recitation remained with him. Jaishankar Prasad was a contemporary of some other literary greats of that time like Acharya Ram Chandra Shukla and Munshi Premchand.

Language and Influence

His initial poetry (*Chitraadhar* collection) was done in the Braj dialect of Hindi, but later he switched to the *Khadi* dialect or Sanskritized Hindi.

In his earlier days, he was influenced by Sanskrit dramas, but later the influence of Bengali and Persian dramas is evident on his works. Prasad's most famous dramas include *Skandagupta*, *Chandragupta* and *Dhruvaswamini*.

Style of Poetry

He is considered one of the four pillars (*Stambh*) of Chhayavad in Hindi Literature along with Sumitranandan Pant, Mahadevi Verma and Suryakant Tripathi 'Nirala'. His style of poetry can at best be described as touching (*maarmic*). Art and philosophy has been exquisitely amalgmated in his writings. He used mainly Tatsam and Tatdbhav words-some of them made really exquisitely by himself.

The subject of his poetry spans the entire horizon of subjects of his era, from romantic to nationalistic. He in a way signifies the epitome of classical Hindi poetry. One of his patriotic poems, 'Himadri Tung Shring Se', won him many accolades in the era of Indian independence movement. However, Kamayani undoubtedly remains his best creation.

Kamayani

Kamayani is widely considered the best of his works. Majority of critics agree that it is the best work of poetry (*Mahakavya*) in Hindi. Though Kamayani has portrayals of divergent subjects, in entirety, it depicts the development of human culture in metaphoric style. Kamayani tells the story of the great flood and the central characters of the epic poem are Manu (a male) and Shradha (a female). Manu is representative of the human psyche and Shradha represents love. Another female character is Ida, who represents rationality. Some critics surmise that the three lead characters of Kamayani symbolizes a synthesis of knowledge, action and desires in human life.

Dramas and other Writings

His dramas are considered to be most pioneering ones in Hindi. Majority of them revolvs around historical stories of Ancient India. Some of them were also based on mythological plots.

He wrote short stories as well. The subjects were mixed-ranging from historical and mythological to contemporary and social. *Mamta* (motherly love) is a famous short-story based on an incident where a Mughal Badshah gets refuge in a Hindu widow's home whose father was killed by Badshah's army. Another one of his well-known short-storie called *chhota jadugar* (little magician) portrays the life of a child who learns to earns his own living by performing small skits with his dolls on streets.

He also wrote a small number of novels.

Major Literary Works

Poetry

- Kamayani(1935)
- Kanan
- Kusum
- Prem Pathik
- Jharna
- Aansoo
- Lehar
- Maharana ka Mahattva
- Arun yeh madhumay desh hamara

Short Story Collections

- Chhaya
- Pratidhvani
- Akashdeep
- Aandhi
- Indrajaal
- Shivendra

Some Famous Short Stories

- Mamta
- Bandi
- Akashdeep(Katha Sangrah)
- Puraskar
- Chhota Jaadugar

Dramas

- Samudragupta
- Dhruvswamini
- Sajjan
- Parinaya
- Ek Ghoont
- Karunalaya
- Praayashchit
- Taskiyya
- Rajyashri
- Vishakh
- Ajaatshatru
- Kamana
- Janamejaye ka Naagyagya
- Skandagupta
- Chandragupta (Contains the famous patriotic poem-*Himadri Shring Tunga se*)
- Dhruvaswamini

Novels

- Titali
- Kankaal
- Iravati

MUNSHI PREMCHAND

Munshi Premchand (July 31, 1880-October 8, 1936) was one of the greatest literary figures of modern Hindi and Urdu literature.

Biography

Premchand,whose original name was Dhanpat Rai Srivastava, was born on 31 July 1880, in village Lamahi near Varanasi, where his father was a clerk in the post office. Premchand's parents died young-his mother when he was seven and his father while he was fourteen and still a student. Premchand was left responsible for his step-mother and step-siblings. Early in life, Premchand faced immense poverty. He earned five rupees a month tutoring a lawyer's child. He was married at the early age of fifteen but that marriage failed, later he married again, to Shivrani Devi, a balavidhava, (child widow), and had several children, she supported him through life struggles.

Premchand passed his matriculation exam with great effort in 1898, and in 1899 he took up school-teaching job, with a monthly salary of eighteen rupees.

Later, Premchand worked as the deputy sub-inspector of schools in what was then the United Provinces.

In 1910, he was hauled up by the District Magistrate in Jamirpur for his anthology of short stories *Soz-e-Watan* (Dirge of the Nation), which was labelled seditious. The first story of the anthology was *Duniya ka Sabse Anmol Ratan* (The Most Precious Jewel in the World), which according to him was "the last drop of blood shed in the cause of the country's freedom". All the copies of *Soz-e-Watan* were confiscated and burnt. Initially Premchand wrote in Urdu under the name of *Nawabrai*. However, after the confiscation of *Soz-e-Watan*. He started writing under the pseudonym *Premchand*. Before Premchand, Hindi literature consisted mainly of fantasy or religious works. Premchand brought realism to Hindi literature. He wrote over 300 stories, a dozen novels and two plays. The stories have been compiled and published as *Maansarovar*.

In 1921, he answered Mahatma Gandhi's call and resigned from his government job. Then he worked as the proprietor of a printing press, editor of literary and political journals (*Jagaran* and *Hans*). Briefly, he also worked as the script writer for the Bombay film world. He didn't think much of the film world and once remarked about film *Mazdoor* (The Labourer)-"The director is the all in all in cinema. The writer may be the king of his pen, but he is an ordinary subject in the director's empire...Idealism creeps into the plots I conceive and I am told there is no entertainment value in them."

Premchand's first marriage was a disaster. The second time, he married a child widow, Shivarani Devi, which was a considered a taboo in India at that time. Premchand had three children-Sripat Rai, Amrit Rai and Kamla Devi Srivastava.

Premchand lived a life of financial struggle. Once he took a loan of two-and-a-half rupees to buy some clothes. He had to struggle for three years to pay it back.

When asked why he doesn't write anything about himself, he answered: "What greatness do I have that I have to tell anyone about? I live just like millions of people in this country; I am ordinary. My life is also ordinary. I am a poor school teacher suffering family travails. During my whole lifetime, I have been grinding away with the hope that I could become free of my sufferings. But I have not been able to free myself from suffering. What is so special about this life that needs to be told to anybody?".

Premchand chaired the first all-India conference of the Indian Progressive Writers' Association in April 1936 at Lucknow.

During his last years,he became terribly ill. The money his wife used to give for his treatment was used in running his press "The Saraswati". He was also writing a book "Mangalsutra" which would never be completed. All this had serious impact on his health leading to his early death on 8th October 1936, at the age of 52.

Writing Style

The main characteristic of Premchand's writings is his interesting story-telling and use of simple language. His novels describe the problems of the rural peasant classes. He avoided the use of highly Sanskritized Hindi (as was the common practice among Hindi writers), but rather he used the dialect of the common people.

Premchand called literature a work that expresses the truths and experiences of life impressively. Presiding over the Progressive Writers' Conference in Lucknow in 1936, he said that attaching the word "Progressive" to writer was redundant, because "A writer or an artist is progressive by nature, if this was not his/her nature, he/she would not be a writer at all."

Before Premchand, Hindi literature was confined to the *raja-rani* (king and queen) tales, the stories of magical powers and other such escapist fantasies. It was flying in the sky of fantasy, until Premchand brought it on the grounds of reality. Premchand wrote on the realistic issues of the day-communalism, corruption, zamindari, debt, poverty, colonialism etc.

Some criticize Premchand's writings as full of too many deaths and too much of misery. They believe Premchand does not stand anywhere near contemporary literary giants of India-Sharat Chandra Chattopadhyay and Rabindranath Tagore.

But it should be noted, that many of Premchand's stories were influenced by his own experiences with poverty and misery. His stories represented the ordinary Indian people as they were, without any embellishments. Unlike many other contemporary writers, his works didn't have any "hero" or "Mr. Nice"-they described people as they were.

Premchand was a contemporary of some other literary giants of that era like Acharya Ram Chandra Shukla and Jaishankar Prasad.

Literary Works

Premchand has written about 300 short stories, several novels as well as many essays and letters. He has also written some plays. He also did some translations. Many of Premchand's stories have been translated into English and Russian.

Godaan (The Gift of a Cow), his last novel, is considered the finest Hindi novel of all times. The protagonist, Hori, a poor peasant, desperately longs for a cow, a symbol of wealth and prestige in rural India. Hori gets a cow but pays with his life for it. After his death, the village priests demand a cow from his widow to bring his soul to peace.

In *Kafan* (Shroud), a poor man collects money for the funeral rites of his dead wife, but spends it on food and drink.

Famous Stories

- *Panch Parameshvar*
- *Idgah*
- *Nashaa*
- *Shatranj ke khiladi*
- *Poos ki raat*
- *Atmaram*
- *Boodhi Kaki*
- *Bade Bhaisahab*
- *Bade ghar ki beti*
- *Kafan*
- *Dikri Ke Rupai*
- *Udhar Ki Ghadi*
- *Namak Ka Daroga*
- *Panch Phool*
- *Prem Purnima*
- *Ram Katha*

Novels

- *Gaban*
- *Sevasadan*
- *Godaan*
- *Karmabhoomi*
- *Kaayakalp*
- *Manorma*
- *Mangalsootra*, incomplete
- *Nirmala*
- *Pratigya*
- *Premashram*
- *Rangbhoomi*
- *Vardaan*

Plays

- *Karbala*

Films based on Premchand's work

Satyajit Ray filmed two of Premchand's works — *Sadgati* and Shatranj Ke Khiladi. *Sadgati* (Salvation) is a short story revolving around poor Dukhi, who gets exhausted to death while hewing wood for a paltry favor. *Shatranj ke Khiladi* (The Chess Players) revolved around the decadence of nawabi Lucknow, where the obsession with a game consumes the players, making them oblivious of their responsibilities in the midst of a crisis.

Sevasadan (first published in 1918) was made into a film with M.S. Subbulakshmi in the lead role. The novel is set in Varanasi, the holy city of Hindus. *Sevasadan* ("House of Service") is an institute built for the daughters of courtesans. The lead of the novel is a beautiful, intelligent and talented girl called Suman. She belongs to high caste. She is married to a much older, tyrannical man. She realizes that marriage is just like prostitution except that there is only one client. Bholi, a courtesan, lives opposite Suman. Suman realizes that Bholi is "outside purdah", while she is "inside it". Suman leaves her husband and becomes a successful entertainer of gentlemen. But after a brief period of success, she ends up as a victim of a political drama played out by self-righteous Hindu social reformers and moralists.

He also worked with the film director Himanshu Rai of Bombay Talkies, one of the founders of Bollywood.

Films and TV Serials

- Sadgati (1981) (TV)
- Shatranj Ke Khilari (1977)
- Godhuli (1977)
- Oka Oori Katha (1977)
- Gaban (1966)
- Godaan (1963)

- Seva Sadan (1938) (based on the novel *Bazaar-e-Husn*)
- Mazdoor (1934)
- Nirmala (TV Series, 1980s)

RAJENDRA YADAV

Rajendra Yadav (born 1929) is one of the eminent Hindi fiction writers. He was born in Agra, Uttar Pradesh in a traditional Yadav family. He completed M.A in Hindi from Agra University. He has by now edited the famous magazine HANS for 20 years. HANS, was founded by Munshi Premchand. He is the author of a number of Hindi books. Rajendra Yadav is regarded as principal architect of the 'New Wave' phenomenon in post-Independence Hindi fiction. He is one of the pioneers of this movement, which comprised in absorbing the spirit of the con-temporary and presenting it starkly. His wife Mannu Bhandari is also a famous Hindi fiction Writer.

His first novel, *Pret Bolte Hain* (that is, the Howling Pretas) (later renamed as *Sara Akash*, the Infinite Cosmos) has reportedly sold about one mil-lion copies, an enviable figure for any book published in India, and has been translated into almost all Indian languages, and several other languages of the world. *Sara Akash* is considered the first Hindi novel which at-tempts to shock and shake Indian culture out of its centuries-old somno-lence. Basu Chatterjee made a film out of it, which, along with Mrinal Sen's Bhuvan Shome, launched Parallel Cinema in Hindi.

Ukhre Huey Log, (that is, *The Rootless People*) his next novel, depicts the trauma of a couple arising out of socio-economic condition which forced them to desert the conventional path-and, still they failed to ac-climatize themselves to a corrupt and dev-ilish world. This novel envisages "living in" concept for the first time.

He wrote two more novels, *Kulta* (that is, *The Way-ward Wife*), and *Shaah aur Maat* (*Check and Mate*). He also wrote several stories and translated into Hindi many works of Russian language writers like Turgenev, Chekhov, and Lermontov (A Hero of Our Times), as also Albert Camus (The Outsider).

Ek Inch Muskaan (that is, *A Little Smile*) which Rajendra Yadav and wife Mannu Bhandari wrote together, is a love tragedy of schizophrenic indi-viduals.

Besides being a writer, Rajendra Yadav was also nominated as a board member of Prasar Bharti in 1999. He retired from that position in November 1999.

SHAILESH MATIYANI

Shailesh Matiyani (Oct 14, 1931-April 24, 2001), is a Hindi writer from Uttarakhand, most known for his works depicting the struggles and the fighting spirit of the Indian lower and lower-middle class, which gave him the title People's writer or 'Jankathakar'

Biography

Shailesh Matiyani was born on 14 October 1931, in Barechhina, Almora, Uttarakhand, it was here that studied up to High School.

In his career spanning five decades, he wrote numerous short stories, novels and published many collections of stories and essays. He was also known for his stories for children. He remained the editor of two publications, Janpaksh and Vikalp, for many years .

He died on April 24, 2001, in Delhi and was cremated at Haldwani .

After his death, 'Shailesh Matiyani Smriti Katha Puraskar' was established by Madhya Pradesh Government.

SHIVANI

Gaura Pant 'Shivani' (October 17, 1923-21st March 2003), better known as Shivani, was one of the most popular Hindi authors of the 20th century and a pioneer in writing Indian women based fiction .

She achieved a large following in the pre-television times of the 60s and 70s, as her works like the novel, 'Krishnakali', were serialised in Hindi magazines like Dharmayug and

Saptahik Hindustan, leading to her cult status as a Hindi novelist. Through her writings, she also made the culture of Kumaon, popular with Hindi-speaking Indians across the country.

Upon her death, Government of India released in a press note described her contributions to Hindi literature as, "...in the death of Shivani the Hindi literature world has lost a popular and eminent novelist and the void is difficult to fill"

Biography

Early Life and Education

Gaura Pant 'Shivani' was born on October 17, 1924, the Vijaya Dasami day in Rajkot, Gujarat, where her father, Ashwini Kumar Pande was a teacher with princely state of Rajkot, her mother was a Sanskrit scholar. Later her father became the Diwan with the Nawab of Rampur and the member of Viceroy's Bar Council, thereafter the family moved to the princely state of Orcha, where her father held an important position. Thus Shivani's childhood had influences of these varied places, and an insight into high class women, which reflected in much of her work.

As she grew older, she along with her brother and a sister, went to live with her grandfather, a Sanskrit scholar and a founding member of Banaras Hindu University.

In 1935, Shivani's first story was published in the Hindi Children's magazine 'Natkhat', at age twelve. That was also when, the three siblings were sent to the study at Rabindranath Tagore's Visva-Bharati University at Shantiniketan. Rabindranath Tagore even visited their ancestral home in Almora several times.

Shivani remained at Shantiniketan for another 9 years, left as a graduate in 1943. It was this period that she took to writing wholeheartedly and had the most profound influence in her writing sensibilities, a period she recounts vividly in her book, 'Amader Shantiniketan' .

Career

In 1951, her short story, 'Main Murga Hun' (I am a Chicken Man) was published in Dharmayug, and she became Shivani, from Gaura Pant.

Her first novel, Lal Haveli, established her reputation in the early sixties, and in the next ten years she produced several major works which were serialized in the Hindi magazine, Dharmayug. Proficient in many other languages including Sanskrit, Gujarati, Bengali, Urdu, and English, Shivani received the Padma Shri for her contribution to Hindi literature in 1982.

She was a prolific writer, her oeuvre consists of over 40 novels, many short stories and hundreds of articles and essays. Her most famous works include Chaudah Phere, Krishnakali, Lal Haveli, Smashan Champa, Bharavi, Rati Vilap, Vishkanya, Apradhini (a collection of interviews with women lifers); travelogues: 'Yatriki', based on her London travels and 'Chareivati', based on her travels to Russia.

Towards the end of her life, Shivani took to autobiographical writings, first sighted in her book, 'Shivani Ke Shryaas Kahaniyan', followed by her two-part memoir, 'Smriti Kalash' and 'Sone De', whose title she borrowed from the epitaph of a 15th Century Urdu Poet:

Thak Gaya Hoon Neend Aa Rahi Hai Sone De

Bahut Hein Zindagi Mene Diya Hai Saath Tere

(I am tired, sleep overtakes me, let me rest

I have been long enough with you in the journey of life)

Shivani continued to write till her last days, and passed away on 21st March 2003 in New Delhi. In 2005, Her daughter, Hindi writer, Ira Pande, published a memoir based on Shivani's life, titled 'Diddi' My Mother's Voice. 'Diddi' in Kumaoni means elder sister, and that's what her children used to address her, as she really was a friend to them.

Thematic Style

"Shivani's fiction proclaims a quiet, warm humanism. Characters who might seem pale and uninteresting in real life—an undistinguished, very orthodox Brahmin priest in a village up in the foothills of the Himalayas, his traditional wife, the village idiot, the widowed mother—take on a human glow and their lives an unexpected resonance. It is the small events, little gestures, nondescript people, that suffuse the world of Shivani's fiction with hope, and the future is something one enters with courage. Shivani's feminism is like a gentle humanism that does not stop short when it meets the female. Within the world-view of her fiction, there are few contradictions or problems that cannot be transcended with a little sympathy and a belief in the goodness of humankind."-'Women Writing in India', *Vol II, by Susie Tharu & K. Lalitha* .

Family

She was married to S.D. Pant, a teacher who worked in the Education Department of Uttar Pradesh, this lead to the family travelling to various places including Allahabad, before settling in Lucknow, where she stayed till her last days. She had four children, six grandchildren and two great-grandchildren.

Unforturnately her husband died at an early age, leaving her to take care of the four children, but a defiant Shivani chose to stay by her self, and raised them to be successful in their own right. Her two daughters, Mrinal Pande, Ira Pande are established writers in themselves. Her other two children are Veena, Muktesh (Micky) Pant.

SRI LAL SUKLA

Shrilal Shukla (born 1925) is a Hindi writer notable for his satire. He also worked as an Indian Administrative Service (IAS) officer. His major works include *"Umraonagar men Kuchh Din"* and *"Suni Ghati ka Suraj"*.

Shukla has highlighted the falling moral values in the Indian society in the post independence era through his novels. His writings expose the negative aspects of life in the rural and urban India in a satirical manner. His novel Raag Darbari has been translated into English (see below).

Shukla received the Sahitya Academy Award, the highest Indian literary award, for his novel *Raag Darbari* and has been declared to be bestowed with padma bhushan. A soap opera based on this continued for several months the national TV network in 1980s.

It is a little known fact that he also wrote a *jasoosi novel* entitled *Aadmi ka Zahar* which went generally unnoticed by his fans and critics alike.

He received the Vyas Samman award in 1999 for the novel *"Bisrampur ka Sant"*.,

Literary Works

- Raag Darbari (novel written in the 1960s), original is in Hindi; an English translation was published under the same title on April 15, 2003 by Penguin Books.
- *Vishrampur ka sant*
- *Umraawnagar mein kuchh din*

BHAGWATI CHARAN VERMA

Bhagwati Charan Verma was one of the leading literary limelights in Hindi during the later half of the twentieth century. He wrote many novels but his magnum opus was Chitra Lekha which was made into two successful movies in Hindi.

Writings

- Bhule Bisre Chitra
- Chitralekha
- Kahi na Jay ka Kahiye
- Rekha
- Sabhin Nachavat Ram Gosai
- Samarthya Aur Seema
- Sampooran Natak
- Sidhi Sachchi Baten
- Tedhey Medhey Rastey
- Vah Phir Nahi Aai

VISHNU PRABHAKAR

Vishnu Prabhakar (b. 1912) is a Hindi writer. He has written several short stories, novels, plays and travelogues to his credit.

Early Life

He was born in Mirapur village of Muzaffarnagar district in Uttar Pradesh. He completed his metric from Hisar in 1929 and joined government service. Even with his work he pursued his interest in literature. He also joined a Natak company in Hissar. He wrote in 1939, Hatya Ke Baad, his first play.

For some time he took writing as his full time career. After independence he worked as a drama director in Aakashvani, New Delhi. He came into news when in 2005 he threatened to return his Padma Bhushan award after he allegedly had to face misconduct at Rashtrapati Bhavan.

Writing Style

His works has elements of patriotism, nationalism and messages of social upliftment.

Major Works

- Novels: Dhalti Raat, Swapnmayi
- Drama: Nav Prabhat, Doctor
- Story Collection: Sangharsh Ke Baad
- Plays: Prakash aur Parchhaiyan, Barah Ekanki, Ashok
- Misc: Jane-Anjane, Awara Maseeha

Awards and Honours

He won Padma Bhushan and the Sahitya Akademi Award for his novel Ardhanarishvara (The Androgynous God or Shiva).

VRINDAVAN LAL VERMA

Dr. Vrindavan Lal Verma was a prominent Hindi novelist, famous for his novels Jhansi Ki Rani, Mrignayani, Amarbel and Kachnar.He has been singularly responsible for reviving the glory of mediaeval Bundelkhand in the public mind through his well researched historical novels.

YASHPAL

Yashpal (December 3, 1903–December 26, 1976) was a Hindi author renowned for *Jhutha Sach (The False Truth,* 1958–1960), which is regarded as one of the best Hindi novels ever written. He won the prestigious Sahitya Academy award for his novel *Meri Teri Uski Baat*. He served as an editor of *Viplav* for many years. His works have been translated into many languages.

Yashpal, a revolutionary fighting for India's freedom, was twenty-eight years old when he was caught, tried and sentenced to fourteen years to life at hard labour. There was little expectation at the time that he would emerge as one of India's outstanding writers of fiction.

He had led two lives, and in each of them had made important contributions to his country. His first life was dedicated to her freedom, his later life to her literature. As India celebrates the centenary of his birth (1903), scholars and public alike are re-evaluating his life and work in the light of changing social and political values.

Yashpal grew up at a time of ferment and agitation for Indian independence. In his school days he was drawn at first to Mahatma Gandhi's non-cooperation movement, but later felt that such movements were unresponsive to the needs of the poor and that non-cooperation with the British was ineffective. He joined National College, Lahore, a hotbed of nationalist sentiment, which was founded by Lala Lajpat Rai, the venerable leader of pre-partition Punjab. There he met Bhagat Singh who was hanged for his role in the assassination of policeman J.P. Saunders in Lahore (1928), and for exploding a bomb in the Central Legislative Assembly in New Delhi (1929).

Yashpal wrote in his reminiscences Sinhavalokan, "One day I and Bhagat Singh got a chance to practice rowing in the Ravi river. Just two of us, no one else was there. I don't remember how the subject came up, but in that solitude I said to Bhagat Singh, trusting him implicitly: Let us pledge our lives to our country.

"Bhagat Singh's face turned very serious, and extending his hand to me he said: I do pledge."

At first Yashpal took part in the activities of Naujawan Bharat Sabha organized by Bhagat Singh, but after the Lahore Bomb Factory was unearthed in 1929, he too went underground and never looked back. As an active member of the Hindustan Socialist Republican Army (HSRA), he came into contact with another well-known revolutionary, Chandra Shekhar Azad, who was killed (1931) in a shootout with police in Allahabad.

During the next two years, Yashpal made explosives at several secret factories, blew up the train carrying Viceroy Lord Irwin in 1929, took part in an attempt to free Bhagat Singh from Borstal Jail in Lahore, shot and grievously wounded two police constables in Kanpur when they tried to block an attempt by his group to escape. He also met his future wife, 17-year old Prakashvati who had left home to join the revolutionary party.

Yashpal was arrested in Allahabad in 1932 when his bullets ran out after an armed encounter with the police. He was one of the main accused in the concluded Lahore and Delhi conspiracy cases, but after a lengthy trial the government decided not to reopen these cases in view of the expenses involved. Some other charges against him could not proven for the lack of witnesses. In the end, he was given a life sentence.

In prison Yashpal taught himself enough French, Russian and Italian to read original works in those languages. He also wrote and re-wrote short stories that were later published as Pinjare ki Uran (Flights of a Caged Mind). In this life of discipline and contemplation came a surprise in the form of a petition by Prakashvati to the jail authorities that she wanted to marry Yashpal, the prisoner serving a life sentence.

Since the jail manual did not forbid a prisoner from getting married, the British superintendent gave his consent. The police did not want the notorious revolutionary to go to the civil court without handcuffs and leg irons, and Yashpal refused to get married tied up like a criminal. A compromised was reached when the Deputy Commissioner agreed to perform the marriage inside the prison. After the ceremony, Yashpal was returned to his cell to serve his life sentence, and Prakashvati went back to Karachi to finish her studies to become a dental surgeon which she had begun after her own arrest and subsequent release by the police.

Their's might be the only marriage ever to take place inside a prison in India. When the news of the marriage leaked outside, the newspapers seized upon the novel idea, provoking the government to add a section to the Indian Jail Manual forbidding a sentence-serving prisoner to be married in the prison in future.

India moved toward self-government in 1938. As part of the election campaign, the Congress Party promised to release of all political prisoners. Workers of Gandhi's movement were released immediately, but assurances were sought from the revolutionaries that they no longer believed in violence. Yashpal refused on the ground that it would appear that he had bargained with the government for his release. He was the last to be set free, on the condition that he would not be permitted to go back to Punjab. He then decided to make Lucknow, the capital of United Provinces (UP) where he was serving his sentence, his home.

Yashpal and Prakashvati, as he wrote in his reminiscences, were penniless. After a few months of hardship, Yashpal founded the Hindi monthly Vipalava (revolution) while Prakashvati worked as a dentist. Her dental practice was flourishing in those days of few women dentists, but she gave it up to help her husband. Soon they brought out the magazine's Urdu edition, Baagi. The masthead of their publication said it all: "You may preach the message of peace and equality. Let revolution sing its fiery song."

Viplava was a milestone in Hindi and Urdu political journalism. Besides being immensely popular, it was also a forum where staunch Gandhians and avowed believers in non-violence and satyagraha (civil disobedience) debated social and political issue with equally staunch Marxists and hardcore revolutionaries. When Yashpal was put in prison for seditious writing, Prakashvati filled in as editor.

In an attempt to muzzle the fiery enthusiasm of the couple, the government demanded huge security deposits from the magazine. The two closed down Viplava and Baagi, and began publishing Viplavi Tract. But police raids and constant harassment took its toll, and it all came to an end after five years of trend-setting journalism. Viplava reappeared briefly in 1948, but could not survive the censorship laws in a free India!

Yashpal, his own freedom regained and India's on the horizon, soon made his mark as a writer. Mahadevi Verma, the eminent Hindi poet, summed it up: "When other writers were praying to Saraswati, the muse of literature, for her blessing, Yashpal was making bombs in a dark, secret cellar. When he arrived on the literary scene much behind others, it was him that Saraswati gave her undivided attention."

If the literature of social reform and social protest in Hindi found a worthy advocate in Yashpal, he wielded a sledgehammer when writing about the exploited and the economically deprived in his fiction, and in the editorials and columns he wrote for Viplava.

Yashpal set about immediately on one his life-long missions: repudiation of what he considered to be backward and unrealistic in the Indian society. But unlike most people devoted to causes, he went about it with gentle humour and tongue-in-cheek wit. His criticism of ancient Hindu ideals as a basis for contemporary society can be seen in his story Dharmraksha (To Uphold Righteousness) where a man denying his normal instincts under the discipline of brahmacharya (celibacy), attempts to rape his 19-year old daughter. Such questioning of long-practiced religious rites and rituals, of the Hindu doctrine of karma and reincarnation as preached by the orthodox often earned him threats to his life.

Yashpal never hid his preference for Marxist ideals, and the inefficacy of the movement led by the Congress Party and

Mahatma Gandhi. His Gandhiwad ki Shav-pariksha (Post-mortem on Gandhiism), written in 1941 when Gandhi was alive, continues to be among his best-selling works. Although some of his early works showed the Communist Party as the saviour of Indian people, he himself never joined the party; in fact, the Communists later turned against him for his criticism of comrades who sacrificed free will and independent judgment to the Party's dictates.

Another consistent feature of Yashpal's writing is his compassion for women and his special concern for the inferior position of women in India. The women protagonists in his writings often break free, or try to, from the traditions of society that keep them in total dependence upon their family. Divya (1944), his novel set in the 1st century BC when there was a wide mingling of Indian and Hellenic cultures in northern India, is about Divya from an aristocratic Brahmin family who tries to find her identity in a male-dominated society. Assertions by Divya such as "the mistress of a noble family is not a free woman; she is not independent like a disreputable courtesan" outraged many of Yashpal's contemporaries.

Others tried to ignore it because they felt that a story about India's so-called Golden Age could not be considered 'literature' if it expounded an unacceptable political ideology. Fortunately, a core of young critics and scholars of successive generations has continued to stand-and even swear-by Divya's yearning for independence when she decides to be a prostitute, so as to be a free woman and have ownership rights over her body. The work showed Yashpal's deep knowledge of Indian classics and his command of Sanskrit.

His novel Jhootha Sach (1958 & 1960), similar in scope and breadth to Tolstoy's War and Peace, and has been compared to the works of Balzac and Victor Hugo. Probably the only work of its kind in any language and often acclaimed as the definitive novel on India's partition, it chronicles the ups and downs in the lives of two families (a brother and sister, and his girlfriend/wife) in pre-and post-partition India. Critics praised the novel for its balanced depiction of both Hindus and Muslims, and readers loved its merciless portrayal of the Congress Party leaders on the make in British-free India. That portrayal was so merciless that Yashpal was blatantly passed over for the Sahitya Akademi Award given by the government. The issue of Congress Party criticism, and of Jawaharlal Nehru, resurfaced a decade later when his name was on the national honours list. Indira Gandhi, then prime minister, reportedly read the 'objectionable' pages of Jhootha Sach and found nothing objectionable. Yashpal, the born anti-establishment rebel, was finally bestowed Padma Bhushan in 1970. The Sahitya Akademi tried to make amends by giving him the denied award in 1976 for his last novel Meri Teri Usaki Baat. It's not known if he'd have accepted it; he was too unwell to say either yes or no.

Yashpal's more than fifty books of short stories, essays, novels, a play and his 3-vol. reminiscences had a profound influence on Hindi literature, and on social and political philosophy in India. Corinne Friend, translator of several works by him, said it all in her book Yashpal: Author and Patriot: "Yashpal, in his concern for the common man and commitment to social justice, his understanding of the quirks of human nature and ability to portray human beings with compassion and humour, and in his simple and powerful writing style, is heir to Prem Chand," the greatest Hindi writer of pre-independence India.

Yashpal died in 1976 while writing the fourth volume of his reminiscences. Praskashvati, who had been the publisher of her husband's books for 60 years, died at age 88 in September 2002.

In the year 2003-2004, events to celebrate Yashpal's birth centenary were held across the length and the breadth of nation with an enthusiasm not seen except at the time of Prem Chand's birth centenary celebrations: from national seminars organized by the Sahitya Akademi (India's National Academy of Letters) at Shimla and at Kolkata, and by the Kerala Sahitya Akademi at Cochin, to local affairs in small towns in the Hindi-speaking heartland of India.

These events were marked by a forceful and unequivocal acknowledgment of Yashpal being the towering figure in the post-Prem Chand era, as well as of the author's importance and his impact on Hindi literature and on the successive generations of young writers. The Government of India issued a commemorative Yashpal Centenary postage stamp.

Books by Yashpal in English translation ·Yashpal: Author and Patriot, Corinne Friend, 1969, University of Pennsylvania Press, Philadelphia, USA [1] · The Essence of Love, Yashpal, 1975, Arnold Heinnemann, New Delhi, India ·Amita, Yashpal, 1977, Arnold Heinnemann, New Delhi, India · Yashpal Looks Back (Sinhavalokan), Yashpal, 1988, Vikas Publishing House, New Delhi, India ·The Second Nose and Other Stories, Yashpal, 2005, Rupa & Co., New Delhi, India · Divya, Yashpal, 2005, Sahitya Akademi, New Delhi, India · The Colour of Truth (Jhootha Sach), Sahitya Akademi, New Delhi, India (in press)

Literary Works

Yashpal has also written RAH BEETI(the story of the journey/Travel Diary) and also "DEKHA SOCHA SAMJHA"(Saw Thought Understood). Those are based on his travels via Eastern Europe (Czechoslovakia etc. and give a vivid and most enchanting description of the life there.)

Novels

- Divya,
- Deshdrohi aswin
- Jhutha Sach
- Dada comrade
- Amita
- Manushya ke roop
- Meri Teri Uski Baat

Story Collections

- Pinjare ki Udaan
- Phulo Ka Kurta
- Dharmayudha
- Sach

SACHCHIDANANDA HIRANANDA VATSYAYAN

Sachchidananda Hirananda Vatsyayana (1911–1987), popularly known by his pen-name Ajneya (or Agyeya), was a pioneer of modern trends not only in the realm of Hindi poetry, but also fiction, criticism and journalism. He was one of the most prominent exponents of the 'Nayi kavita' (New Poetry) in Hindi, and edited the 'Tar Saptaks'. Agyeya also translated some of his own works, as well as works of some other Indian authors to English.

Biography

Sachchidananda Hirananda Vatsyayana was born on March 7, 1911. His father was an archaeologist, and an expert in the Sanskrit language. His childhood was spent in many different places, including Lucknow, Jammu, and Srinagar.

Agyeya travelled extensively, both in India and abroad. Between 1961 and 1964, he held a visiting faculty position at the University of California, Berkeley. In 1965, he returned to India and became editor of the weekly 'Dinmaan'. He remained in India till 1968, before embarking on a trip to Europe. In 1969 he returned to Berkeley as Regents Professor, and continued there till June, 1970. In 1976, he had an 8 month stint at Heidelberg University as visiting professor.

Literary Works

Poetry Anthologies:

- Bhagnadoot (1933)
- Chinta (1942)
- Ityalam (1946)
- Hari ghaas par kshan-bhar (1949)
- Baawra Aheri (1954)
- Indradhanu raunde hue ye (1957)
- Ari o karuna prabhamaya (1959)
- Aangan ke paar dvaar (1961)
- Poorva (Ityalam & Hari ghaas par kshan-bhar) (1965)

- Sunahale Shaival (1965)
- Kitni naavon mein kitni baar (1967)
- Kyonki main use jaanta hoon (1969)
- Saagar-mudra (1970)
- Pahle main sannata bunta hoon (1973)
- Mahavriksha ke neeche (1977)
- Nadi ki baank par chhaya (1982)
- Prison days and other poems (in English) (1946)
- Agyeya Kavya Saptak
- Tar Saptak
- Doosra Saptak
- Teesra Saptak

Novels:

- Shekhar: Ek Jeevani I (1941)
- Shekhar: Ek Jeevani II (1944)
- Nadi ke dweep (1952)
- Apne-apne ajnabi (1961)

Stories Anthologies:

- Sampurn Kahanian (2005)
- Jaidol
- Meri Priya Kahaniyan (2004)

Critic:

- Atmanepad

Travelog:

- Ek Boond Sahsa Uchli Si (2003)
- Smrati Ke Galiyaron Se (2000)

Translations:

- First Person, Second Person, A Selection of Poems from the Work of "Agyeya" (with Leonard Nathan) (1971)

Awards and Honours

- Sahitya Akademi Award

- Jnanpith Award in 1978 (for the anthology 'Kitni Naavon mein kitni baar')
- Bharatbharati Award
- International Golden Wreath Award for poetry in 1983.

BHISHAM SAHNI

Bhisham Sahni (August 8, 1915-July 11, 2003) was a Hindi writer, playwright, and actor, most famous for his novel and television screenplay *Tamas* ("Darkness"), a powerful and passionate account of the Partition of India. He was awarded the Padma Bhushan for literature in 1998, and Sahitya Akademi Fellowship in 2002. He was the brother of the noted actor Balraj Sahni.

Biography

Bhisham Sahni was born on Aug 08, 1915 in Rawalpindi. Later he earned a master's degree in English at Government College in Lahore, and also attended Khalsa College, Amritsar.

He joined the struggle for Indian independence, and was jailed for his participation in the Quit India Movement of 1942. Upon Partition, he and his Punjabi Hindu family were forced to move to Amritsar.

In the late 1940s, he worked with his brother as a stage performer in Mumbai with the Indian People's Theatre Association. In 1950, he became a lecturer in English at Delhi College.

From 1957 to 1963, he lived in Moscow and worked as a translator from Russian to Hindi, during the period he translated twenty-five books from Russian into Hindi, including Tolstoy's Resurrection. In addition to those languages, Sahni was fluent in English, Urdu, Sanskrit, and Punjabi.

He was general secretary of the Progressive Writers Association, and was the founder and chairman of 'SAHMAT', an organization promoting cross-cultural understanding, founded in memory of the murdered theatre artist and activist Safdar Hashmi.

Late in life, he appeared in several films, including Saeed Mirza's *Mohan Joshi Hazir Ho!* (1984), *Tamas* (1986), Kumar Shahani's *Kasba* (1991), Bernardo Bertolucci's *Little Buddha* (1993) and Aparna Sen's *Mr. and Mrs. Iyer* (2002).

Literary Works

Based on the 1947 Partition of India riots he witnessed at Rawalpindi, Bisham Sahni wrote his epic work *Tamas*(Darkness, 1974), a novel portraying the terror-stricken Hindu exodus from Muslim majority areas, though the overall theme remained the human-story behind the entire carnage. It has been translated to English, and several Indian languages including Gujarati, Kashmiri, and Manipuri.

Tamas won the 1975 Sahitya Akademi Award for literature, and was later made into a television film in 1987 by Govind Nihalani. Two of his masterpiece stories 'Chief ki davat' and 'Amritsar aa gaya hai' are also based on the Partition.

Sahni's prolific career as a writer also included five other Hindi novels, over hundred short stories spread over nine collections of short stories, (including Bhagya Rekha (1953), Pahla patha (1956), Bhatakti rakha (1966), and Nischar (1983)); a collection of children's short stories 'Gulal ka khel', six plays including Hanusa (1977), Kabira khara bazar mein (1981), Madhavi (1982) and Muavze (1993), his autobiography "Aaj ke Ateet" (Pasts of the Present), and the biography of his brother Balraj Sahni, "Balraj My Brother," (English).

During his life time, Bisham Sahni won several wards including Shiromani Writers Award, 1979, Uttar Pradesh Government Award for Tamas, 1975, Madhya Pradesh Kala Sahitya Parishad Award, for his play 'Hanusa', 1975 the Lotus Award from the Afro-Asian Writers' Association, 1981 and the Soviet Land Nehru Award, 1983, and finally the Padma Bhushan for literature in 1998, and India's highest literary award the Sahitya Akademi Fellowship in 2002 .

Quote

"If people knew each other, they would find it hard to hate."

NIRMAL VERMA

Nirmal Verma (3rd April 1929, Shimla-25 October 2005) is a Hindi writer and novelist. Nirmal Verma did M.A. in History from Delhi University and studied the Czech language at the Oriental Institute in Prague.

Awards and Milestones

- Nirmal Verma won the Jnanpith award in 1999, the highest literary award for Indian writers.
- A collection of short stories 'Kavve aur Kala Pani' won the Sahitya Akademi award in 1985 .
- He was a fellow with the International Institute for Asian Studies.
- Library of Congress catalogues most of the works of Nirmal Verma in its collection.

The Nai Kahani Movement

Nirmal Verma, together with Mohan Rakesh, Bhisham Sahni, Kamleshwar, Amarkant, Rajendra Yadav and others, is the founder of the *Nai Kahani* (new short story) in Hindi literature.

Nirmal Verma is best known for his short stories and his best known story, 'Parinde' is supposed to be the pioneer of the *Nai Kahani Movement*. Nirmal Verma's other notable stories are *Andhere Mein*, *Dedh Inch Upar*, and *Kavve Aur Kala Pani.*

Nirmal Verma's last story was published in "Naya Gyanodaya" August 2005 issue, titled "Ab Kuchh Nahin".

Nirmal Verma experimented vividly with theme as well as technique of the Hindi short story in the 60s and 70s.

A collection of his letters written to Ramkumar (well known artist and his brother) has been published by Bhartiya Jnanpith, titled "Priya Ram" (Dear Ram).

Major Works

- Kala Ka Jokhima-investigation of the Indic arts in the 20th century

- Dhundha Se Uthati Dhun-written like a diary addressing issues related to Hindi literature
- Ve Din-Nirmal Verma's first novel, set in Prague, Czechoslavakia
- Antima Aranya-novel
- Rata Ka Reporter-novel
- Ek Chithara Sukh-novel
- Lal Teen Ki Chhat-novel

RAJKAMAL CHAUDHARY

Rajkamal Chaudhary (1929-1967), (also spelled as Rajkamal Chaudhari) was an Indian poet, short story writer, novelist, critic and thinker in Hindi, Maithili and Bangla languages.

Biography

Raj Kamal was born at Mehsi village in Saharsa district of Bihar.

Writing Style

Major Works

- Machhali Mari Hui (A Fish Dead), novel
- Nadi Bahati Thi (There Flowed a River), novel
- Mukti Prasang (a long poem prescribed in many colleges and universities including University of Delhi)
- Kankawati
- Das Kavita
- Agni-snaan
- Paththar ke neeche dabe hue haath
- Tash ke patton ka shahar

BIBLIOGRAPHY

Abrams, M. H and Stephen Greenblatt: *The Norton Anthology of English Literature*, W.W. Norton, New York, 2000.

Agarwal, Beena : *The Plays of Rabindra Nath Tagore : A Thematic Study*, New Delhi, Satyam Pub., 2003.

Alter, Stephen and Wimal Dissanayake: *The Penguin Book of Modern Indian Short Stories*, Penguin Books, New Delhi, 1991.

Andrews, C.F. : *Rabindranath Tagore : Selected Stories*, New Delhi, Srishti, 2004.

Badshahi Angti: *The Emperor's Ring*, Ananda Publishers, Calcutta 1969.

Bakso Rahashya: *The Mystery of the Box*, Ananda Publishers, Calcutta 1973.

Balachandra Rajan : *Milton and the Climate of Reading: Essays*, University of Toronto Press, Toronto, 2006.

Beatina, Mary: *Narayan: A Study in Transcendence*, Oxford: Peter Lang Publishing, New York, 1994.

Bhattacharya, Sabyasachi : *Vande Mataram : The Biography of a Song*, New Delhi, Penguin, 2003.

Bond, Ruskin : *Delhi is Not Far : A Novel*, New Delhi, Penguin, 2005.

Bose, Aurobindo : *Later Poems of Rabindranath Tagore*, New Delhi, Rupa & Co., 2002.

Chakrabarti, Santosh : *Studies in Tagore : Critical Essays*, New Delhi, Atlantic, 2004.

Chatterjee, Indira : *A Thematic Study of Tagore's Novels*, Gurgaon, Shubhi Pub., 2007.

Chaudhuri, Sukanta : *Rabindranath Tagore : Selected Poems*, New Delhi, Oxford Pub., 2004.

Chhinnamastar Abhishap: *The Curse of Kali*, Ananda Publishers, Calcutta 1981.

Das, Sisir Kumar and Sukanta Chaudhuri : *Rabindranath Tagore : Selected Writings on Literature and Language*, Delhi, Oxford University Press, 2001.

Gangtokey Gandagol: *Confusion in Gangtok*, Ananda Publishers, Calcutta 1971.

Gorosthanev Sabdhan: *Caution in the Graveyard*, Ananda Publishers, Calcutta 1979.

Goyal, Bhagwat S.: *R. K. Narayan's India: Myth and Reality*, South Asia Books, Lahore, 1993.

Hariprasanna, A.: *The World of Malgudi: A Study of R. K. Narayan's Novels*, South Asia Books, Lahore, 1997.

Howlader, Chinmoy : *Influence of Kalidasa on Rabindranath Tagore*, Delhi, Bharatiya Kala Prakashan, 2003.

Jha, Gauri Shankar : *Current Perspectives in Indian English Literature*, New Delhi, Atlantic Pub., 2006.

Jha, Radhika : *The Elephant and the Maruti : Stories*, New Delhi, Penguin, 2003.

Jha, Rama: *Gandhian Thought and Indo-anglian Novelists: Mulk Raj Anand, Raja Rao, R. K. Narayan, & Bhabani Bhattacharya*, Chanakya Publications, Delhi, 1983).

Joi Baba Felunath: *Glory to Baba Felunath*, Ananda Publishers, Calcutta 1976.

Joseph, T. and S. Francis : *Edmund Spenser : A Critical Study*, New Delhi, Anmol Pub., 2005.

Kailashey, Kelenkari: *Chaos in Kailash*, Ananda Publishers, Calcutta 1974.

Kain, Geoffrey: *R. K. Narayan: Contemporary Critical Perspectives*, Michigan State University Press, East Lansing, 1998).

Magnus, Laurie : *A Dictionary of European Literature : Designed as a Companion to English Studies*, New Delhi, Cosmo, 2006.

Marathe, Sudhakar : *The Elephant's Child and Other Stories : The Delightful World of Rudyard Kipling*, New Delhi, Penguin, 2005.

Mittal, C.R. : *Eliot's Early Poetry in Perspective*, New Delhi, Atlantic, 2001.

Nayan Rahashya: *Mystery in Nayan*, Ananda Publishers, Calcutta 1991.

Paul, S.K. : *The Complete Poems of Rabindranath Tagore's Gitanjali : Texts and Critical Evaluation*, New Delhi, Sarup, 2006.

Pousse, Michel: *R. K. Narayan: A Painter of Modern India,* Peter Lang Publishing, Oxford, 1995.

Prakash Kona : *Pearls of an Unstrung Necklace*, Fugue State Press, New York, 2005.

Prasad, V. V. N. Rajendra: *Five Indian Novelists: B. Rajan, Raja Rao, R. K. Narayan, Arun Joshi, Anita Desai,* South Asia Books, Lahore, 1997.

Royal Bengal Rahashya: *The Royal Bengal Mystery*, Ananda Publisher, Calcutta 1975.

Sanyal, Lopa : *Daniel Defoe : The Novelist*, New Delhi, Sonali, 2006.

Selvadurai, Shyam: *Story-Wallah: A Celebration of South Asian Fiction*, Houghton Mifflin, New York, 2005.

Sonar Kella: *The Golden Fortress*, Ananda Publishers, Calcutta 1971.

Susham Bedi: *Gatha Amerbel Ki (Song of the Amerbel)*, National Publishing House, Delhi, 1999.

Tiwary, R.S. : *Current Indian Creativity in English*, Jaipur, Book Enclave, 2003.

Walsh, William: *R. K. Narayan: A Critical Appreciation,* University of Chicago Press, Chicago, 1983.

Wilbur L.Cross : *The Development of the English Novel*, New Delhi, Atlantic, 2001.

Yadav, Ajay Singh : *Darkness Before Dawn*, Bhopal, Light House Books, 2000.

Zaman, Niaz : *Didima's Necklace and Other Stories*, Dhaka, Writers.Ink, 2005.

INDEX

A

Accounts, 105, 149, 211.
Achievement, 125, 126, 184.
Adaptation, 9, 10, 72, 123.
Agency, 117.
Altaf Fatima, 72, 73.
Amitav Ghosh, 76, 166.
Approach, 60, 116, 148.
Arrangements, 169.
Arundhati Roy, 57, 143, 144, 148, 149, 150.
Authority, 180.
Authors, 8, 10, 22, 44, 45, 57, 58, 61, 64, 67, 68, 124, 203, 217, 240, 253.

B

Baby Halder, 4.
Bankim Chandra Chattopadhyay, 47.
Bhisham Sahni, 220, 255, 257.
Brahmacharya, 249.
Buddhism, 81, 138.
Business, 13, 58, 167, 200, 201, 211.

C

Christian, 2, 18, 101, 143, 155, 168, 169, 170, 218.
Climate, 134, 163.
Commission, 36, 77, 140, 202.
Committee, 77, 79, 80, 120.
Conference, 2, 61, 142, 200, 235.
Contribution, 2, 39, 40, 69, 109, 117, 184, 190, 208, 215, 224, 242.
Cooperation, 1, 85, 246.
Costumes, 181.
Crisis, 31, 67, 68, 127, 182, 199, 238.
Culture, 10, 23, 28, 36, 37, 70, 77, 80, 108, 113, 115, 125, 126, 130, 137, 142, 150, 159, 164, 194, 224, 231, 239, 241.

D

Department, 24, 76, 81, 101, 114, 125, 126, 184, 199, 211, 243.
Deterioration, 162.
Devaki Nandan Khatri, 215.
Development, 6, 47, 66, 88, 118, 145, 159, 211, 212, 231.

F

Fakirs, 50.
Finance, 179.
Foundation, 78, 109, 118, 164.
Freedom, 2, 4, 5, 9, 13, 17, 19, 35, 36, 44, 48, 55, 56, 85, 86, 127, 143, 146, 148, 151, 155, 156, 181, 183, 189, 228, 234, 246, 249.

G

Ganga basin, 14.
Government, 15, 30, 47, 48, 61, 77, 79, 117, 118, 125, 130, 136, 140, 169, 177, 182, 185, 186, 187, 188, 189, 196, 199, 234, 240, 241, 245, 247, 248, 249, 251, 252, 255, 256.

H

Hinduism, 102, 130, 136, 216.

I

Industry, 79, 134, 210, 217.
Institute, 22, 44, 62, 63, 83, 92, 120, 134, 203, 210, 238, 257.
Internet, 25, 38, 91, 160, 193.
Islam, 216.

J

Jaishankar Prasad, 230, 236.
Journalism, 4, 5, 30, 65, 72, 83, 84, 93, 94, 96, 209, 217, 248, 249, 253.
Journalist, 8, 23, 48, 65, 71, 72, 75, 77, 82, 85, 169, 172, 186, 196, 198, 201, 202, 216, 217.
Justice, 76, 83, 105, 118, 148, 149, 165, 169, 251.

K

Khushwant Singh, 58, 172, 186, 188.

L

Languages, 16, 24, 25, 27, 32, 35, 47, 66, 67, 69, 76, 77, 78, 94, 111, 127, 151, 161, 177, 190, 204, 209, 213, 242, 258.
Laws, 118, 249.
Leadership, 36, 115, 179.
Liberation, 30, 158.
Literature, 6, 7, 8, 10, 18, 24, 25, 27, 28, 29, 31, 33, 34, 39, 40, 47, 48, 49, 50, 55, 59, 62, 63, 66, 67, 68, 69, 76, 77, 78, 86, 88, 89, 91, 95, 96, 101, 102, 106, 108, 109, 114, 115, 116, 117, 119, 120, 121, 130, 134, 136, 137, 140, 141, 157, 158, 159, 162, 193, 194, 196, 197, 201, 203, 206, 209, 211, 212, 217, 220, 224, 225, 226, 227, 230, 231, 233, 234, 235, 236, 241, 242, 245, 246, 249, 251, 252, 255, 256, 257, 258.

M

Management, 5, 22, 92, 128.
Methodology, 133, 152.
Mulk Raj Anand, 1, 112, 121.

N

Network, 75, 76, 123, 201, 221, 244.

O

Operations, 36, 199.
Opportunity, 26, 36, 103.
Organization, 2, 69, 137, 203, 255.

P

Pankaj Mishra, 101.
Philosophy, 50, 101, 106, 113, 138, 159, 166, 181, 216, 224, 231, 251.
Policy, 146, 176.

Politics, 4, 16, 17, 46, 50, 86, 90, 145, 149, 158, 159, 160, 161, 166, 172.
Prakash Kona, 91.
Production, 60, 110, 174, 177, 202.
Projects, 11, 23, 147, 199.

R

Rahi Masoom Raza, 131.
Raj Kamal Jha, 82.
Rana Dasgupta, 57.
Reincarnation, 249.
Religion, 51, 86, 102, 103, 140, 141.
Research, 8, 25, 37, 38, 66, 95, 140, 193.
Rituals, 249.

S

Salvation, 238.
Samit Basu, 22.
Sarnath Banerjee, 8.
Scholarship, 28, 75, 78, 136, 150, 162, 163, 188.
Sharat Chandra Chatterji, 53.
Shashi Deshpande, 65.
Shiva, 245.
Sikhism, 189.
Society, 1, 6, 18, 31, 45, 52, 53, 63, 64, 77, 78, 88, 89, 103, 105, 110, 120, 124, 126, 129, 137, 140, 141, 151, 158, 159, 161, 163, 179, 182, 190, 198, 202, 210, 243, 249, 250.
Suchitra Bhattacharya, 31.
Sufis, 46.
Susham Bedi, 24, 25, 27.
Swadesh Deepak, 58, 59, 60, 61.

T

Technology, 2, 44, 62, 63, 83, 92.
Tradition, 41, 110, 119, 127, 151, 153.

U

University, 1, 3, 8, 22, 24, 25, 28, 30, 31, 32, 33, 42, 43, 44, 45, 46, 48, 54, 55, 57, 62, 63, 64, 66, 68, 69, 73, 76, 77, 78, 80, 81, 82, 83, 84, 88, 92, 93, 94, 96, 99, 100, 101, 109, 110, 111, 114, 115, 118, 120, 121, 125, 126, 128, 132, 133, 134, 136, 138, 139, 141, 153, 157, 162, 163, 166, 167, 176, 183, 184, 185, 186, 196, 197, 199, 202, 209, 210, 220, 225, 226, 228, 239, 241, 252, 253, 257, 258.
Upamanyu Chatterjee, 46, 57.

V

Vedas, 230.
Vikram Chandra, 42, 57.
Vikram Seth, 57, 76, 164.

W

Writers, 1, 8, 15, 29, 31, 43, 50, 55, 82, 89, 91, 92, 118, 121, 124, 125, 133, 139, 147, 155, 164, 175, 176, 180, 183, 186, 187, 194, 211, 218, 220, 221, 227, 235, 236, 239, 243, 246, 249, 252, 255, 256, 257.